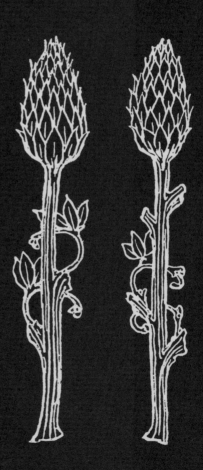

BERNARD SHAW AND THE AESTHETES

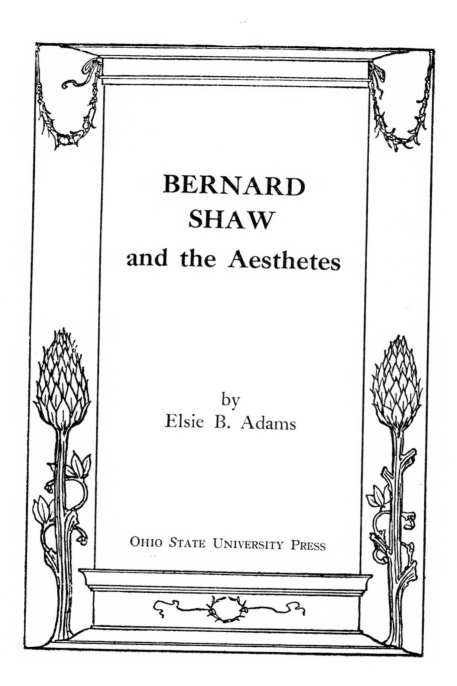

BERNARD SHAW

and the Aesthetes

by
Elsie B. Adams

OHIO STATE UNIVERSITY PRESS

Library of Congress Catalogue Card Number: 76-153421
Standard Book Number: 8142-0155-5
Manufactured in the United States of America

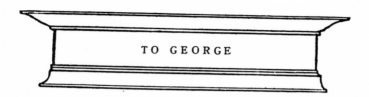

TO GEORGE

Table of Contents

Preface

HEN I FIRST EMBARKED on a study of Bernard Shaw and the aesthetes, my research yielded only negative results. The answer to the question, What is Shaw's relationship to the aesthetes? seemed to be, None. Then another problem arose, even more basic than the first: how to define *aesthete*. Literary historians and observers of the fin-de-siècle scene use the term *aesthete* somewhat indiscriminately to refer to Rossetti, Morris, Swinburne, Wilde, Pater, Beardsley, and a variety of others. Finding a definition inclusive as well as accurate proved to be the most difficult task of my research. The definitions of *aesthete* and *aesthetic movement* which I suggest in my introduction are, admittedly, tentative.

After I had working definitions and an outline of the major art theories held by the aesthetes, another problem arose: whereas before there had been very little to say about Shaw and the aesthetes, suddenly there was too much to say. My study is therefore less detailed than I might wish. For example, I devote one chapter to Ruskin, Morris, and Shaw; but I am convinced that only monograph- or book-length studies of Shaw and Ruskin or Shaw and Morris could reveal the full extent of Shaw's debt to either. So, too, do I see the need for a separate study of Shaw and Wilde, or Shaw and Swinburne, of Shaw and Yeats, of even such unlikely companions as Shaw and Pater. My major purpose in this work has been to demonstrate that the subject of Shaw and the aesthetes is in fact a rich, though previously unexplored, territory. The approach to Shaw through his artistic milieu not only reveals the importance of a segment of nineteenth-century thought to his theory of art but also emphasizes a side of Shaw—the artistic side—which has in the past often been neglected.

In the following pages all of my quotations from Shaw are from the Standard Edition of the *Works of Bernard Shaw,* published by Constable and Company Limited (London, 1931–52), unless I specify otherwise. Whenever page references appear in parentheses in my text, they are to the Standard Edition.

For permission to quote from the works of Bernard Shaw, I make grateful acknowledgment to The Society of Authors on behalf of the Bernard Shaw Estate.

For permission to use other material excerpted in this book, I am grateful to the following:

Vanguard Press, Inc., and Hutchinson and Company, Ltd.: for excerpts from Stephen Winsten, *Days with Bernard Shaw* (New York: Vanguard Press, 1949); The Macmillan Company: for excerpts from the *The Autobiography of William Butler Yeats, Consisting of Reveries over Childhood and Youth, The Trembling of the Veil, and Dramatis Personae* (New York: The Macmillan Company, 1953). COPYRIGHT 1916, 1936, BY THE MACMILLAN COMPANY. COPYRIGHT, 1944, BY BERTHA GEORGIE YEATS; and for excerpts from "Sailing to Byzantium," from *The Collected Poems of W. B. Yeats* (New York: The Macmillan Company, 1956). Copyright, 1903, 1906, 1907, 1912, 1916, 1918, 1919, 1924, 1928, 1931, 1933, 1934, 1935, 1940, 1944, 1945, 1946, 1950, 1956, by THE MACMILLAN COMPANY. Copyright, 1940, by GEORGIE YEATS. Definitive Edition, with the author's final revisions, © The Macmillan Company 1956; and to M. B. Yeats and Macmillan & Co. (London): for excerpts from *The Autobiography of William Butler Yeats* and from "Sailing to Byzantium," in *The Collected Poems of W. B. Yeats.*

Portions of this study have appeared elsewhere: "Bernard Shaw's Pre-Raphaelite Drama." Reprinted by permission of the Modern Language Association of America from *PMLA* 81 (October, 1966): 428–38. © by The Modern Language Association of America. "The Portrait of the Artist in Bernard Shaw's Novels" was originally published in *English Literature in Transition* 10, no. 3 (1967) : 130–49.

I am personally indebted to Professor A. J. Fritz, who directed *Bernard Shaw and the Aesthetes* in its first draft—a dissertation at the University of Oklahoma—and to other professors who made my study at the University of Oklahoma particularly rewarding, especially Professors J. L. Kendall, William Maehl, Roy R. Male, and Calvin G. Thayer. My husband, George R. Adams, who originally suggested the subject of Shaw and the aesthetes to me, deserves special thanks for research assistance, helpful commentary, and baby-sitting. I am grateful to Mrs. Donna Lewis, English Department secretary at Wisconsin State University-Whitewater, who efficiently and cheerfully assisted with manuscript typing. I am also grateful to the libraries at Columbia University, Cornell University, and SUNY-Binghamton, for allowing me to use their research facilities during my work. Finally, I wish to thank Wisconsin State University-Whitewater for reducing my teaching load from twelve to nine hours during my revision of the manuscript.

A final word: throughout the researching and writing of *Bernard Shaw and the Aesthetes,* I have been reminded of Shaw's criticism of Dixon Scott's *Men of Letters.* Scott had analyzed Shaw's style and Shaw had complained, "It was very much as if I had told him the house was on fire, and he had said, 'How admirably monosyllabic!' and left the nursery stairs burning unheeded. My impulse was to exclaim, 'Do you suppose, you conceited young whelp, that I have taken all that trouble and developed all that literary craft to gratify your appetite for style? Get up at once and fetch a bucket of water; or, at least, raise an alarm, unless you wish me to take you by the scruff of the neck and make you do it. You call yourself a critic: you are a mere fancier.' " I realize that the house still burns, and with an ever more destructive blaze, and that people to sound the alarm and organize the bucket brigade are needed more than ever. It is therefore with an apology to Shaw that I offer the following results of my study.

List of Abbreviations

Shaw's Works

The Admirable Bashville	*Bashville*
Androcles and the Lion	*Androcles*
Back to Methuselah	*Methuselah*
As Far as Thought Can Reach	*AFT*
Caesar and Cleopatra	*C&C*
The Dark Lady of the Sonnets	*Dark Lady*
The Devil's Disciple	*Disciple*
The Irrational Knot	*IK*
Love among the Artists	*LAA*
Major Critical Essays	*Essays*
The Perfect Wagnerite	*Wagnerite*
The Quintessence of Ibsenism	*Quintessence*
The Sanity of Art	*SA*
Man and Superman	*M&S*
Mrs. Warren's Profession	*Mrs. Warren*
Our Theatres in the Nineties	*OTN*
Pen Portraits and Reviews	*Portraits*
Saint Joan	*Joan*
The Shewing Up of Blanco Posnet	*Blanco Posnet*
Sixteen Self Sketches	*Sketches*
Three Plays for Puritans	*Three Plays*
Translations and Tomfooleries	*T&T*

Periodicals

American Scholar	A Sch
College English	CE
Comparative Literature	CL
Dalhousie Review	DR
Drama Survey	Dram S
English Literature in Transition	ELT
Journal of Aesthetics and Art Criticism	JAAC
Journal of English and German Philology	JEGP
Modern Drama	MD
Modern Language Review	MLR
Notes and Queries	N&Q
Prairie Schooner	Pr S
South Atlantic Quarterly	SAQ
Shaw Review	Shaw R
Tulane Drama Review	TDR
Texas Studies in Literature and Language	TSLL
University of Toronto Quarterly	UTQ
Victorian Studies	VS

Introduction

BERNARD SHAW'S STATEMENT that " 'for art's sake' alone I would not face the toil of writing a single sentence" has served as an effective deterrent to any attempts to place Shaw in the English aesthetic movement. Although few critics of Shaw would concur in James Huneker's opinion that Shaw "refuses to be an artist. He loathes art,"[1] most agree that Shaw is outside the movement of "art for art's sake." Max Beerbohm, reviewing Shaw's novel *Cashel Byron's Profession,* expresses precisely the predominant critical opinion of Shaw's relationship to the aesthetes: "As a passage by steam is to a voyage by sail, so is Mr. Shaw's fiction to true fiction. A steamboat is nice because it takes us quickly to some destination; a sailing-yacht is nice in itself, nice for its own sake. Mr. Shaw's main wish is to take us somewhere."[2] Most other critics less metaphorically, but no less emphatically, separate Shaw and the aesthetes. G. K. Chesterton's comment in his biography of Shaw is typical: "No one can understand Bernard Shaw who does not give full value to this early revolt of his on behalf of ethics against the ruling school of *l'art pour l'art.*"[3] Literary historians also place Shaw outside the aesthetic movement. In one of the best literary histories of the 1890s, Holbrook Jackson offers what has become almost a cliché in Shaw criticism: Shaw, he says, belongs to a movement of "art for life's sake," universal, communal, and collective rather than intensive and individual.[4]

These opinions are supported by Shaw's own consistent and

emphatic refutation of art for art's sake. The most frequently quoted of these refutations occurs in his attack on the "bellettrist," the "mere virtuoso in literature," in the Epistle Dedicatory to *Man and Superman* (p. xxxiv), an attack echoed in Shaw's preface to *Three Plays by Brieux*: "Now great art is never produced for its own sake. It is too difficult to be worth the effort" (p. xx). An even stronger attack occurs in Shaw's speech of 1908 on "Literature and Art": "I say that all art at the fountainhead is didactic, and that nothing can produce art except the necessity of being didactic. I say, not in the spirit of vulgar abuse, but in the solemnest Scriptural use of the terms, that the man who believes in art for art's sake is a fool; that is to say, a man in a state of damnation."[5] Shaw's admiration of Ibsen's drama and Wagner's music focuses on both artists' ability to transcend art for art's sake. Shaw values most the socially oriented plays of Ibsen's middle period, described in *The Quintessence of Ibsenism* as "realistic prose plays of modern life, abandoning all production of art for art's sake" (*Essays,* p. 60) ; and he distinguishes Wagner from those composers "in which the music was trying to exist ornamentally for its own sake and had no real content at all."[6] Throughout his long career, Shaw never abandoned this attitude toward art for art's sake; in one of his last works, the preface to *Farfetched Fables*, he points to his active political life—"the Shavian idiosyncrasy" which "disgusts the Art For Art's Sake faction" (p. 71).

In addition to Shaw's contemptuous references to art for art's sake, his comments about—or, to be more exact, the absence of comments about—key figures in the aesthetic movement suggest his separation from it. If literary historians had only Shaw's work from which to reconstruct a picture of the literary scene of the 1880s and 1890s, they would know of Ruskin and Morris but would be almost unaware of Swinburne and Moore, and totally unaware of Pater, Symons, Dowson, or Johnson. They would know of Rossetti, other Pre-Raphaelites, and Whistler from Shaw's art criticism of the 1880s. They would know of Wilde and James from Shaw's drama criticism of the 1890s, but they would know little about the nondramatic works of these two artists. And their opinion of all the aesthetes, if based on Shaw's usually unfavorable judgments of them (Ruskin and Morris excepted), would be low.

But Shaw's silence about figures in the movement is certain to have been from choice, not ignorance. As John Gassner has noted, the "art-for-art's sake phenomena at the turn-of-the-century could not but be noticed and in some way or other reflected by Shaw, who was equally conscious of art and sociology."[7]

My attempt to define Shaw's place in the aesthetic movement is encouraged by the recent trend in Shaw criticism which emphasizes Shaw the artist over Shaw the philosopher and social critic. For example, Edmund Wilson denigrates Shaw's ideas but calls him "a considerable artist"; W. H. Auden says, "For all his theater about propaganda, his writing has an effect nearer to that of music than the work of any of the so-called pure writers"; Arthur H. Nethercot maintains that Shaw sacrificed his revolutionary views for the sake of making plays palatable to the public; and Eric Bentley stresses Shaw's artistry over his didactic or "naturalistic" tendencies, saying that "the platform satisfied only a fragment of his nature."[8] But only recently have any critics begun to suggest a close relationship between Shaw and the aesthetes. J. I. M. Stewart says, "Shaw's statement that for art's sake alone he 'would not face the toil of writing a single sentence' is simply untrue, for the art of the plays is elaborated not to give us something more persuasive than the prefaces but simply something more delightful." And Harold Fromm agrees: "Although he thought he did not care for art for art's sake, he was an esthete like Matthew Arnold, like Ruskin, like Schopenhauer, like many other nineteenth-century thinkers whose main concern was with order and beauty and their application to daily life."[9]

To call a statement by Shaw "simply untrue," as Stewart does, is risky. A safer procedure is to assume that Shaw always means what he says, and then to try to determine exactly what he has said. But in order to decide what was said, one needs a working definition of *aesthete* and *aesthetic* movement. A particularly helpful starting point for such definitions is provided by Helmut E. Gerber, who says that the period from 1880 to 1920 ("or, more flexibly, between 1870 and 1930") is the interweaving of "decadence, aestheticism, naturalism, impressionism, symbolism, neo-romanticism, late Victorianism, modernism, and a host of other isms."[10] Whether one defines aestheticism narrowly as a cult of art or broadly as a concern (overshadowing all others) for creating or comprehending beauty, the aesthetic movement can be seen as encompassing a number of the "isms" of the late nineteenth century. Aestheticism may be compatible with decadence, with impressionism, or even with naturalism, as the career of George Moore suggests. Whistler, who is undeniably a part of English art for art's sake, is also an impressionist; he has also been called an aesthete, a Pre-Raphaelite, and a decadent, though he refused to consider himself a part of any movement. Likewise, Pater can be seen as an aesthete, a decadent, or an impressionist, as can Oscar Wilde.

The picture which the term *aesthete* calls up for most of us—if it calls up anything at all—is the aesthete of late nineteenth century satire, a composite image combining the characteristics of Arnold, Swinburne, Pater, the Pre-Raphaelites, Whistler, and Wilde. For example, in W. H. Mallock's *The New Republic* (1877), Pater, satirized as Mr. Rose, is introduced as a "pre-Raphaelite" who speaks on "self-indulgence in art." Mr. Rose is first seen gravely discoursing on the "infinite and passionate beauties" of a flower; he believes that the aim of life "is life," i.e., "the consciousness of exquisite living," and he delivers long speeches on the aim of culture ("to make the soul a musical instrument"), on the vulgarity of the city, and on "modern aestheticism," which "holds nothing common or unclean" (pp. 11, 15, 21, 123, 165–69, 171).

In the most famous satire on the aesthetes, Gilbert and Sullivan's *Patience* (1881), the aesthete Bunthorne is "a Fleshly Poet" who affects medievalism, belongs to the "Inner Brotherhood," writes Swinburnean verse, describes himself as "an apostle in the high aesthetic band," wears his hair long, and attitudinizes. He is a combination of Pre-Raphaelite, Swinburne, Arnold, and possibly Pater; but he was immediately associated with Wilde. Bunthorne's rival, Archibald Grosvenor, is a parody of young Oscar Wilde— "an Idyllic Poet," "a trustee for Beauty," "the Apostle of Simplicity," a "broken-hearted troubadour, / Whose mind's aesthetic and whose tastes are pure!"[11] Whereas Bunthorne and Grosvenor affect innocence, purity, and an indifference to worldly affairs, Esmé Amarinth in *The Green Carnation* (1894) is the epitome of worldly sophistication, condemning innocence, naturalness, and sincerity as "bourgeois." Amarinth, satirizing Wilde's decadent phase, represents perversion and abnormality, a perversion originating with the pose of the lily-carrying, transcendental young man depicted in *Patience,* for Mr. Amarinth says that he once was "an aesthete. I have lain upon hearth-rugs and eaten passion-flowers. I have clothed myself in breeches of white samite, and offered my friends yellow jonquils instead of afternoon tea."[12] But, he explains, after aestheticism became popular, he traded the aesthetic "passion-flowers" for the green carnation. An aesthete who combines the innocence of Grosvenor with the worldliness of Amarinth is the hero of G. S. Street's *The Autobiography of a Boy* (1894)—an absurd but harmless aspirant to wicked words and deeds whose worldly pose, attempts to shock, and condescending advice to his elders are borne with amused tolerance by most of his associates.

The aesthete portrayed by *Punch* in the 1870s and 1880s is one of several hypersensitive types. Jellaby Postlethwaite, introduced as "the great Poet, you know, who sat for Maudle's 'Dead Narcissus,' " prefers to contemplate a lily instead of eating lunch, supplies adjectives such as "supremely consummate" to the fashionable world, and confesses, "I never bathe. I always see myself so dreadfully *foreshortened* in the water, you know." He has affinities with Wilde, but he is sometimes drawn to look like Whistler.[13] His artist friend is Maudle, primarily modeled on Swinburne and Wilde; Maudle writes Swinburnean verse in "a Maudle-In Ballad. To His Lily," but he resembles Wilde in "Maudle on the Choice of a Profession," where he asks why a *"consummately* lovely" boy should *"be* anything? Why not let him remain for ever content to *Exist Beautifully?"*[14] Swinburne, Pater, and Burne-Jones are satirized as the successful champions in "Clowning and Classicism . . . Being the Opening Scene of a New and Original Great-god-Pan-tomime, entitled, Harlequin King Cultchaw; Or, The Three Champions of Paganism and the Sleeping Beast" (*Punch,* 7 Jan. 1882). Instructed by King Cultchaw, "a Modern Evil Genius," the three go to awake "the Sleeping Beast" by calling up Wilde and "the *Spirit of the Hair"*; they are all reviled by "the Good Fairy Ruskin" for perverting his doctrine, but at the end they enter "the Realms of Professional Beauty."

Though *Punch* attacked Arnold, Ruskin, Burne-Jones, Swinburne, Whistler, and Wilde in personal satire, the magazine concentrated on the amateur aesthete. "Affiliating an Aesthete" (19 June 1880) shows Postlethwaite, Maudle, and Mrs. Cimabue Brown, *Punch's* type of the "aesthetic" lady, encouraging "a promising young Pharmaceutical Chemist" named Pilcox to become a sculptor; this chemist-sculptor becomes so sure of himself that in a few months he is expressing scorn for Michelangelo ("A Reaction in Aesthetics," 9 Oct. 1880). According to *Punch*, the aesthetic movement included all social classes; it reached up to the Duke of Bedford (shown in "Punch's Fancy Portraits—No. 30," 7 May 1881) and down to John Smaulker Junior, a servant at "Peacocke Pleasaunce," a "new Igh Art Willa," who describes to his friend Mary ("among the Philistians") a proposed "society for bringing Beauty ome to the Pantry."[15] By 1882, however, the popular phase of the aesthetic movement was dying; "The Academy Soirée" in an 1882 issue of *Punch* says that "we scarce turn to stare / At the specimen Aesthetes, now happily rare."

In *Punch* and other satires of the period, then, *aesthete* refers to a number of artistic types—to the dreamy, languid, soft-voiced Mr. Rose; to "the Fleshly Poet," Rossetti or Swinburne or an indeterminate Pre-Raphaelite; to the apostle of high-art or culture; to the Kyrle Man determined to bring a dado, "a simple-sweet toon," or "a sniff of this Lily" to the lower classes; or to the "aesthetic" lady, with her flowing gown, languorous pose, and "intense" expression. What these types have in common is affectation and unnaturalness—the pose of the aesthete, who may be either innocent and absurd or evil and dangerous.

Nonsatiric definitions of the aesthete also stress his affectation. For example, a review of Wilde's *Poems* (1881) defines an aesthete as one "who pretends to derive the same moral satisfaction from a certain pattern or color in china that other people do from the contemplation of an heroic or virtuous action; who declines to have his hair cut by a barber because it is 'part of himself'; with whom an ill-assorted marriage does not mean incompatibility of temper, but of complexion; and who orders a restaurant waiter to bring him, not roast beef and potatoes, but an all-satisfying lily."[16] The editorial statement "in earnest" in *Punch* (7 Jan. 1882), presumably by F. C. Burnand, who was editor at the time, reads:

> The word "Aestheticism" has been perverted from its original meaning; *i.e.* the perception of all that is good, pure, and beautiful in Nature and in Art, and, as now vulgarly applied, it has come in a slang sort of way to stand for an effeminate, invertebrate, sensuous sentimentally-Christian, but thoroughly Pagan taste in literature and art, which delights in the idea of the resuscitation of the Great God Pan, in Swinburnean songs at their highest fever-pitch, in the mystic ravings of a BLAKE, the affectation of a ROSSETTI, the *Charmides* and revoltingly pan-theistic *Rosa Mystica* of OSCAR WILDE, the *Songs of Passion and Pain* and other similar mock-hysterical imitations of the "Mighty Masters." VICTOR HUGO, OUIDA, SWINBURNE, BURNE-JONES, have much to answer for.

Another definition hostile to the aesthete is that of Frederic Harrison: "What is it to be an Aesthete? Is it not to air one's zeal for Art, not out of genuine love of beauty, but out of fashion and love of display, in order to be like our neighbours or to be unlike our neighbours, in the wantonness of a noisy life and a full pocket?"[17] To these may be added James McNeill Whistler's attack on the aesthetic movement in his "Ten O'Clock" lecture of 1885. Using *aesthete* in *Punch's* sense of "dilettante" or "amateur," Whistler warns, "The Dilettante stalks abroad. The amateur is loosed. The voice of the aesthete is heard in the land, and the catastrophe is upon us." Whistler, who was himself frequently satirized as an aesthete, on another occasion used *aesthete* to designate a kind of agreeable loafer; he called a former houseguest "the prince of parasites! . . . A genius, a musician, the first of the 'Aesthetes,' before the silly name was invented. He hadn't anything to do—he didn't do anything for me—but decorate the dinner-table, arrange the flowers, and then play the piano, and talk, and make himself amiable."[18]

Though attacked and parodied, the aesthetes were in the early 1880s receiving some critical acclaim. Pater used *aesthetic* to refer to the detached, sensitive, flexible education required by the New Cyrenaicism.[19] Swinburne criticized Whistler's comments in the "Ten O'Clock" lecture, noting that Whistler himself can be called an aesthete, for "not merely the only accurate meaning, but the only possible meaning, of that word is nothing more, but nothing less, than this—an intelligent, appreciative, quick-witted person; in a word, as the lexicon has it, 'one who perceives.' "[20] Appreciative allusions to the aesthetes were appearing in reviews of around 1880, one expressing gratitude to Ruskin, Morris, and the Pre-Raphaelites, who taught us "that it is only by following Nature that we can ultimately conquer her," that "the Aesthetic Revolution is an accomplished fact," for it has aroused the public to the need for beauty, "and the era of culture has at last set in."[22] A review of Burnand's *The Colonel*, which attacked aesthetic fanaticism, complains that "the satire is rather ill-directed":

> It is impossible to feel very indignant with an honest fellow's wife because she is subdued to admiration of a particular school in art. It is impossible to feel that the adventurer himself has committed any deadly sin, or is deserving of condign punishment, because he is the author of "Lady Mine" or of "Sir Tristram"—because the women of his choice are limp and melancholy—because he dines, somewhat slily, at an excellent restaurant, when he is professing that he "seldom eats," and that a heavy-headed flower is "all he wants."

Similarly, a review of *Patience* shows appreciation for the aesthetes, "who have had the beauty," though "the Philistines . . . have had the wit" and "must consider themselves fortunate in having both Mr. Gilbert and Mr. Burnand upon their side."[23]

A book-length study of the aesthetes, Walter Hamilton's *The Aesthetic Movement in England* (1882), appeared during the aesthetic movement; like other critics sympathetic to the aesthetes, Hamilton believes that "too many people know of the aesthetes only through *Patience* or *The Colonel.*" He admits that some "over-enthusiastic apostles" of aestheticism make themselves absurd, but the true aesthetes "are they who pride themselves upon having found out what is really beautiful in nature and art." According to Hamilton, the movement originated with Ruskin and the Pre-Raphaelite Brotherhood (P.R.B.); its poets include Dante Gabriel Rossetti, William Michael Rossetti, Thomas Woolner, William Morris, Algernon Swinburne, Arthur O'Shaughnessy, and Oscar Wilde. Hamilton dislikes the term "Aesthetic Movement," and uses it, interestingly enough, only "because it is generally accepted and understood"; he prefers to call the movement "a Renaissance of Mediaeval Art and Culture." Drawing on his knowledge of the aims of the P.R.B., the works exhibited at the Grosvenor Gallery from 1878 to 1881, and the contemporary debates on art, Hamilton lists the following characteristics of the aesthetic movement: (1) a rejection of conventional approaches to art and a desire to work faithfully from nature; (2) a hatred of vulgarity; (3) a "union of the arts of poetry and painting"; (4) influences from both medieval and Japanese art; (5) subdued and melancholy tones; and (6) a tendency to sensuous subjects (pp. vi–viii, iii, 23–30).

By 1882 the aesthetes had achieved a kind of respectability in the eyes of their critics. Even Robert Buchanan, who in 1871 had written an extremely abusive review of Rossetti and "The Fleshly School of Poetry," declared in 1882 that the fleshly school had grown "saner, purer, and more truly impassioned in the cause of humanity." As examples, he offers Swinburne, who left "the pastoral region shepherded by the impeccable Gautier" and rose "to heights of clear and beautiful purpose"; Morris, who "needs no apology"; and Rossetti, who "never was a fleshly poet at all; never, at any rate, fed upon the poisonous honey of French art."[24]

The objects of abuse in the 1890s were no longer called "aesthetes" but "decadents." In *Punch* the worshippers of the peacock feather and the lily were replaced by "The Decadent Guys," who contemplated not passion flowers but rotting "cabbage-stalks that lay dreaming themselves daintily to death in the gutter at their feet."[25] Generally it was assumed that in England the decadence was an outgrowth of aestheticism, so that the term *aesthetic*, when it appeared, was often associated with abnormality and perversion. More than one critic, especially after the trial of Wilde, pointed to the "aesthetic craze" as the source of the "morbid, uncleanly, and unnatural" in art.[26] Thus Frank Harris refers to "epicene aesthetes" in his biography of Wilde, and G. K. Chesterton accuses the aesthetes of having a "diseased pride," praising social decay "as the decay of a corpse is praised by worms."[27]

If one looks for the element these disparate definitions of aesthete have in common, he finds the idea of a person devoted to beauty above all else, one to whom art takes precedence over religious faith or social and political concerns. It can be argued that all artists fit this definition, but what distinguishes the aesthete from other artists is the degree of his devotion to art. The "religion of art" is a cliché, but a useful one. For example, Arnold can be called an aesthete; Browning can not. Although in *The Ring and the Book* Browning says that "art remains the one way possible / Of speaking truth," by telling it "obliquely" and thus representing truly, as nothing else can, the ambiguity of human experience; and although he assigns to the artist the exalted role of shaping the book (the fact of experience) into the ring (art), Browning's final faith is not in art, but in love, also symbolized by the ring. On the other hand, in *Culture and Anarchy* Arnold not only assigns to art the place of providing form to otherwise chaotic experience but he also says that art and intellect—not religious faith or human love—are the sources of sweetness and light. In finally placing art above other human concerns, Arnold, Ruskin, Rossetti, Morris, Whistler, Pater, Wilde, Moore, James, and a host of artists of the 1890s, including Beardsley, Symons, and Yeats, are aesthetes; and the major Romantic poets (with the possible exception of Keats)—Carlyle, Tennyson, and Browning—are not; nor is Bernard Shaw.

With this tentative definition of aesthete in mind, one must, I think, then divide the aesthetes into two groups: one which sees the purpose of art as essentially a moral one; the other that divorces the purpose of art from morality. The first derives almost directly from the English Romantic movement and looks to the Middle Ages as the last great flowering of art; it includes Ruskin, Rossetti, the Pre-Raphaelites, and Morris. The latter group also can be seen as a part of English Romanticism, but it is French influenced and eclectic, absorbing elements from impressionism, symbolism, and decadence. Swinburne, Whistler, and Pater are the major English influences of this branch of the aesthetic movement, which also includes Moore, Wilde, Beardsley, Symons, and various other "decadent" contributors to *The Yellow Book* and *The Savoy*. The aesthetic movement was made up of both groups of artists who, in spite of widely varying techniques and allegiances to other artistic movements, had one belief in common: that, in a world where religious, social, and moral values had collapsed, art was, if not an absolute, at least a tentative answer to the need for a faith. The essential doctrinal point separating the two groups is whether or not art has a moral function. Though neither group believes that art should be overtly didactic, those whom I will call the moral aesthetes see the purpose of art to be ultimately a moral one, i.e., of social value, capable of producing reforms in society. Those whom I will call the fin-de-siècle aesthetes insist on a separation of art and morality.[28] They believe that art is of no social use: it will not promote brotherly love or social awareness, or make mean lives lovelier, or produce happier workers, or create more beautiful cities. It may incidentally serve a moral function in that it refines the senses, ennobles, or, as Baudelaire says, gives man an idea of the perfection forever lost to him; but this function is not a part of the poet's intention.

An examination of Shaw's relationship to both branches of this movement constitutes the remainder of my study. I do not mean to imply that Shaw was an aesthete, because his faith was never in art alone; he sought not artistic but political or religious answers to social and metaphysical problems. Nor do I wish to join the trend of praising Shaw's artistry at the expense of his ideas: I would not like to be a part of the compact by which great works of art are revered "in consideration of abrogating their meaning; so that the reverend rector can agree with the prophet Micah as to his inspired style without being committed to any complicity in Micah's furiously Radical opinions" (Epistle Dedicatory, *M&S*, p. xxxiii). But it is my belief that those opinions are better understood if one comprehends the milieu out of which they arose.

A Beardsley poster, drawn in 1894 as an advertisement for Shaw's *Arms and the Man* at the Avenue Theatre, suggests that the lives of the fin-de-siècle aesthetes and Shaw touched; and on at least one occasion Shaw directly linked himself with the *Yellow Book* era: he called himself "a relic of a bygone phase of affectation marked by Yellow Books, Keynote novels, Beardsley, John Lane and other dusty relics of the day before yesterday."[29]

PART I

SHAW AND THE MORAL AESTHETES

Chapter I

RUSKIN, MORRIS, AND SHAW

ERNARD SHAW can easily be seen as akin to the moral aesthetes and as part of the "art for the sake of social betterment" movement. This "moral" and, in general, early phase of the aesthetic movement traces its immediate origins to John Ruskin, whose theories furnished a foundation for Pre-Raphaelite beliefs, including those of the artist-socialist, William Morris. Shaw regarded both Ruskin and Morris as poet-prophets with "a great power of seeing through vulgar illusions, and a capacity for a higher morality than has yet been established in any civilized community" (Preface, *Androcles*, p. 31). Though he praised their social consciousness over their efforts on behalf of art, much of his theory of art is based on the ideas of Ruskin and Morris.

In the preface to *Major Barbara* Shaw calls Ruskin and Morris "aristocrats with a developed sense of life," who "have enormous social appetites and very fastidious personal ones," and who demand a social change for aesthetic reasons.

They are not content with handsome houses: they want handsome cities. They are not content with bediamonded wives and blooming daughters: they complain because the charwoman is badly dressed, because the laundress smells of gin, because the sempstress is anemic, because every man they meet is not a friend and every woman not a romance. They turn up their noses at their neighbor's drains, and are made ill by the architecture of their neighbor's houses. Trade patterns made to suit vulgar people do not please them (and they can

3

get nothing else) : they cannot sleep nor sit at ease upon "slaughtered" cabinet makers' furniture. The very air is not good enough for them: there is too much factory smoke in it. They even demand abstract conditions: justice, honor, a noble moral atmosphere, a mystic nexus to replace the cash nexus. Finally they declare that . . . to rob and pill by the hands of the policeman, the bailiff, and the soldier, and to underpay them meanly for doing it, is not a good life, but rather fatal to all possibility of even a tolerable one. (Pp. 213–14)

Significantly, the complaints and demands which Shaw attributes to Ruskin and Morris are also those Shaw himself made. He advocated dress reform, temperance, and improved sanitation; he called for economic and religious reform which would in turn lead to more beautiful houses and cities; he even found "the very air . . . not good enough" and spoke out against air pollution at the Annual Meeting of the Coal Smoke Abatement Society in 1911.[1]

Shaw's most extensive commentary on Ruskin occurs in "Ruskin's Politics" (1919). In this speech Shaw finds Ruskin's progress from artist to social critic to prophet illustrated in the portraits at the Ruskin Centenary Exhibition of the Royal Academy. In the early portraits of Ruskin, Shaw sees a resemblance to Mozart; later he detects a likeness to social critics (his examples are John Stuart Mill and Grant Allen); finally he sees a resemblance to "God as depicted in Blake's Book of Job." Ruskin began, Shaw says, "as an artist with an interest in art—exactly as I did myself, by the way—[and] was inevitably driven back to economics, and to the conviction that your art would never come right whilst your economics were wrong." He concludes that Ruskin's politics were a kind of antidemocratic communism and that Ruskin can therefore be described as the prophet of Bolshevism.[2]

Although Shaw does not discuss it, he also agreed with numerous of Ruskin's aesthetic theories. Probably the single most important idea about art that Shaw shared with Ruskin was the conviction that "if a great thing can be done at all, it can be done easily. . . . If a man can compose at all, he can compose at once, or rather he must compose in spite of himself."[3] One of Shaw's earliest and cleverest expressions of this idea occurs in his novel *Cashel Byron's Profession* (1882) when Cashel, a prizefighter, delivers a long extemporaneous speech correcting Herr Abendgasse's paper on "The

True in Art." Cashel, who thoroughly understands the art of fighting, contends that "a man that understands one art understands
every art"; and he offers this advice to all artists:

> Striving and struggling is the worst way you could set about doing any-
> thing. It gives a man a bad style, and weakens him. It shews that he
> dont believe in himself much. . . . Now, nothing can be what you
> might call artistically done, if it's done with an effort. If a thing cant
> be done light and easy, steady and certain, let it not be done at all. . . .
> In all professions any work that shews signs of labor, straining, yearn-
> ing . . . or effort of any kind, is work beyond the man's strength that
> does it, and therefore not well done." (Pp. 91–92)

As an example, Cashel points to the poor fighting stance of a figure
in a Pre-Raphaelite painting, who clearly "doesnt know how to
fight . . . because he's all strain and stretch; because he isnt at
his ease; because he carries the weight of his body as foolishly as
one of the ladies here would carry a hod of bricks; because he isnt
safe, steady, and light on his pins, as he would be if he could forget
himself for a minute and leave his body to find its proper balance of
its own accord" (p. 93). Cashel's criticism here echoes Ruskin's
complaint that the Pre-Raphaelites were "working too hard" at
their art and thus producing an overwrought effect.[4] That Shaw
was in accord with Ruskin's and Cashel's theory that great art is
effortless can be demonstrated by the frequent occurrence of the
idea in Shaw's essays and speeches. He characteristically maintains that "fine art of any sort is either easy or impossible." To a
group of school children he explained, "To me there is nothing in
writing a play: anyone can write one if he has the necessary natural
turn for it; and if he hasnt he cant: that is all there is to it." And
Stephen Winsten records Shaw's saying that "I only like to do
things that I find easy, like writing plays. William Morris was like
that."[5]

Shaw was also in sympathy with Ruskin's theory that art has
an ethical basis. In the 1883 preface to *Modern Painters* Ruskin
wrote that "beautiful things are useful to men because they are
beautiful, and for the sake of their beauty only." However, his defense of beauty for its own sake is to separate art from commercialism, not from morality, which for Ruskin was the end of art. In

Modern Painters he distinguished between "Aesthesis," beauty appealing to the senses alone, and "Theoria," beauty concerned with "the moral perception and appreciation of ideas of beauty"; he denied "that the impressions of beauty are in any way sensual; they are neither sensual nor intellectual, but moral."[6] He also believed that great art arises out of an ethical nature, that nobility of subject is the first requisite for artistic greatness, and that only a noble soul can produce great art, for an artist's faults of character show in his work.[7] Shaw did not, as we shall see in later chapters, agree with the details of Ruskin's art theories; for example, he accepted the primarily sensual nature of fine art and believed that an unscrupulous man such as Louis Dubedat or the Shakespear of *The Dark Lady of the Sonnets* could produce art. But, like Ruskin, he was convinced that art should produce a moral effect, which to Shaw sometimes meant social reform and sometimes religious faith.

Ruskin's greatest influence on Shaw was exerted indirectly, through William Morris. A follower of Ruskin, Morris lamented the disappearance of art in a materialistic, exploitative, and ugly age, and turned to social reform as the necessary first step to artistic health. Just as Ruskin came to believe "that your art would never come right whilst your economics were wrong," Morris came to believe that only a revolution abolishing social classes and giving all "a fair share of the good and evil of life" could provide a healthy atmosphere in which art could thrive.[8] The aesthetic utopia depicted in his *News from Nowhere* (1890) began, significantly, with revolution and economic reform. With such reform Morris hoped to mend the present "fatal schism between art and daily life," so that all men could become artists, with creative, fruitful work and pleasant leisure.[9] Although he distinguished between intellectual arts, such as paintings and sculpture, which are of no material use and which "address themselves wholly to the mind of man," and decorative and ornamental arts—such as pottery-making, glasswork, weaving, and printing—which have a material use in one's daily life, he insisted that "in all times when the Arts were in a healthy condition there was an intimate connexion between these two kinds of art."[10]

Predictably, Shaw respected Morris's socialism more than his aestheticism. Shaw's final estimate of Morris is clear in a 1934 letter to *The New Statesman and Nation*. To H. G. Wells's description of Morris as "a poet and decorator" Shaw answered, "That is not the significance of William Morris to us; there are plenty of poets and decorators about. Morris's significant specialty was his freely expressed opinion that idle capitalists are 'damned thieves.' And the word damned was more than mere decoration."[11] Shaw especially took to heart Morris's statement that "no man is good enough to be another man's master"; he quotes it in his repudiation of imperialistic rule in the preface to *John Bull's Other Island* (p. 63) and refers to it in a speech "Property or Slavery?" (1913), in which he calls Morris "the greatest man who came forward in the nineteenth century to champion Socialism."[12] Reviewing J. W. Mackail's biography of Morris (1899), Shaw finds fault with Mackail for emphasizing Morris's artistic over his socialistic side, for seeing Morris "too much from the Burne-Jones point of view" and not enough in terms of Morris's socialistic "street corner exploits" (*Portraits*, pp. 208–9). For example, Mackail says that translating the *Odyssey* turned Morris away from revolutionary socialism, but Shaw says that witnessing the battle of Trafalgar Square in 1887 did it. Shaw consistently maintained that Morris's socialism provided mental stimulation not offered by his artistic endeavors. In *William Morris As I Knew Him* (1936) Shaw explains that Morris's art was effortless: "The knowledge that he could go on writing lovely lines for ever as the idle single of an empty day must have finally changed that exultant phrase to a self-criticism." Even the sagas offered no challenge: "All this was literature, romance, art for art's sake, done with a natural facility that cost him nothing." Socialism, on the other hand, exercised his mind and changed "the idle singer" to a "prophet and a saint" (pp. 47–52). Thus in Morris, Shaw found another living example of the poet-prophet—one influenced by Ruskin and akin in purpose to Shaw himself.

Nevertheless, Shaw respected Morris's artistic endeavors and praised them in his art criticism. In a review of an arts and crafts exhibit of 1888 he says that Morris's illuminated manuscript pages show "what Mr. Morris can do with his valuable time in his serious moments, when he is not diverting himself with wall-decoration, epic story-telling, revolutionary journalism and oratory, fishing and other frivolities of genius." In this review Shaw approves of the arts and crafts movement and deplores "the silly British pictures, the vicious foreign pictures, signboards all of them of the wasted talent and perverted ambition of men who might have been passably useful as architects, engineers, potters, cabinetmakers, smiths, or bookbinders."[13] In "William Morris as Actor and Dramatist" (*OTN*, 2:209–13) he praises Morris's musical ear, the modernity of his tastes in furnishings and book designs, and his "prose wordweaving"; he says that "Morris would have written for the stage if there had been any stage that a poet and artist could write for" and that he had, in fact, written a play which was a highly entertaining "topical extravaganza" for the Socialist League. Morris figures in a conjecture by Shaw about "What Socialism Will Be Like": Morris and Company is used as an example of the expensive hobby a great man could pursue in a socialistic state. Shaw argues that, after every man is prosperous enough "to buy good bread and good clothes," a rich man could, as Morris did in a nonsocialistic state, spend "his superfluity of income on something no government could do."[14]

Morris's efforts to make creative artists or artisans of all people make up a part of Shaw's own social vision. For example, in his defense of an aesthetic education in the preface to *Misalliance* (1910), where he maintains that "we all grow up stupid and mad to just the extent to which we have not been artistically educated," Shaw presents a Morrisian argument for an art-conscious world (pp. 86 ff.). Because we are so accustomed to boredom and ugliness, he says, we suspect that fine art is somehow lascivious; as a result we are ignorant of art, and "all the wholesome conditions which art imposes on appetite are waived: instead of cultivated men and women restrained by a thousand delicacies, repelled by ugliness, chilled by vulgarity, horrified by coarseness, deeply and sweetly moved by the graces that art has revealed to them and nursed in them, we get indiscriminate rapacity in pursuit of pleasure and a parade of the grossest stimulations in catering for it." The present hope for art lies in the fact that modern technology—producing the pianola, photography, book printing, and the phonograph—puts "a vast body of art now within the reach of everybody." Implicit in this argument is Morris's contention that, until art becomes a way of life for everyone, society will suffer. It is no accident that in this essay Shaw uses Morris's definition of art—"the expression of pleasure in work" (p. 100).

A similar argument appears in Shaw's last completed novel, *An Unsocial Socialist* (1883), where the protagonist, Sidney Trefusis, envisions aesthetic as well as economic reform. Trefusis hopes for a future in which art is no longer a luxury, available only to the rich, but is instead a part of every man's daily life.

> Photography perfected in its recently discovered power of reproducing color as well as form! Historical pictures replaced by photographs of *tableaux vivants* formed and arranged by trained actors and artists, and used chiefly for the instruction of children! Nine-tenths of painting as we understand it at present extinguished by the competition of these photographs, and the remaining tenth only holding its own against them by dint of extraordinary excellence! Our mistuned and unplayable organs and pianofortes replaced by harmonious instruments, as manageable as barrel organs! Works of fiction superseded by interesting company and conversation, and made obsolete by the human mind outgrowing the childishness that delights in the tales told by grown-up children such as novelists and their like! An end to the silly confusion, under the one name of Art, of the tomfoolery and make-believe of our play hours with the higher methods of teaching men to know themselves! Every artist an amateur, and a consequent return to the healthy old disposition to look on every man who makes art a means of money-making as a vagabond not to be entertained as an equal by honest men! (Pp. 160–61)

Trefusis is sometimes taken to be Shaw's anti-artist,[15] but this speech does not come from a man who hates art, but from one who refuses to enjoy an art which caters to the values of a corrupt society. Nor does Trefusis hate artists: one of his best friends is the Pre-Raphaelite and socialist, Donovan Brown, whose character is probably drawn from that of William Morris.

The artist Donovan Brown is referred to not only in *An Unsocial Socialist* but also in Shaw's first novel, *Immaturity* (1879), where the aesthete Hawkshaw argues with the young clerk Smith about the merits of Browne's art. (Browne loses the final *e* in his name in the later novel.) Hawkshaw says that Browne's pictures "overflow" with "the intense devotion of the Byzantine painters"; Smith disagrees:

9

On the contrary . . . they dont contain one scrap of it. Angelico and Filippo Lippi and the rest of them painted as if they were sent on earth to glorify God. Mr Donovan Browne paints as if he were self-dedicated to the task of painting beautiful pictures, or, in other words, of ennobling his fellow-creatures; and if we were not tired of the part of his genius which belongs to our own age, and blind to that which belongs to the infinite epoch of the highest art, we should draw a triumphant contrast instead of an apologetic comparison between him and an admirable but obsolete school which owed its concentration to mental narrowness. (*Immaturity*, p. 270)

That Browne is, as Morris was, a "Pre-Raphaelite" painter is obvious from Hawkshaw's reference to Browne's medieval intensity and from Smith's reference to the "apologetic comparison" drawn between Browne and medieval artists. The reference to Browne's desire to ennoble mankind rather than to glorify God might also apply to Morris. The identification of Browne with Morris becomes less conjectural in *An Unsocial Socialist,* where we learn that Donovan Brown has become a socialist, as had Morris and Shaw between the writing of *Immaturity* and *An Unsocial Socialist.*[16] Brown is, in fact, the author of the socialist petition Trefusis is circulating for signatures. Trefusis explains that he and Brown became friends in an economic dispute over the value of a painting, and that "subsequently [Brown] fell into my views" (p. 215).

Shaw later created a dramatic portrait of Morris in the character of Apollodorus in *Caesar and Cleopatra.* Though Apollodorus was clearly not designed in every detail as a faithful portrait of Morris,[17] there are nevertheless unmistakable allusions to Morris. Like Morris, Apollodorus (the names rhyme) is a "patrician," a "carpet merchant," and a shop-keeper whose shop (i.e., Morris and Company) is "a temple of the arts." Apollodorus is, as Morris was in his early career, a self-confessed aesthete; his "motto is Art for Art's sake," which he calls "a universal password." Apollodorus is not only a devotee of art but also a devotee of Cleopatra, singing of the pangs of love and serving his lady with knightly gallantry, just as Morris dedicated himself to Jane Burden (Mrs. Morris), who came to represent in Morris's and Rossetti's art another type of female beauty. Among Apollodorus's attributes are some characteristics of the man of action. He is an excellent swordsman, though his valor is in defense of Cleopatra's honor and thus in Shaw's view equal to inglorious brawling. But he is bold, strong, and quick to forget a quarrel (*C&C*, p. 143). He is also generous, "overpowering" the porters by his liberal tip (p. 147). His dive into the sea at the end of act 3 inspires even Caesar's admiration. And, after the murder of Pothinus, he deserts Cleopatra and pledges his "heart and life" to Caesar (p. 184). Apollodorus's skill with the sword, the daring example of his plunge into the sea, and his friendship with Caesar are no doubt a tribute to Shaw's good friend and fellow socialist, Morris, the former "idle singer of an empty day" turned revolutionary socialist, a man of action. Therefore, though Apollodorus represents the idolater of art and love attacked in the preface to *Three Plays for Puritans,* he does not receive the savage treatment Shaw threatens in that preface.[18]

Morris, and Ruskin before him, were for Shaw not only living examples of poet-prophets but also formulators of a theory of Pre-Raphaelite art. Neither Ruskin nor Morris was a member of the original Pre-Raphaelite Brotherhood; but both were associated with the Pre-Raphaelite movement, Ruskin as sponsor and perhaps original inspiration of it,[19] and Morris as one of the perpetuators of it in the 1870s and 1880s. And both were "Pre-Raphaelite" in that they were convinced that the last period of ethical health and artistic productivity was the Middle Ages. In "The Nature of Gothic" Ruskin outlines three stages of architectural ornament: (1) "Servile" (Greek, Ninevite, and Egyptian), where the workman was a slave executing his master's orders; (2) "Constitutional" (medieval), where each workman expressed the individuality of his soul while admitting his imperfection and testifying to "God's greater glory"; and (3) "Revolutionary" (Renaissance), where each man admitted of no greater power than his own personality and the resulting loss of faith led to his enslavement to false political, economic, and aesthetic ideals.[20] Morris traces similar periods of art in an 1882 lecture, "Architecture and History"; he describes (1) the classical period, in which a slave society produced simple original art; (2) the feudal period, in which a genuine craftsmanship grew out of the guild system, and the artist "worked for no master save the public, . . . made his wares from beginning to end him-

self, and sold them himself to a man who was going to use them";
and (3) the modern period, an era of religious, social, and artistic
decline beginning with the Tudors.[21]

Both Ruskin and Morris demand an end to the degrading, ma-
chine-like existence brought about by capitalism and the factory
system. Ruskin speaks of the corruption and perversion arising
from the "degradation of the operative into a machine": "It is not
that men are ill fed, but that they have no pleasure in the work by
which they make their bread, and therefore look to wealth as the
only means of pleasure. It is not that men are pained by the scorn
of the upper classes, but they cannot endure their own; for they
feel that the kind of labour to which they are condemned is verily
a degrading one, and makes them less than men." By encouraging
a workman to express his uniqueness and thus accepting his human
imperfection, society loses the "engine-turned precision" of modern
buildings, furniture, and dress, but it gains a genuine art, arising
out of reverence for human life.[22] Morris similarly argues that
"England has of late been too much busied with the counting-house
and not enough with the workshop," that the "greed of unfair gain"
has replaced art with "luxury and show." But whereas Ruskin
pleads for a return to medieval ideals of "noble reverence" and
noblesse oblige, Morris wants a society which has no poverty, no
masters and servants, and no unrewarding division of labor—a
society which provides men pleasurable work.[23]

Shaw essentially agrees with the Ruskin-Morris analysis of medieval and modern life. In "William Morris as Actor and Dramatist" (OTN, 2: 210) he says that the thirteenth century was "the
most advanced point" in art and that the nineteenth was "the most
backward one"; and his essay "On Going to Church," in the first
issue of Arthur Symons's The Savoy (1896), is heavily indebted to
the medievalism of Ruskin and Morris. At the beginning of this
essay, Shaw rejects art "produced by the teapot, the bottle, or the
hypodermic syringe" and recommends, instead of such stimulants,
going to church for the rest and recreation artistic productivity requires. But only a beautiful church offers aesthetic stimulation,
and most modern churches are ugly—conventional, barren monuments to commerce. Shaw prefers medieval churches which were
sanctuaries "shielded by God's presence from pride and glory and

all the other burdens of life." Like Ruskin and Morris, Shaw sees the Renaissance as the beginning of a decline in art. With capitalism and religious scepticism came a loss of artistic power, so that today "under modern commercial conditions, it is impossible to get from the labour in the building-trade that artistic quality in the actual masonry which makes a good mediaeval building independent of applied ornament." One can find, however, evidence of a reawakening of religion and art in certain village churches built in modern times by the faithful, and in the stained glass of Morris and Burne-Jones, who show that "the decay of religious art from the sixteenth century to the nineteenth was not caused by any atrophy of the artistic faculty, but was an eclipse of religion by science and commerce."[24]

This essay, linking medieval art and a living religion, suggests Shaw's major debt to Ruskin and Morris and at the same time points up the major difference between them. To Shaw the religious impulse was crucial; to Ruskin and Morris, art was both the reason for, and the result of, social or moral change. After the revolutionary restructuring of society, Morris envisions healthy, beautiful men and women; gorgeous landscapes; attractive buildings and furnishings; and generous, hearty good-fellowship. Notably, Shaw's utopia is not one of sensuous beauty but of contemplation, where art is abandoned with the toys of childhood.

Chapter II

THE PRE-RAPHAELITES AND SHAW

HOUGH SHAW'S CONCEPT of "Pre-Raphaelite" was influenced most by Ruskin and Morris, it was also influenced by the Pre-Raphaelite Brotherhood. Founded in 1848, the P.R.B. had seven original members—the painters William Holman Hunt, John Everett Millais, F. G. Stephens, and James Collinson; Dante Gabriel Rossetti and his brother, William Michael Rossetti; and a sculptor and poet, Thomas Woolner. They were united in opposition to Academy art; and they were also dedicated, Holman Hunt says, to following the "innocent spirit," the "simplicity," the "frank expression and unaffected grace" of Italian art before "the showy followers of Michael Angelo had grafted their Dead Sea fruit on the vital tree" of art.[1] By 1856 the original P.R.B. had lost its unity: Millais was elected to the Royal Academy; Collinson, a convert to Roman Catholicism, had resigned and gone into seclusion; and Rossetti turned to new disciples—Morris, Burne-Jones, and their coterie at Oxford. However, though the brotherhood itself quickly dissolved, the Pre-Raphaelite movement continued as Hunt, Millais, and Rossetti gained fame and as Morris and Burne-Jones perpetuated it in a new and more exotic phase.

In the 1880s and early 1890s, Shaw reviewed Pre-Raphaelite art. These reviews, which appeared in *The World* and in Annie Besant's journal, *Our Corner,* stress the serious intentions of the Pre-Raphaelites as well as their passion for color, meticulous attention to detail, and naïveté in point of view. According to Shaw, Holman

Hunt paints with a childlike vision, moral earnestness, conscientious workmanship, and glowing color. But he is too "matter of fact"—too literal and too conventional; for example, "The Light of the World" is not a symbol of anything "but a picture of a symbol taken literally," presenting "the ideal Christ of pure superstition in his prettiest shape."[2] Similarly, Millais is an excellent workman who, unfortunately, sacrifices intellectual content for richness of color, so that his landscapes "tempt one to declare that no man has ever seen anything that Millais could not paint, although many men have painted things that he cannot see."[3] Shaw praises Burne-Jones but finds fault with him, as Ruskin had, in his tendency toward an overwrought effect. In an *Art Journal* article of 1891, Shaw speaks of the "transcendant expressiveness" of the work of Burne-Jones's studio assistant, J. M. Strudwick, who, being unable to concentrate on technique alone—"execution for execution's sake"—exercised his genius in inventive and carefully conceived art. Shaw also praises Rossetti, whose "wealth of color, poetic conception, and the fascination of the faces" is marred only by his "want of thoroughness as a draughtsman" and his stylized treatment of female figures.[4]

Shaw's fascination with the Pre-Raphaelite lady is evident in his description of his "Mystic Betrothal" to William Morris's daughter, May Morris,[5] and in his dramatic representation of a former Pre-Raphaelite lady, Henry Higgins's mother in *Pygmalion*, who "was brought up on Morris and Burne Jones." In her drawing room are Morris wallpapers and fabrics, "a few good oil-paintings from the exhibitions in the Grosvenor Gallery thirty years ago (the Burne Jones, not the Whistler side of them)," and "a portrait of Mrs. Higgins as she was when she defied fashion in her youth in one of the beautiful Rossettian costumes which, when caricatured by people who did not understand, led to the absurdities of popular estheticism in the eighteen-seventies" (*Pygmalion*, p. 244). In "How I Became a Public Speaker" Shaw refers presumably to one of the "absurdities" in his account of his first speaking success: at the Zetetical Society he answered a paper on art "by a lady in the esthetic dress momentarily fashionable in Morrisan cliques just then." He furnishes no details about the content of this speech, but admits that he "wiped the floor with that meeting" (*Sketches*, p. 57).

Though Shaw objected to the "popular estheticism in the eighteen-seventies," to Hunt's conventional morality, to Millais's lack of intellectual content, to Burne-Jones's overwrought effect, and to Rossetti's want of draftsmanship and stylized females, he nevertheless was willing to identify himself with the Pre-Raphaelite movement in the preface to *Plays Pleasant*. In this preface he says that *Candida* was written after his 1894 trip to Florence, "where I [like Ruskin and Morris before him] occupied myself with the religious art of the Middle Ages and its destruction by the Renascence." On a previous trip to Birmingham, he attended a Pre-Raphaelite exhibit; observing the church windows of Morris and Burne-Jones, he found that "on the whole, Birmingham was more hopeful than the Italian cities; for the art it had to shew me was the work of living men." The preface continues, "When my subsequent visit to Italy found me practising the playwright's craft, the time was ripe for a modern pre-Raphaelite play. Religion was alive again, coming back upon men, even upon clergymen, with such power that not the Church of England itself could keep it out" (p. vi). What this claim to be a Pre-Raphaelite dramatist means can best be understood by comparing Pre-Raphaelite art theory with Shaw's, which encompasses virtually every belief of the P.R.B.

The major principle of the P.R.B. was that announced in the first issue of *The Germ*: "to encourage and enforce an entire adherence to the simplicity of nature." Essays in *The Germ* admonish the artist to make "pure transcripts and faithful studies from nature, instead of conventionalities and feeble reminiscences from the Old Masters."[6] Ruskin likewise maintains that "the Pre-Raphaelites imitate no pictures: they paint from nature only,"[7] as did William Michael Rossetti, who in his introduction to an 1899 reprint of *The Germ* explained the name "Pre-Raphaelite."

It would be a mistake to suppose, because they called themselves Praeraphaelites, that they seriously disliked the works produced by Raphael; but they disliked the works produced by Raphael's uninspired satellites, and were resolved to find out, by personal study and practice, what their own several faculties and adaptabilities might be, without

16

being bound by rules and big-wiggeries founded upon the performances of Raphael or of any one. They were to have no master except their own powers of mind and hand, and their own first-hand study of Nature. (P. 6)

The meaning of "adherence to . . . nature" varies among the Pre-Raphaelites: to Hunt it means a faithful rendering of physical nature, often as background in a painting which is otherwise based on a purely imaginative image; for example, for his scriptural subjects he made trips to the Holy Land to observe "oriental proprieties" (i.e., exactness of costume, terrain, climate, etc.), so that he could paint "from Nature, . . . not indirectly from sketches, but direct from the scene itself on to the canvas of the final picture."[8] To F. G. Stephens the return to nature implies looking at "the poetry of the things about us," observing and capturing modern life instead of looking to the past.[9] D. G. Rossetti does not limit "painting from nature" to contemporary subjects but applies it to medieval subjects as well when he says that Morris's painting of Sir Tristram "is being done all from nature of course," just as Morris says that Rossetti's "The Blessed Damosel" is "strong, unforced and full of nature."[10] Ruskin correctly observed that the paintings produced by adherents to the Pre-Raphaelite principle "will be as various as the kinds of truth which each artist will apprehend."[11]

Just as this relativism allowed Ruskin to write about Turner in his essay on "Pre-Raphaelitism," so it allowed Shaw to call himself a Pre-Raphaelite dramatist, advocating a return to nature and expressing hatred of academicism. His first art review for *Our Corner* (June, 1885) significantly begins with an attack on the Academy: "During the past month Art has suffered an unusually severe blow at the hands of the Royal Academy by the opening of the annual exhibition at Burlington House." And his statement that " 'for art's sake' alone I would not face the toil of writing a single sentence" is a part of an assault on academicism in art in the Epistle Dedicatory to *Man and Superman*. Shaw explains that his objections to "literary virtuosity" stem from a conviction that style is impossible without opinions. The old masters, he says, were master artists because they had something to say, and, though their ideas were eventually disproved, the effective form resulting

17

from them remained. On the other hand, academicians neglect ideas and try to paint or write or compose according to rules.

> Your Royal Academician thinks he can get the style of Giotto without Giotto's beliefs, and correct his perspective into the bargain. Your man of letters thinks he can get Bunyan's or Shakespear's style without Bunyan's conviction or Shakespear's apprehension, especially if he takes care not to split his infinitives. And so with your Doctors of Music, who, with their collections of discords duly prepared and resolved or retarded or anticipated in the manner of the great composers, think they can learn the art of Palestrina from Cherubini's treatise. . . . Your academic copier of fossils offers them to you as the latest outpouring of the human spirit, and, worst of all, kidnaps young people as pupils and persuades them that his limitations are rules, his observances dexterities, his timidities good taste, and his emptinesses purities. (P. xxxv)

This passage is a paraphrase of Pre-Raphaelite doctrine.

Following the Pre-Raphaelite distinction between realism and rules in art, Shaw distinguishes between "real" and "literary" in his rejection of conventional techniques and his defense of artistic integrity. For example, he compares Shakespeare unfavorably with Bunyan because Shakespeare's heroes and heroics are often of "paper origin," bookish and classical, whereas Bunyan's originate out of sincere conviction (*OTN*, 3: 1–3). He accuses Swinburne of expressing "in verse what he finds in books as passionately as a poet expresses what he finds in life" (*OTN*, 2: 181).[12] He condemns dramatic characters based on books rather than life, and, as if in anticipation of his own Major Barbara and Saint Joan, attacks G. Stuart Ogilvie's *The Sin of St. Hulda* because the heroine is based on other artistic renderings, when "the nearest Salvation Army barrack or London Mission will supply half a dozen saints of infinitely greater sanctity and heroism than the waxwork angel" (*OTN*, 2: 98–99). In short, his plea for dramatic characters "whose fortunes we can follow as those of a friend or enemy" (*OTN*, 2: 118), his praise of Ibsen for "the inevitable return to nature which ends all the merely technical fashions" (*Essays*, p. 139); his defense of the realism of his own characters and situations; and his attacks on formula plots, especially the "well-made" play, all stress the need for "pure transcripts . . . from nature, instead of . . . from the Old Masters." The Pre-Raphaelite doctrine advanced by Stephens could stand as a statement of Shaw's own: "Nothing can be more humble than the pretension to the observation of facts alone, and the truthful rendering of them. If we are not to depart from established principles, how are we to advance at all?"[13] In "A Dramatic Realist to His Critics" Shaw says that "all my audacious originalities are simple liftings from stores of evidence which is ready to everybody's hand. . . . I simply discovered drama in real life."[14]

Though Holman Hunt and other members of the P.R.B. denied any slavish or "prosaic reproduction" of realistic detail, their methods and their finished works often show a concern for laborious reproduction of minute detail. Ford Madox Brown complains in a diary notation of 1854 that Rossetti is "getting on slowly with his calf [in 'Found']. He paints it all like Albert Durer, hair by hair."[15] Even Rossetti in an early letter (25 November 1847) admitted that "the seed of the flower of Pre-Raphaelism was photography. . . . The execution was to be like the binocular representations of leaves that the stereoscope was then beginning to show."[16] This concern for detail made itself apparent in "Pre-Raphaelite" drama, according to an article of 1856 equating Pre-Raphaelite drama with realistic staging and "the specification of little traits and details that serve to realise the character as much as possible."[17]

Though it can be argued that Shaw's drama aims primarily at the essence rather than at the "little traits and details" of character and action, Shaw expresses a preference for minute detail in art, a preference he attributes to his "normal" eyesight. In the preface to *Plays Unpleasant* he explains that, when an eye test revealed that he had normal vision, he "naturally took this to mean that it was like everybody else's"; but he was assured instead that he "was an exceptional and highly fortunate person optically, normal sight conferring the power of seeing things accurately, and being enjoyed by only about ten per cent of the population, the remaining ninety per cent being abnormal" (p. vi). Shaw's "normal" vision is illustrated by the following anecdote from *The Sanity of Art*.

Once I had a discussion with an artist who was shewing me a clever

19

picture of his in which the parted lips in a pretty woman's face revealed what seemed to me like a mouthful of virgin snow. The painter lectured me for not consulting my eyes instead of my knowledge of facts. "You dont see the divisions in a set of teeth when you look at a person's mouth," he said: "all you see is a strip of white, or yellow, or pearl, as the case may be. But because you know, as a matter of anatomic fact, that there are divisions there, you want to have them represented by strokes in a drawing. That is just like you art critics, &c., &c." I do not think he believed me when I told him that when I looked at a row of teeth, I saw, not only the divisions between them, but their exact shape, both in contour and in modelling, just as well as I saw their general color. (*Essays*, p. 293)

Shaw would no doubt have disagreed with the critic of an 1857 Pre-Raphaelite exhibit who complained that Holman Hunt, with a "monomaniacal" love for nature, had violated visual, mental, and pictorial law by rendering "with utmost pains and detail, the eye, the beak, and the plumage of a swallow swiftly upon the wing!"[18] Shaw would have said that the critic's vision, not Hunt's painting, was at fault. He would also have defended, as Burne-Jones did in the Whistler-Ruskin trial (1878), "completeness" and detail in art over Whistler's impressionism, for Shaw criticized impressionist art on the grounds that the impressionists could not see well. In an art review of 1889, he says that "there must be many people who can see a pin where Mr. Walter Sickert cannot see a tenpenny nail."[19]

This preference for minute realistic detail does not suggest Shaw's Pre-Raphaelitism as precisely as does his belief in the moral function of art. The critical essays in *The Germ* suggest that Pre-Raphaelite art was considered, by Pre-Raphaelite theorists at least, highly moral. John Lucas Tupper in "The Subject of Art (No. 1)" uses the appeal to "mental and moral faculties" as the criterion for distinguishing between "high" and "low" art; after listing subjects suitable to the high purpose of art, he concludes, "every thing or incident in nature which excites, or may be made to excite, the mind and the heart of man as a mentally intelligent, not as a brute animal, is a subject for Fine Art." In "The Purpose and Tendency of Early Italian Art," F. G. Stephens, echoing Ruskin, says, "The Arts have always been most important moral guides. Their flourishing has always been coincident with the most wholesome period of a nation's: never with the full and gaudy bloom which but hides corruption."[20] These opinions, however, represent the more conservative element in the P.R.B. Though Holman Hunt believes that art "should unite with other powers to promote orderly purpose, and should denounce the pride of irresponsibility together with that dissectional spirit which proclaims that art has no connection with morals"; and though his pilgrimages to the Holy Land were not simply searches for authentic background for religious paintings but also expressions of religious purpose "to use my powers to make more tangible Jesus Christ's history and teaching," he also admits that art is not of necessity moral.[21] And Rossetti's parable, "Hand and Soul," which appeared in the first issue of *The Germ*, suggests that a conscious moral purpose may destroy art. "Hand and Soul" traces the career of a thirteenth-century Italian painter, who sees one by one fame, faith, and moral intent fail as guides in his art. Finally the image of his own soul appears to explain to him why his art has failed: he has listened to his mind and not to his heart. His soul assures him that real faith cannot fail him; he made a mistake in consciously attempting to do God's work. When he wanted to depict "some moral greatness that should impress the beholder," he failed because he "wouldst say coldly to the mind what God hath said to the heart warmly."[22] Thus Rossetti conceives of a divinely inspired and moral, even religious, art; but he believes that a consciously moral aim will ruin the ultimately moral effect of it. This concept of morality in art is, as we shall see in later chapters, basic in Shaw's theory of art. Whenever Shaw portrays an artist who is devoted to improving morality, that character is an unsuccessful artist; only the artist who, in Rossetti's words, does what God "hath set in thine heart to do, . . . even though thou do it without thought of Him," produces great art.

But for the major influence on Shaw's concept of Pre-Raphaelite morality one turns not to the essays in *The Germ* but to the shapers of his attitude toward medieval art. Shaw's medievalism combined the Pre-Raphaelitism of Hunt, who saw the P.R.B. as an attempt "to emulate the courageous independence of ancient art," and of Ruskin and Morris, who saw the Middle Ages as an age of faith, of social stability and artistic vitality. In his use of a modern subject in what he conceives to be a medieval spirit of independence from prescribed forms, Shaw is closer to the original aims of the P.R.B. than the second generation of Pre-Raphaelites were, with their love of what Ford Madox Ford says is best suggested by the phrase "long necks and pomegranates."[23] Shaw is in agreement with the idea that "Pre-Raphaelitism is not Pre-Raphaelism";[24] instead of using predominantly medieval subjects, as Rossetti, Morris, and Burne-Jones did, Shaw uses religious themes in a modern milieu. That Shaw considered the essence of medieval art to be the religious impulse governing it is apparent in his essay (discussed above, pp. 12-13), "On Going to Church."

Shaw's commentary on religious art culminates in the thesis developed in "The Religious Art of the Twentieth Century" and the succeeding sections of the preface to *Back to Methuselah*, where Shaw maintains that "art has never been great when it was not providing an iconography for a live religion" (p. lxxviii). Reiterating the ideas from "On Going to Church," Shaw asserts that the Middle Ages produced great art; but, after Raphael (and this choice of the dividing point between medieval and modern art is significant), an interval of unbelief caused a decline in art. Shakespeare, for example, "could not become the conscious iconographer of a religion because he had no conscious religion" (p. lxxx). However, certain artist-prophets—Michelangelo, Beethoven, and Goethe—anticipated the next religion and kept art alive; now the concept of creative evolution makes great art again possible. The preface ends with Shaw's "hope that a hundred apter and more elegant parables by younger hands will soon leave mine as far behind as the religious pictures of the fifteenth century left behind the first attempts of the early Christians at iconography" (p. lxxxvi).

According to Shaw, the new living religion is a catholic one: "There is only one religion, though there are a hundred versions of it."[25] The artist is to express this living religion in the theater, the equivalent of the medieval cathedral. The theater-church analogy, one of Shaw's favorites, is more than an analogy to him; for Shaw the theater *is* the church in which the living religion is preached: "The theatre is really the week-day church; and a good play is essentially identical with a church service as a combination

of artistic ritual, profession of faith, and sermon" (*OTN*, 1: 264).
In "Church and Stage" (*OTN*, 2: 28) he defends the representation of religious ritual on the stage, maintaining that "it is better
to tolerate the catholicly religious people who are claiming for the
theatre its share in the common spiritual heritage than to put a
weapon into the hands of the sectarianly religious people who
would make an end of the theatre altogether if they could."
Though he would save the theater from "the sectarianly religious
people," he would not save it from puritanical purging when it
defiles its holy purpose; accordingly, in the preface to *Three Plays
for Puritans* he begs that the theater be rescued from "profaneness
and immorality" by a realistic drama (p. xx). He condemns the
romantic drama which substitutes "sensuous ecstasy for intellectual
activity and honesty," the pseudoreligious and all-for-love plays
popular in the Victorian theater. Finally, Shaw was able to see
a "sterner virtue" in the theater than in the church. "Church and
Theatre" (Preface, *Heartbreak House*, pp. 34–35) contrasts "the
Theatre: that stuffy, uncomfortable place of penance in which we
suffer so much inconvenience on the slenderest chance of gaining
a scrap of food for our starving souls," with the church and its
well-dressed women, its erotic literature, sensuous music, gorgeous
stained glass, painting, sculpture, and architecture. The fact that
Shaw's catholic religion was also a puritan religion led him eventually to prefer his modern Pre-Raphaelite drama to the religious
art of the Pre-Raphaelites, since "in point of appeal to the senses
no theatre ever built could touch the fane at Rheims." This sense
of the religious mission of the theater is the key to understanding
Shaw's reference in the preface to *Plays Pleasant* to Pre-Raphaelite
drama. In his words, "the time was ripe for a modern pre-
Raphaelite play. Religion was alive again."[26]

Chapter III

PRE-RAPHAELITE DRAMA: *CANDIDA*

 PRE-RAPHAELITE PLAY may be defined as a drama which, like medieval art, arises out of a genuine religious impulse. It is in this sense, then, that all of Shaw's drama devoted to suggesting the infinite possibilities of the ever-changing and progressing Life Force—especially *Man and Superman, Major Barbara, The Shewing Up of Blanco Posnet, Back to Methuselah,* and *Saint Joan*—can be considered Pre-Raphaelite drama. But *Candida* is uniquely "a modern pre-Raphaelite play": not only does it return, as does all of Shaw's drama, to the nature of "if not everyday, at least every-life" situations;[1] but also it demands a reevaluation of the nature and function of the artist, as the P.R.B. itself had done, and it offers a modern analogue to medieval religious art. The subtitle, "A Mystery," suggests at once the play's religious import and its medieval analogues.

Candida is specifically a Shavian mystery play about Madonna and Child, with Candida as Shaw's portrait of the Holy Mother. In a letter to Ellen Terry, Shaw says that Candida "is the Virgin Mother and nobody else,"[2] a confidence borne out in the stage direction describing Candida: "A wise-hearted observer, looking at her, would at once guess that whoever had placed the Virgin of the Assumption over her hearth did so because he fancied some spiritual resemblance between them" (*Plays Pleasant*, p. 89). Marchbanks, we are told, has perceived the resemblance and given the Morells the picture, just as Shaw perceives a resemblance

24

between his heroine and the Holy Mother. In understanding his intention to create in *Candida* "THE Mother Play,"[3] Shaw's reference to the Holy Mother in his letters to the Abbess of Stanbrook are helpful. Just as he believes in a catholic religion, he believes in a universal Madonna, whom he calls "Our Lady of Everywhere." He writes to the Abbess that he is "always saying Hail, Mary! on my travels" as he encounters Her in many forms. "Our Lady of Everywhere," significantly, is not the Madonna captured by Raphael, whose Dresden Madonna Shaw calls "the ideal wet nurse, healthy, comely, and completely brainless." In fact, he says, most Christian representations of Mary tend to be failures.[4]

If a division of critical opinion is evidence of artistic failure, Candida may be another failure to represent Mary. Pronouncements on Candida vary from Beatrice Webb's view of her as a "sentimental prostitute" to Shaw's assertion that she is the Holy Virgin. The critics who agree with Shaw's analysis of Candida emphasize her instinctive, direct, self-sufficient nature, her combination of the Philistine-realist temperament, and her embodiment of the Life Force. In a much-quoted letter to James Huneker, Shaw calls her "that very immoral female," "as unscrupulous as Siegfried," "without 'character' in the conventional sense," yet free "from emotional slop," with "unerring wisdom on the domestic plane."[5] Notably, he compares her to Siegfried, whom he considered "a type of the healthy man raised to perfect confidence in his own impulses," representative of "the unfettered action of Humanity doing exactly what it likes."[6] Because Candida, like Siegfried, is above conventional notions of good and evil, she appears from the conventional point of view immoral, insensitive to others' feelings, harsh, intimidating. (She issues commands to the two men without reference to their wishes; she is not aware, as Marchbanks is, of the pain her frankness causes Morell.) However, she is not cruel but genuinely unconscious of the more conventional, less "natural," reactions of others. To Morell's hurt and shocked reaction when she says that her love and not his morality bind her to him, she answers, "How conventional all you unconventional people are!" (p. 118) To Shaw, her "immoral" and "unscrupulous" nature is simply evidence of her indifference to convention, a quality Shaw found worthy of reverence rather than censure.

If Candida is "THE Mother," her children are, of course, Morell and Marchbanks. The play furnishes ample evidence that she looks on both as her children, to be protected and guided by her loving care. Of Eugene she says, "Oh, he's a dear boy! We are very fond of him"; "Do you know, you are a very nice boy, Eugene"; "You great baby, you!" (p. 90, 93). She also orders him about and pets him[7] as a mother would her child. She likewise calls Morell her "boy": "My boy is not looking well. Has he been overworking?" "You silly boy" (p. 114, 115). Finally, though Marchbanks is closer to actual childhood, Morell is the "boy" who acknowledges dependence on Candida as "my wife, my mother, my sisters: . . . the sum of all loving care to me" (p. 140).

The fact that Morell proves the weaker of the two suitors and thus in greater need of Candida's love does not imply that Shaw meant him to be contemptible. Morell, a preacher and lecturer, a socialist with "the gift of the gab," is the sort of man Shaw liked and, in many ways, the sort of man Shaw was. If Shaw's own socialist activities did not suggest his regard for Morell, his adjectives describing Christian socialism would: "clear, bold, sure, sensible, benevolent, salutarily shortsighted" (Preface, *Plays Pleasant*, p. viii). Moreover, Morell, symbolically named, exemplifies the kind of morality which Shaw claims changed Ruskin, Morris, and Shaw himself from mere artists to prophets; Morell's Christian socialism makes him a part of the "one religion" with which the modern Pre-Raphaelite artist deals, the religion "coming back . . . even upon clergymen." On the realistic level, Candida's care frees Morell for his work of lecturing and preaching, just as Charlotte Shaw was later to free Shaw for his work by protecting him from the cares of mundane domestic affairs. A generally ignored section of Shaw's letter to the Rugby boys about the "secret" of *Candida* is his closing admission that, though the poet has no business "with the small beer of domestic comfort and cuddling and petting at the apron-string of some dear nice woman," Eugene probably eventually discovered that "he had to keep his feet on the ground as much as Morell, and that some enterprising woman married him and made him dress himself properly and take regular meals."[8] Any reader of *Man and Superman* knows that Shaw did not find female domination of the male contemptible but rather the natural state of affairs, necessary for the propagation of the race. Morell is merely a domesticated John Tanner, except that what Tanner knows all along about the nature of woman Morell has to learn; and, instead of rebelling against her domination, Morell acquiesces in it, as Tanner does in the final scene of *Man and Superman*.

Another dramatic representation of the mother-child relationship is Shaw's portrayal of Henry Higgins and his mother in *Pygmalion*. The fact that Mrs. Higgins was in her youth a Pre-Raphaelite lady and that she still lives in the atmosphere of Morris and Burne-Jones is no doubt Shaw's rather esoteric allusion to his earlier treatment of a similar mother-child relationship in his "pre-Raphaelite play." Higgins is a combination of both Morell and Marchbanks. He is babied and accepts the babying, as Morell does. But, whereas Morell finds a mother-substitute in his wife, Higgins finds a substitute for a wife in his mother. Shaw explains in his epilogue to *Pygmalion* that Higgin's aesthetic education changed his sexual to intellectual passion: "When Higgins excused his indifference to young women on the ground that they had an irresistible rival in his mother, he gave the clue to his inveterate old-bachelordom. . . . If an imaginative boy has a sufficiently rich mother who has intelligence, personal grace, dignity of character without harshness, and a cultivated sense of the best art of her time to enable her to make her house beautiful, she sets a standard for him against which very few women can struggle" (p. 296). As a wifeless artist, the Pygmalion of the title, Higgins is most like Marchbanks; notably, both achieve their independence from female involvement through the mother-woman's influence.

Candida will baby Morell all his life; Marchbanks she leads to independence. She first protects him from learning "what love really is" from another woman, possibly a wicked woman. When he becomes a gallant worshipper of love, who proposes that Morell and he "go on a pilgrimage . . . in search of a worthy lover for her" (p. 129) and who sentimentally volunteers to "die ten times over sooner than give [Candida] a moment's pain" (p. 131), Candida, with her "divine insight" (Marchbanks's term, p. 127), allows Eugene "to stay and learn" why Morell is master of his home. Thus she frees Eugene for his development as an artist by allowing him to see that woman's purpose and the artist's are irreconcilable.

However, Shaw is not primarily concerned in *Candida* with depicting the struggle between the artist-man and the mother-woman, though that is a part of the conflict. His major aim is "to distil the quintessential drama from pre-Raphaelitism" (Preface, *Plays Pleasant*, p. vii). According to Shaw, the central struggle in *Candida* is Pre-Raphaelitism "at its best in conflict with the first broken, nervous, stumbling attempts to formulate its own revolt against itself as it develops into something higher" (p. vii). This statement is, to say the least, obscure; and the first question to be answered in dealing with it is, What is Pre-Raphaelitism "at its best"? It might be the idealizing of woman and love, the worship of the "stunner" peculiar to the Rossettian branch of the Pre-Raphaelite movement. If so, Eugene's idealizing of Candida and his horror at her subjection to everyday chores and Morell's sermons are aspects of the Pre-Raphaelite reverence for female beauty and the love it inspires; and the development "into something higher" is his recognition that Candida is not a woman to sail away in "a tiny shallop . . . far from the world, where the marble floors are washed by the rain and dried by the sun" (p. 111), but a woman who fills the lamps, scrubs the floors, peels onions, and mothers children—in short, a Shavian woman, not at all like a Rossetti or a Burne-Jones. Another possibility is that Pre-Raphaelitism "at its best" is the desire of the artist to base his art on his own observations and his own vision of truth—a desire which requires freedom from the "greasy fool's paradise" of domestic life, freedom to explore "Tristan's holy night."[9] It is likely that Shaw had in mind both the idealizing of woman and sincerity of artistic purpose as elements of Pre-Raphaelitism "at its best"; certainly Marchbanks's glimpse of the Shavian Life Force woman and his realization that he must be free from her is part of the lesson ("secret") he learns from Candida. And in the sense that Candida guides him to both recognitions she is truly the Mother of Genius, which to Shaw is another way of saying Mother of God.[10]

An additional interpretation of "the secret in the poet's heart," one not acknowledged by Shaw in any of his numerous letters on the subject, is the secret alluded to by Thomas Carlyle in "The

Hero as Poet" in *Heroes and Hero-Worship*. Carlyle says that the poet and prophet are fundamentally alike and in some ages synonymous because both are "Hero-souls" sent by nature to penetrate "into the sacred mystery of the Universe; what Goethe calls 'the open secret.' 'Which is the great secret?' asks one.—'The *open* secret,'—open to all, seen by almost none! That divine mystery, which lies everywhere in all Beings, 'the Divine Idea of the World,' that which lies at 'the bottom of Appearance,' as Fichte styles it."[11] According to Carlyle, the poet or prophet makes "this divine mystery . . . more impressively known to us"—the prophet revealing the moral, and the poet, the aesthetic side of it. This concept of the poet-prophet is very similar to Shaw's description of the artist-genius, who sees "the distant light of the new age" and "keeps on building up his masterpieces until their pinnacles catch the glint of the unrisen sun" (Preface, *Plays Pleasant*, p. vii). Though Carlyle's hero-poet looks inward and Shaw's looks forward, both have a unique mystical purpose; and it is highly probable that Marchbanks's secret, especially in a play subtitled "A Mystery," owes something to this passage from Carlyle. This interpretation of the secret would explain why Morell and Candida do not know it and why the poet goes out into the mysterious night, "the true realm of the poet."[12]

If the poet's secret is "that divine mystery, which lies everywhere in all Beings," a third explanation of what Shaw means by Pre-Raphaelitism "at its best" suggests itself—an explanation based on Shaw's analysis of medieval art in "On Going to Church." The "best" of Pre-Raphaelitism may be the genuinely religious impulse which dictates the creation of all great art, and the development "into something higher" the evolutionary development of art in order to express the constantly evolving religion of creative evolution. In the preface Shaw is careful to point out that a prosaic explanation of the dialectical process of thesis (Pre-Raphaelitism "at its best"), antithesis ("its own revolt against itself"), and synthesis (development "into something higher") is possible only after the synthesis; the artist cannot explain the "divine mystery" until it is "a story of yesterday" and life has become again something higher, something not yet perceptible even to the man of genius:

> Let Ibsen explain, if he can, why the building of churches and happy homes is not the ultimate destiny of Man, and why, to thrill the unsatisfied younger generations, he must mount beyond it to heights that now seem unspeakably giddy and dreadful to him, and from which the first climbers must fall and dash themselves to pieces. He cannot explain it: he can only shew it to you as a vision in the magic glass of his artwork; so that you may catch his presentiment and make what you can of it. (Pp. vii–viii)

This is, Shaw continues, "the higher but vaguer and timider vision . . . which offered me a dramatic antagonist for . . . Christian Socialist idealism" (p. viii). In *Candida* this vision (the "secret") is caught by Marchbanks at the end of the play. According to Shaw, when Eugene says, "I no longer desire happiness; life is nobler than that," he is speaking "the language of the man recreated by a flash of religion."[13] This religious vision also controls the theme of the play itself. Marchbanks is only a youth; he is just starting out into the night, and his poetry is yet to be written. Shaw, however, has caught the vision of the future and wishes to express it in "a modern pre-Raphaelite play," a drama which returns to the religious impulse controlling the art of the Middle Ages.

Candida is not primarily an expression of Shaw's religion; he was yet to write a "parable of Creative Evolution" (*Man and Superman*) and a "Metabiological Pentateuch" (*Back to Methuselah*). *Candida* defines the nature and purpose of the artist who, after his sojourn in the night, may be able to create "an iconography of a live religion." In suggesting the religious nature of the art of the future, Shaw employs in *Candida* an elaborate analogy to medieval art. The subtitle of the play, "A Mystery," too often taken by critics to refer to the play's troublesome and elusive theme, states its genre. It is a modern mystery play of the Madonna and Child, which will be performed in the modern equivalent to the medieval cathedral, the theater, where the catholic religion of creative evolution lives.

PART II

SHAW
AND THE FIN-DE-SIECLE
AESTHETES

Chapter IV

THE DEVELOPMENT OF
FIN-DE-SIECLE AESTHETICISM

HE ROMANTIC CONCEPT of a nonstatic universe, a universe in the process of "becoming," and the romantic faith in the creative imagination are at the basis of subsequent art movements throughout the nineteenth century. Just as the Pre-Raphaelite rebellion against academy rules and the attempt to "adhere to nature" are manifestations of romantic individualism and artistic experimentation, so, too, later art movements—realism, naturalism, impressionism, symbolism, decadence—are often a result of the romantic search for value in a changing, imperfect, and diverse universe.

Although fin-de-siècle aestheticism did not grow directly from the Pre-Raphaelite movement, the Pre-Raphaelites at least prepared the way for it. Ruskin's and Morris's emphasis on the importance of art to life, the Pre-Raphaelite defiance of artistic convention, and Rossetti's suggestion that a moral intention is not only irrelevant but positively harmful to art foreshadow later developments in the aesthetic movement. The Pre-Raphaelites and the exponents of a moral art are peculiarly English, deriving their aesthetic from the English romantics and their artistic models from the Middle Ages; but the fin-de-siècle aesthetes formed an aesthetic heavily influenced by the French movement of *l'art pour l'art*.

The later nineteenth century might be seen as a period of, to use Morse Peckham's terminology, "negative romanticism"[1]—a period in which disillusion and world-weariness led not to spiritual rebirth, to affirmation, to Carlyle's "Everlasting Yea," but to feelings of guilt, despair, and alienation. Walter Pater provides an explanation of how such romantic disillusion can lead to a faith in art for art's sake: the disillusioned man, "cut off from certain ancient natural hopes," demands an "artificial stimulus," having lost the medieval "all-embracing prospect of life as a whole." With only empirical knowledge and subjective experience to guide him, he turns to art or science or experience as an exceptional thing, "almost as men turn in despair to gambling or narcotics, and in a little while the narcotic, the game of chance or skill, is valued for its own sake. The vocation of the artist, of the student of life or books, will be realised with something—say! of fanaticism, as an end in itself, unrelated, unassociated."[2] Though Pater is referring specifically to a nineteenth-century French artist, his remarks apply also the English fin-de-siècle aesthetes, who, as Granville Hicks notes, believed in beauty "as artists of all ages have done, but they believed in it more intensely, for it was all they believed in."[3]

Influenced by what the poet laureate of England had called the "poisonous honey stol'n from France,"[4] the fin-de-siècle aesthetes insisted on the separation of art and morality and the importance of form over content. These ideas were derived particularly from Gautier and Baudelaire, acknowledged influences on Swinburne and Moore and obvious sources of many of the ideas of Whistler, Pater, and Wilde. In his preface to *Mademoiselle de Maupin* (1835), Gautier had attacked critics who demand morality or utility in art; the pretense of morality in art is wearisome, he says, hypocritical, and absurd: "On ne se fait pas un bonnet de coton d'une métonymie, on ne chausse pas une comparaison en guise de pantoufle; on ne se peut servir d'une antithèse pour parapluie; malheureusement, on ne saurait se plaquer sur le ventre quelques rimes bariolées en manière de gilet. . . . Il n'y a de vraiment beau que ce qui ne peut servir à rien; tout ce qui est utile est laid, car c'est l'expression de quelque besoin, et ceux de l'homme sont ignobles et dégoûtants, comme sa pauvre et infirme nature.—L'endroit le plus utile d'une maison, ce sont les latrines."[5] Baudelaire praised Gautier's *Mademoiselle de Maupin* for encouraging an "excessive love of beauty," and he insisted that "la poésie ne peut pas, sous peine de mort ou de défaillance, s'assimiler à la science ou à la morale; elle n'a pas la Vérité pour objet, elle n'a qu'Elle-même."

Speaking in "Notes nouvelles sur Edgar Poe (1857) of *"l'hérésie de l'enseignement,* laquelle comprend comme corollaires inévitables l'hérésies de la *passion,* de la *vérité* et de la *morale,"* he says that the public erroneously thinks that poetry should strengthen conscience, perfect manners, or fulfill a useful purpose; poetry, he insists, has no other object than itself. Baudelaire does, however, find a kind of use for poetry in that it brings beauty to an otherwise vulgar and incomplete existence: he does not say "que son résultat final ne soit pas d'élever l'homme au-dessus du niveau des intérêts vulgaires. . . . Je dis que si le poëte a poursuivi un but moral il a diminué sa force poétique."[6] In divorcing art from moral purpose, the followers of *l'art pour l'art* could concentrate on form and on style as the determinant and the ultimate justification of art.

The movement of *l'art pour l'art* came to public notice in England with the publication of Swinburne's *Poems and Ballads* (1866) and his subsequent essay, "Notes on Poems and Reviews," in which, answering his outraged critics, he denied that questions of morality are relevant to art. He had earlier expressed the necessity of separating artistic and moral realms in his essay of 1861 defending Baudelaire, where he attacked critics for forgetting "that a poet's business is presumably to write good verses, and by no means to redeem the age and remould society."[7] In "Notes on Poems and Reviews" he defends his own poetry, including "Dolores," which had been singled out as "especially horrible." This poem, he says, was written "with no moral or immoral design; but the upshot seems to me moral rather than immoral, if it must needs be one or the other, and if (which I cannot be sure of) I construe aright those somewhat misty and changeable terms" (16: 373). In *William Blake* (1868) Swinburne maintains that the artist's concern should be for form alone. In a passage reminiscent of Rossetti's "Hand and Soul," Swinburne says, "Save the shape, and art will take care of the soul for you"; the artist's creed should be, "Art for art's sake first of all, and afterwards we may suppose all the rest shall be added to her." Like Baudelaire, he does not say that art never produces a moral effect, but he does say that a moral intention will probably spoil a work of art and that any moral effect is accidental and "beside the question" (16: 134–40).

Like Swinburne, the painter James McNeill Whistler emphasized the divorce of morality from art, because art "is selfishly occupied with her own perfection only—having no desire to teach." He believes that "the masterpiece should appear as the flower to the painter . . . with no reason to explain its presence—no mission to fulfill." He also believes that art is solely an effect of color and form, not of subject or detail. For example, in a letter to *The World* of 1878 he criticized the English inability to separate picture and story, explaining that in his "Harmony in Grey and Gold" he cared nothing "for the past, present, or future of the black figure, placed there because the black was wanted at that spot. . . . The subject-matter has nothing to do with harmony of sound or of colour. . . . Art should be independent of all clap-trap—should stand alone, and appeal to the artistic sense of eye or ear, without confounding this with emotions entirely foreign to it, as devotion, pity, love, patriotism, and the like."[8]

Not only does Whistler oppose Ruskin's linking of ethics and art and his linking of a noble subject and a great style, he also insists in the "Ten O'Clock" lecture that "there never was an artistic period," for the artist seeks and finds beauty "in all conditions and in all times." Therefore, Whistler argues, art is not a product of progress or decay but "is limited to the infinite." Opposing the idea that art is for the people, he begins the "Ten O'Clock" with an attack on popular aestheticism: "The people have been harassed with Art in every guise. . . . Their homes have been invaded, their walls covered with paper, their very dress taken to task." Art is not, he insists, for the middle classes or for the majority of people, who have only vulgarity in common: "Art seeks the Artist alone."[9] In short, Whistler's comments on art as divorced from didactic or moral purpose; as arrangement, line, color, form alone; as universal, requiring not a right time but only an artist; as exclusive, i.e., not democratic; as the result of hard work and skillful execution, not "natural" inspiration, all point up clearly the direction the aesthetic movement had taken: away from that of Ruskin, the Pre-Raphaelites, and Morris.

That direction was profoundly influenced by Walter Pater, who, according to Richard Le Gallienne, "was virtually the founder of the Aesthetic Movement."[10] Pater's art theory rests on that Epicurean philosophy expressed in the conclusion to *The Renaissance* (1873) and in *Marius the Epicurean* (1885), a belief in perpetual change and in the reality of subjective consciousness. All experience, Pater explains, is "a group of impressions," limited by human consciousness and by time, each impression being but "a single moment, gone while we try to apprehend it, of which it may ever be more truly said that it has ceased to be than that it is" (*Works*, 1:235). Because fixed knowledge is impossible, success in life depends on keeping the senses alert to aesthetic moments, relying on one's own impression, and, above all, keeping a "constantly renewed mobility of character" (2:139). One must attempt to "be present always at the focus where the greatest number of vital forces unite in their purest energy," or, in somewhat less obscure terms, to get "as many pulsations as possible into the given time." Because art gives "the highest quality to your moments as they pass," the good life is, then, the aesthetic life (1:236–39). Pater is careful to explain that his Epicureanism is not mere hedonism. Not only did he suppress the conclusion to *The Renaissance* in the 1877 edition because he "conceived it might possibly mislead some of those young men into whose hands it might fall" (1:233); but in *Marius the Epicurean* he explains that, although this philosophy could result in "a languid, enervating, consumptive nihilism," for Marius (as for Pater) it resulted instead in a desire to beautify the soul and body, in a desire to attain "not pleasure, but a general completeness of life" (2:137, 143).

This Epicurean ideal draws on Matthew Arnold's philosophy of art. Arnold's culture, like Pater's aesthetic education, implies a spiritual perfection—antimaterialistic, harmonious, flexible, not dependent on wealth or health or morality. When Arnold says that "nothing is more common than for people to confound the inward peace and satisfaction which follows the subduing of the obvious faults of our animality with what I may call absolute inward peace and satisfaction,—the peace and satisfaction which are reached as we draw near to complete spiritual perfection," he is separating conventional morality ("the subduing of the obvious faults of our animality") and culture, which implies, he says, absolute spiritual perfection. Art has for Arnold, as it has for Pater, the highest place in man's spiritual progress; it has as its ideal *"an inward spiritual activity, having for its characters increased sweetness, increased light, increased life, increased sympathy.*"[11]

Just as Arnold's philosophy is an English antecedent of Pater's Epicureanism, so Pater's art theory provides a background for the form and style-consciousness of the fin-de-siècle aesthetes. Like Whistler, Pater often stated that good art is determined primarily by its form, not by its matter. For example, in *The Renaissance* he defines poetry as "all literary production which attains the power of giving pleasure by its form, as distinct from its matter." However, in his essays on "The School of Giorgione" and on "Style," he assigned a relatively important place to matter; "*All art,*" he said, "*constantly aspires towards the condition of music*"; i.e., the form "should become an end in itself, should penetrate every part of the matter," should reduce to a minimum the distinction between matter and form (1:135–37, 250). Finally, in "Style" he distinguishes between "good art," determined by the perfect fusion of form and matter, and "great art," which depends on the nobility of its matter. Expressing a sentiment which could also have come from one of the advocates of "art for morality's sake," Pater says that, if good art is "devoted further to the increase of man's happiness, to the redemption of the oppressed, or the enlargement of our sympathies with each other, or to such presentment of new or old truth about ourselves and our relation to the world as may ennoble and fortify us in our sojourn here, or immediately, as with Dante, to the glory of God, it will be also great art." However, Pater's concept of morality in art is intimately dependent on aesthetic sensibility. His essay on Shakespeare's *Measure for Measure* will serve as illustration: the play conveys, Pater says, "the very intricacy and subtlety of the moral world itself, the difficulty of seizing the true relations of so complex material, the difficulty of just judgment," and it expresses the need for a "finer justice, a justice based on a more delicate appreciation of the true conditions of men and things, a true respect of persons in our estimate of actions." But because art develops "those fine appreciations" which can lead to a "finer justice," Pater's idea of the morality represented by art is that which demands aesthetic sensibility. This concept of morality in art and Pater's comments elsewhere on the relationship of form to matter necessarily modify the distinction between "good art" and "great art" in "Style."[12] In fact, in the midst of his discussion of the morality of *Measure for Measure*, Pater speaks of "that artistic law which demands the predominance of form everywhere over the mere matter of subject handled."

Although Pater's position seems at times to diverge considerably from Whistler's, in actuality the two are close. Both Pater and Whistler consider artistic effect of primary importance. Both insist on the artist's vision as the sole determiner of the kind of reality his art will express. And both say that artistic productivity does not depend on social health; like Whistler, Pater says that art has been produced in all ages. He praises the Renaissance, but he considers it not as an age but as an attitude, which he finds not only in fifteenth-century Italy but also in medieval France and eighteenth-century Germany; to Pater the Renaissance is "a many-sided but yet united movement, in which the love of the things of the intellect and the imagination for their own sake, the desire for a more liberal and comely way of conceiving life, make themselves felt" (1:2). For Pater as for Whistler the artist's temperament, not his age, is the sole source of artistic inspiration.

The aestheticism of Swinburne, Pater, and Whistler was dramatized and advertized by Oscar Wilde, who absorbed almost every tendency in the aesthetic movement and is thus considered by many to be the symbol of the aesthetic movement. At first he was thought to be a follower of the Pre-Raphaelites; Hamilton, who defines the aesthetic movement as the "Renaissance of Medieval Art and Culture," devotes a chapter of *The Aesthetic Movement in England* to Wilde.[13] Later, Wilde was identified with the French-influenced aesthetes and particularly with the decadents. Satires of Wilde depict him as both pure and intense and as wicked and corrupt: in *Patience* (1881) he is the innocent, melancholic Grosvenor, "an Idyllic Poet," "the Apostle of Simplicity"—or "Archibald the All-Right"; but in Robert Hichen's *The Green Carnation* (1894) he is Esmé Amarinth, a corruptor of youth, and an insincere epigrammist, admitting a love for "what are called warped minds, and deformed natures, just as I love the long necks of Burne-Jones's women, and the faded rose-leaf beauty of Walter Pater's unnatural prose."[14] The influences on Wilde were as various as the influences on the aesthetic movement itself: he was devoted to Ruskin's teaching at Oxford; his view of criticism as creating "the intellectual atmosphere of the age" is heavily indebted to Arnold; his costume and pose of the 1880s identified him with popular aestheticism; his artistic creed was so heavily indebted to Whistler that Whistler said that "Oscar . . . dines at our tables and picks from our platters the plums for the pudding he peddles in the provinces";[15] his poetry is sometimes impressionistic; his pose of the 1890s linked him with decadence; and his works *The Soul of Man under Socialism* and *The Ballad of Reading Gaol* reflect a social consciousness which places him in the moral tradition of Ruskin and Morris and link him with the wider social reform impulse of the period. However, though Wilde's life reflected both the moral and amoral streams of the aesthetic movement, his art theory primarily repeated and emphasized the aesthetic theory of Swinburne, Pater, and Whistler. His critical essays develop an already familiar theory of art, including the ideas that the object of art is beauty, not truth; that art is not useful; that style, not subject, determines art; and that art is not produced "naturally" but consciously and deliberately.[16]

The conviction found in Wilde, Swinburne, Whistler, and Pater that the artist's first and only obligation is to produce art is central to the English art for art's sake movement. Though the origins of this fin-de-siècle movement are numerous and complex, one does not mispresent them in seeing it as an outgrowth of romanticism, its way prepared by Ruskin, Arnold, and the Pre-Raphaelites and its course influenced by the French movement of *l'art pour l'art*. The English leaders of art for art's sake were Swinburne, Whistler, and Pater, who by the 1880s had formulated a theory of art which, as Wilde popularized it, became the basis of fin-de-siècle aestheticism. This theory, if condensed into maxims about art like those in Wilde's preface to *The Picture of Dorian Gray*, would take the following form:

Art need not serve a moral or useful purpose. It is the joyous expression of beauty alone.

Art may be experimental and should be free from academic rules and popular demands.

Art is not democratic. It is anti-bourgeois.

In art, form is all-important. Art is not produced "naturally." Treatment of subject and style are more important than choice of subject matter.

Art is subjective. It may thus be "realistic," impressionistic, "naturalistic," or symbolical.

Art is not limited to a particular time or place.

The theories of other aesthetes such as Symons, Moore, or Beardsley are merely variations and refinements of this community of beliefs.

By the 1890s the slogan "art for art's sake" had become a cliché, so that one finds a writer for *The Yellow Book* referring to "that honourable property-piece, the maxim of Art for Art's sake."[17] Nevertheless, the concept of art for art's sake in Swinburne, Whistler, Pater, and Wilde emphasizes the main point of difference between the followers of Ruskin and the followers of Pater. It has been argued that, in advocating a moral art, Ruskin does not mean that art deals with issues of right and wrong, but that he means "that the perception of beauty is not isolated from the rest of human life . . . that it is not an affair of the intellect or purely of the senses, but of the emotions," and that Pater is "essentially of the same party as Ruskin" in his relation of art to all experience.[18] But there is a real difference in emphasis between Ruskin's view of an art which should be produced only by an ethical man and which reflects the ethics of that man and his age, or Morris's view of an art which ultimately performs the social service of restoring the dignity of the laboring class and uniting society in a brotherhood of artisans, and Pater's view of an art which, depending in no way on an ethical artist or a moral age, can provide a "higher morality" in that beauty contributes to "completeness of life." At least one disciple of Pater, Arthur Symons, believed that Pater "did much to rescue us from the dangerous moralities, the uncritical enthusiasms and prejudices, of Mr. Ruskin."[19]

In the final analysis, most of the aesthetes who adopted art for art's sake as an article of faith did not only mean that art's purpose is to create a beautiful object; they also recognized that art serves a higher purpose in its contribution to culture. They never denied that art can elevate the manners or sensibilities of those who come in contact with it. Their major concern in insisting on art for art's sake was not so much to deny to art a moral function—if morality is more broadly defined than usual to include anything, whether or not it clashes with convention, which works for the betterment of mankind—as it was to divorce art from "the heresy of didacticism," to use Poe's term, and to free it from the aims of immediate social improvement. Thus Hubert Crackanthorpe, echoing the sentiments of Arnold, Pater, and Wilde and speaking for many of the avant-garde artists of the 1890s, writes in the second volume of *The Yellow Book* that "the business of art is to create for us fine interests, to make of our human nature a more complete thing: and thus, all great art is moral in the wider and truer sense of the word." But, he continues, "theoretically, Art is non-moral. She is not interested in any ethical code."[20] This latter statement uses *moral* not "in the wider and truer sense" but in the narrower and more common one of "acceptable to society's concept of right." Indeed, one of the primary purposes of the art for art's sake movement was to protest against what Arthur Symons calls "bourgeois solemnity."

"Art for art's sake" in England, then, could mean a number of things—none of them contradictory to the other. It meant, first of all, what the slogan seems to say: the sole purpose of art is the creation of a beautiful object, i.e., art. But it also sometimes carried the implication that such art, by enriching the culture, incidentally serves a moral purpose—in its widest sense. And, as a rallying cry for many of the avant-garde of the 1880s and 1890s, it served as a reminder to Victorian society that art is something other than a reflection of bourgeois values, that by its nature it cannot be "respectable." As we shall see, the art theory of Bernard Shaw owes more to the aesthetic movement in England than his comments on art for art's sake would lead one to believe.

Chapter V

ART FOR ART'S SAKE AND SHAW'S THEORY OF MORAL ART

HEN ASSESSING Shaw's place in the aesthetic movement, one must determine which of the meanings of art for art's sake he had in mind when he wrote that " 'for art's sake' alone I would not face the toil of writing a single sentence." And, in order to do this, one needs to examine Shaw's attitudes toward art and morality, which are summarized in the following statement from *The Sanity of Art*:

> The claim of art to our respect must stand or fall with the validity of its pretension to cultivate and refine our senses and faculties until seeing, hearing, feeling, smelling, and tasting become highly conscious and critical acts with us, protesting vehemently against ugliness, noise, discordant speech, frowzy clothing, and re-breathed air, and taking keen interest and pleasure in beauty, in music, and in nature, besides making us insist, as necessary for comfort and decency, on clean, wholesome, handsome fabrics to wear, and utensils of fine material and elegant workmanship to handle. Further, art should refine our sense of character and conduct, of justice and sympathy, greatly heightening our self-knowledge, self-control, precision of action, and considerateness, and making us intolerant of baseness, cruelty, injustice, and intellectual superficiality and vulgarity. The worthy artist or craftsman is he who serves the physical and moral senses by feeding them with pictures, musical compositions, pleasant houses and gardens, good clothes and fine implements, poems, fictions, essays, and dramas which call the heightened senses and ennobled faculties into pleasurable activity. The great artist is he who goes a step beyond the demand, and, by supplying works of a higher beauty and a higher interest than have yet been

perceived, succeeds after a brief struggle with its strangeness, in adding this fresh extension of sense to the heritage of the race. (*Essays,* pp. 315–16)

The influence of Ruskin and especially of Morris is evident in the statement that art makes us so sensitive to ugliness that we insist on a more beautiful world. The idea at first seems consistent also with Pater's idea of art as a means of enlarging our aesthetic faculties, or of Crackanthorpe's reference to artistic morality "in the wider and truer sense of the word." However, Shaw's vision is social; that of the fin-de-siècle aesthetes is personal. Shaw, like Ruskin and Morris, wants beautiful lives for everyone; the fin-de-siècle aesthetes recoil from ugliness and try to create more beautiful lives for themselves and, at most, for others like them. It is the difference between Shaw's plans for slum clearance and Whistler's designs for the peacock room.

Shaw's second statement of the aim of art ("Further, art should refine . . .") parallels, interestingly, Pater's distinction in "Style" between good and great art. Shaw's "worthy artist," however, does not parallel Pater's "good" artist, who succeeds in fusing form and content into an artistic whole; Shaw's "worthy artist" proceeds on the level of Pater's "great" artist, serving both "the physical and moral senses." And Shaw's "great artist" has a purpose higher than any conceived of by Pater or, for that matter, by anyone: he is to create "works of a higher beauty and a higher interest than have yet been perceived." For an amplification of this idea one turns again to the preface to *Plays Pleasant,* where the artist's function is defined as expression of a vision of a world not yet evolved.

In comparing this with other statements by Shaw about artists who serve a "moral" end, we must note that, like the aesthetes, Shaw uses the word *moral* in at least two senses: (1) "in the wider and truer sense of the word," i.e., tending to the refinement of man's senses or the elevation of his soul through contact with art; (2) in the limited sense of the word, i.e., acceptable to society's standards. Whenever Shaw uses *moral* in the second sense, he always insists, as do the aesthetes, that art is not moral. Because "every step of progress means a duty repudiated, and a scripture torn up," what the world terms "sin" and "immorality" is therefore not only justifiable but necessary. Thus Shaw defends Ibsen's "immoral" tendencies, and calls himself "a specialist in immoral and heretical plays," defining *immoral* as "whatever is contrary to established manners and customs" and asserting that "an immoral act or doctrine is not necessarily a sinful one: on the contrary, every advance in thought and conduct is by definition immoral until it has converted the majority."[1] The Devil's Disciple (Dick Dudgeon, John Tanner, Andrew Undershaft) is a characteristic Shavian hero, and the plays also abound with characters (Candida, Lady Cicely, Joan) who follow their wills without regard to conventional notions of sin. Shaw even praises Swinburne and Wilde, two aesthetes whose work he generally disliked, for their roles as devil's advocates. In "Giving the Devil His Due" he approves of the rebellious attitude toward conventional virtue in Swinburne's book on Blake; similarly, he approves of Wilde as a critic "of morals and manners."[2]

Shaw acted as devil's advocate in his attack on Max Nordau's *Degeneration* (1893), which held that virtually every post-romantic art movement in Europe originated in perversion and mental disease. Shaw's essay, originally entitled *A Degenerate's View of Nordau* (1895), reveals the extent of his kinship to the decadent aspects of fin-de-siècle aestheticism. His major objection is to Nordau's thesis that opposition to customary morality is a malady, a form of mental and physical degeneracy. Shaw regards such opposition as healthy and sane: for example, the impressionist movement, because it substituted "a natural, observant, real style for a conventional, taken-for-granted, ideal one," was "wholly beneficial and progressive, and in no sense insane or decadent"; and Ibsen grasped the fact that abstract rules of conduct are often in conflict with, and inferior to, human passion, which "is the steam in the engine of all religious and moral systems" (*SA*, pp. 291–94, 301–4). Once again Shaw argues that laws and customs, because they are always out of date, must be defined by the thinkers and artists and ultimately replaced by better laws and customs, which will also eventually be out of date and need replacing.

Shaw points out that the great artist's defiance of convention may lead to imitators who "bring out really silly and vicious stuff, which the reviewers are afraid to expose, lest it, too, should turn out to be the correct thing" (p. 312), and he agrees that these imitations need condemnation; but he does not look on these as diseased or decadent, as Nordau does, but as "absurd" (p. 300), "silly" (p. 312), or at worst, "abnormal" (p. 293), or "vicious" (p. 312). Nordau and Shaw both think that some impressionist painters produce "abnormal" pictures. But Nordau attributes this "abnormality" to "*nystagmus,* or trembling of the eyeball," a disease peculiar to psychological degeneracy, or to a "partly insensitive" retina, peculiar to hysteria;[3] characteristically, he assumes that the artist is by nature mentally ill. On the other hand, Shaw uses his "normal" vision as a standard from which to judge the relatively bad vision of some impressionists, "who produce abnormal pictures because they saw abnormally" (*SA,* p. 293).

Shaw protests about the extent of Nordau's attack: "He is so utterly mad on the subject of degeneration that he finds the symptoms of it in the loftiest geniuses as plainly as in the lowest jailbirds" (p. 325). Shaw particularly objects to Nordau's equation of Ruskin, Morris, the Pre-Raphaelites, Wagner, and Ibsen, whom Shaw defends, with Verlaine, Mallarmé, Gautier, Baudelaire, Wilde, and Zola, to mention only a few of those attacked by Nordau, whom Shaw is presumably not inclined to defend. Nordau occasionally offends Shaw personally, as when he says that, "like hypochondriacs and 'hémorroïdaires,' the German hysterical subject is anxiously concerned about his precious health. His crazes hinge on the exhalations of his skin and the functions of his stomach. He becomes a fanatic for Jaeger vests, and for the groats which vegetarians grind for themselves"; or when he says that Ibsen's defenders perversely "discover in his pieces world-pictures of the greatest truth, the happiest poetic use of scientific methods, clearness and incisiveness of ideas, a fiercely revolutionary desire for freedom, and a modernity pregnant with the future."[4] Such comments seem deliberately aimed at Shaw, who wore Jaeger woolens, ate no meat, and praised Ibsen's ideas. Shaw was almost bound to answer these and the attacks on his artistic favorites.

Ironically, Shaw could have agreed with Nordau's moral bias; but he disagreed with his definition of morality. In fact, Shaw's attitude toward decadent art is closer to the Philistine position than to the aesthete's. In "On Going to Church" he deplores the demand for "nightmarish art and literature" produced by "that terrible dream-glamour in which the ugly, the grotesque, the wicked, the morbific begin to fascinate and obsess instead of disgusting."[5] Clearly Shaw would agree with Symons that the decadent movement in literature was unhealthy, but he would never, as Symons does, approve of the unhealthiness.[6] Significantly, Shaw changed the title of his answer to Nordau from *A Degenerate's View of Nordau* to *The Sanity of Art,* thus shifting the emphasis to an intrinsic normality, sanity, and health of art and offering not simply a negation of convention but an affirmation of faith in art and society.

Not only did Shaw reject the decadent's glorification of the abnormal but also he rejected the reasons offered by some fin-de-siècle aesthetes as justification for "immorality" in art. Though their iconoclasm, like Shaw's, is a protest against bourgeois hypocrisy, pettiness, and materialism, it is usually defended on aesthetic grounds. For example, when Pater approves of the "antinomian" quality in the story of "Aucassin and Nicolette," he is approving not so much of the rebellion against Christian values as of the "search after the pleasures of the senses and the imagination, . . . their care for beauty, . . . their worship of the body" which led some artists of the medieval Renaissance (Pater's term) to that rebellion (*Works,* 1:24). Or when Wilde presents an argument in defense of sin as "an essential element of progress," the idea is identical to Shaw's, except that Wilde offers an aesthetic justification: without sin, he says, "the world would stagnate, or grow old, or become colourless."[7]

Another difference between Shaw and the fin-de-siècle aesthetes on the question of art and morality is that Shaw would never, as did Pater, Whistler, Wilde, Symons, Beardsley, and Moore, admit that questions of art and morality are separate; Shaw requires that art be immoral, not amoral. Shaw would agree with one-half of Symons's defense of *London Nights* (1896) against charges of immorality: the idea that "the principles of morality fluctuate with the spiritual ebb and flow of the ages";[8] but he would not accept Symons's conclusion that art, being eternal, therefore has no necessary connection with morality.

Confusingly, the "specialist in immoral and heretical plays" also characterizes himself as a moral and religious playwright. Shaw is very explicit about the didactic and propagandistic purpose of art. He is reported to have said to a Shelley Society meeting in 1887, apropos of a paper on *The Revolt of Islam,* "a poem ought to be didactic, and ought to be in the nature of a political treatise."[9] In the 1893 preface to the edition of *Widowers' Houses* published by Henry and Company, he describes the play as "a propagandist play—a didactic play— a play with a purpose," an "expression of my sense of moral and intellectual perversity rather than of my sense of beauty" (p. xviii). The didactic impulse is often emphasized by the subtitles of his plays: "An Original Didactic Realistic Play," "A Sermon," "A . . . Pamphlet," etc. And in the preface to *Pygmalion* he boasts of the success of the play in spite of "the wiseacres who repeat the parrot cry that art should never be didactic. It goes to prove my contention that great art can never be anything else" (p. 198).

But Shaw never looks on art simply as a sermon or a pamphlet or a tract. Poetry is not a political treatise; it is *"in the nature of a political treatise"* (italics added), "the most artistic way of teaching those things which a poet ought to teach."[10] When Shaw told Stephen Winsten that Shelley's poetry made a radical of him (Shaw), he was referring to the aesthetic as well as the propagandistic qualities of the poetry: "Shelley made his ideas sing" and thus could convert "by the sheer logic of his poetry."[11] Shaw always claims for his own drama an artistic as well as educative quality. *Widowers' Houses* is not only "a propagandist play" but "a technically good practicable stage play" which should be judged not "as a pamphlet in dialogue, but as in intention a work of art." Shaw warns his critics not to consider the play a mere Fabian tract just because it demonstrates a knowledge of modern economics: "Any person who would like to see the difference between an essay on rent and *Widowers' Houses* can buy *Fabian Essays.*"[12] Shaw returns to this point in a letter to the biographer O'Bolger when he asks, "Would anyone but a buffleheaded idiot of a university professor, half crazy with correcting examination papers, infer that all my plays were written as economic essays, and not as plays of life, character, and human destiny like those of Shakespear or Euripides?" (*Sketches,* p. 89) Thus, some subtitles notwithstanding, he does not look on his plays as simply sermons, pamphlets, tracts, but plays which are actable, stageable, and readable as art.

A key to his definition of didactic art is in his distinction between philosophy and didacticism in *The Perfect Wagnerite* (pp. 218–19), where he complains that with *Die Götterdämmerung* the Ring "ceases to be philosophic, and becomes didactic." *Didactic* in this context refers to the offering of a panacea instead of "a dramatic symbol of the world as Wagner observed it"; both Wagner and Shelley "lapse into panacea-mongering didacticism by the holding up of Love as the remedy for all evils and the solvent of all social difficulties." Though this use of *didactic* is unfortunate for those who would have Shaw always consistent, it is helpful in understanding his other comments on didacticism in art. When Shaw demands didactic art, he is clearly not referring to "panacea-mongering" but to a presentation of the world as an artist perceives it; and, because Shaw denies that great art can be produced without a philosophic conviction, didactic art is necessarily a dramatization of a philosophy, or, again, the creation of "an iconography of a live religion."

That the iconography must be interesting enough to reach an audience is self-evident. One of Shaw's leading educational theories, discussed at length in the preface to *Misalliance*, is that a person does not learn what he does not want to learn. And one should note that the statement immediately preceding Shaw's denial of art for art's sake in the Epistle Dedicatory to *Man and Superman* is: "No doubt I must recognize, as even the Ancient Mariner did, that I must tell my story entertainingly if I am to hold the wedding guest spellbound." At times he suggests that the sheer vitality of the message keeps the audience spellbound: "The dramatist knows that as long as he is teaching and saving his audience, he is as sure of their strained attention as a dentist is, or the Angel of the Annunciation" (*Quintessence*, p. 145). At other times he describes art as a sugar-coated pill; the use of stock comic devices and characters, he explains to J. E. Vedrenne in 1907, is "the jam that has carried the propaganda pill down."[13] At still other times he looks on art as requiring neither the platform spell-binder's appeal nor the sugar-coating. In "The Religion of the Pianoforte" (1894), the preface to *Misalliance* (1910), and "The Aesthetic Man" (in

Everybody's Political What's What, 1944) he regards art as a teacher by indirection; the educational function of art is fulfilled whether or not the didactic intention is there: refinement of the senses leads to refinement of the feelings, which in turn eventually leads to refinement of the mind and then, ironically, to a rejection of art because it appeals to a lower faculty. In connection with this theory, which is very close to Pater's ascetic aestheticism, he argues that we must "deliberately reverse our Puritan traditions and aim at becoming a nation of skilled voluptuaries," because "high feeling" leads to "high thinking," and this leads to "plain living";[14] Shaw's examples of artists who have fulfilled this purpose are Shelley and Wagner, whose art expresses the sensory-emotional-intellectual levels and who personally practiced "plain living" (i.e., vegetarianism, teetotalism, and political radicalism). In the preface to *Misalliance* (pp. 87–100) he says that "fine art is the only teacher except torture" and that providing an aesthetic education for a child is the most effective way of guiding him to a religion. This is not to say that art itself is the religion; children must be protected from idolatry of artists and art connoisseurs. But the child needs to be allowed "unfettered access to a whole body of Fine Art," and, if he has not been subjected to boring books, lectures, and sermons, and if his mind has been kept free from secular and conventionally religious indoctrination, he will find his artistic "level" and "demand art everywhere as a condition attainable by cultivating the body, mind and heart." The aesthetic education proposed here duplicates Shaw's account of his own education;[15] and, though he never suggests that constant exposure to good music, painting, and literature will make Shaws of everyone, he does say that it will make sensitive and possibly socially conscious or religious beings of everyone.

Shaw's concept of the social, indeed sacred, purpose of art seems to be contradicted in his occasional disparagement of art. But, as with the term *moral,* so too *art* has several distinct meanings in Shaw's work. Usually *art* refers to Shavian art, an art like that of Wagner or Ibsen, which is not only coherent, organic, meaningful but also by definition philosophic. But *art* also is used as Wilde uses it in "The Decay of Lying," as a synonym for romancing, an escape from life. For example, in Shaw's next-to-last article as drama critic of *The Saturday Review,* he describes his recent anesthetized state, in which he was able to achieve an "artistic and sentimental" character: "For the first time in my life I tasted the bliss of having no morals to restrain me from lying, and no sense of reality to restrain me from romancing. I overflowed with what people call 'heart.' I acted and lied in the most touchingly sympathetic fashion." He concludes that, as a result, "artistically, I was an immense success: morally, I simply had no existence." Now he understands how he "can come to life as an artist and a man of feeling—as everything that I have been reproached so bitterly for not being": the secret is in "a bag of ether" (*OTN,* 3: 381–83). The amoral art referred to here is that which is detached from everyday affairs, the kind that Wilde describes in "The Decay of Lying" as not drawn from life, not useful, more probable and better than nature in that it is true to an imaginative vision. Shaw's comparison of nonrealistic art to an etherized state suggests precisely his objections to such an amoral art: no matter how pleasant the artist's dreamworld may be, he can neither reach nor alter the real world; he is inactive and, what is worse, sick, or he would not require the anesthetic.

Shaw's concept of the "artistic and sentimental" etherized state is identical to the concept of art described in act 3 of *Man and Superman,* where "the romantic man" equals "the Artist," whose milieu is hell—the fashionable, unthinking, pleasure-seeking state. Don Juan acknowledges the debt he owes the artist, who "taught me to hear better, . . . to see better, and . . . to feel more deeply" (p. 111), but Juan rejects him because of his worship of love. This artist is the believer in art for art's sake, the "bellettrist" berated in the Epistle Dedicatory. The artist philosopher is of another kind altogether; the "bellettrist" is damned, but the artist-philosopher, like Rembrandt, Mozart, and Nietzsche, may become one of "the masters of reality" in Heaven. As Martin Ellehauge explains in *The Position of Bernard Shaw in European Drama and Philosophy,* Shaw conceives of three stages of art: (1) art as "plastic and voluptuous beauty," an immature and degenerate stage; (2) art as an expression of "the beauty of intense life," the "intense life" being to Shaw the struggle between the flesh and the spirit, the reverse of the Continental concept of the "life of the senses"; (3) art as the creation of life itself, this stage involving a rejection of the creation of lifeless art (pp. 41–42). This is the stage dramatized in part 5 of *Back to Methuselah.* The master sculptor Martellus has smashed his statues and advises Arjillax to smash his also

> because you cannot give them life. . . . Anything alive is better than anything that is only pretending to be alive. [*To Arjillax*] Your disillusion with your works of beauty is only the beginning of your disillusion with images of all sorts. As your hand became more skilful and your chisel cut deeper, you strove to get nearer and nearer to truth and reality, discarding the fleeting fleshly lure, and making images of the mind that fascinates to the end. But how can so noble an inspiration be satisfied with any image, even an image of the truth? In the end the intellectual conscience that tore you away from the fleeting in art to the eternal must tear you away from art altogether, because art is false and life alone is true. (Pp. 218–19)

This passage has been called Shaw's "death sentence for art." But it does not condemn art in the present. The advice is uttered in a future time "as far as thought can reach," in the year 31,920.

Ellehauge says that Shaw considers himself at the stage of artistic evolution, where "one . . . makes art serve life, and . . . is part of a movement tending towards the total supersession of art by life." Though Ellehauge refers specifically to *Back to Methuselah,* his outline applies also to Shaw's earlier comments on art. The artist damned in *Man and Superman* is in the first stage; the artist-philosopher is in the second. The third stage is reached by "the masters of reality" who in their eons of contemplation, Juan says, are to help "Life in its struggle upward" (*M&S*, p. 101). When Shaw disparages art, he is usually referring to art in the first stage; only when he projects himself "as far as thought can reach" does he condemn a higher art (stage two).

Shaw then differs from the fin-de-siècle aesthetes most emphatically, and crucially, on the question of art and morality; for Shaw art must serve an ultimately moral—i.e., religious—purpose. But when *moral* refers to conventional morality, he argues that art is not moral; however, he never admits that art is separate from morality (conventional or otherwise), but maintains rather that it is in opposition to conventional morality. In his concept of what constitutes didactic art, Shaw approaches, though he does not embrace, the idea of the detachment of art from morality (the freedom of art from overt sermonizing). His didacticism is not the oversimplifications and preachments associated with propaganda; he rejects the didacticism which offers panaceas and insists that the truthful representation of the artist's observed world will reach the emotions, then the intellect, and, hopefully, the spirit of man. For Shaw art is never an end in itself; in fact, once it has served its educative purpose, it should become unnecessary. But, until the Life Force reaches a utopian, or heavenly, stage, it is aided by the art that acts, on the lowest level, to refine the senses and, on the highest level, to refine the mind and soul.

Chapter VI

THE ARTIST, THE CENSOR, AND THE PUBLIC

HE LITERATURE of the aesthetes is rich in documents pleading for artistic freedom. In fact, René Wellek has stated that "much of what is considered 'aestheticism' in England is simply the defense of the artist against the arrogant moral pretensions of his critics, who forbade the treatment of whole areas of human experience and feelings."[1]

The aesthetes had a model for their declaration of freedom from moral censure in Gautier's preface to *Mademoiselle de Maupin;* there Gautier had damned critics for judging literature by the standards of their wives and daughters, who, he notes, could not possibly be so innocent as the critics believe. Swinburne echoed this criticism in "Notes on Poems and Reviews" (1866), particularly objecting to the prudish demands on art imposed out of consideration for "children and girls," saying that "it would seem indeed as though to publish a book were equivalent to thrusting it with violence into the hands of every mother and nurse in the kingdom as fit and necessary food for female infancy" (*Works,* 16: 363). Henry James in "The Art of Fiction" (1884) attacked the English novel for its diffidence and pointed out that "the absence of discussion is not a symptom of the moral passion."[2] And George Moore carried the battle to the circulating library in *Literature at Nurse, or Circulating Morals* (1885).

Shaw is in agreement on the question of the artist's freedom to use forbidden subject matter, to explore new techniques, and to shun prescribed morality. A remarkable number of Shaw's non-dramatic works deal with the question of artistic freedom—notably, *The Sanity of Art;* various articles for *The Saturday Review,* especially "A Purified Play" (16 February 1895), "The Late Censor" (2 March 1895), and "The Living Pictures" (6 April 1895); an article for the *North American Review,* "The Censorship of the Stage in England" (August, 1899); his statement to the Joint Select Committee on Censorship (1909), published as "The Rejected Statement" in the preface to *The Shewing Up of Blanco Posnet;* and a speech, "Censorship as a Police Duty" (8 June 1928). Though Shaw's special crusade is against the censorship of stage plays, he also wants ideological freedom for all the arts. The crusade arose partly out of personal anger, for three of his own plays were censored—*Mrs. Warren's Profession* (written 1893–94) for its subject matter; *The Shewing Up of Blanco Posnet* (1909) for blasphemy; and *Press Cuttings* (1909) for personal satire in Balsquith and Mitchener.

But the crusade also arose out of a reaction to the abusive criticism directed not only at the aesthetes but at all artistic innovators, including Ibsen and Ibsenite dramatists. For example, in the first issue of *The Yellow Book* Arthur Waugh attacks both the aesthetes and the naturalists because neither was concerned with the inculcation of morality. He asks that frankness in art be restrained by "the final test of all art, the necessity of the moral idea," and he opposes the directions modern literature has taken. He especially objects to the new school of literature which introduces the "refinements of lust . . . into the domestic chamber," even depicting childbirth and venereal disease,[3] which Waugh apparently considers equally abhorrent subjects. Though he is referring specifically to women writers of realistic fiction, his objection also obviously extends to the Ibsen-inspired drama of the late nineteenth century. An 1895 attack by Harry Quilter on Wilde and the aesthetes also attacks naturalism (Arthur Morrison's *Tales of Mean Streets* is his primary target) and the entire "neurotic" school, with its "morbid," "erotic," "repellent," "enervating" subjects.[4] In another attack on a neurotic and rebellious age, a critic for *Blackwood's Edinburgh Magazine* links the aesthete and the socialist, and the decadent and the anarchist, because they all hate what is sacred to the majority and their attitudes originate in "exaggerated emotionalism." He finds comfort in the fact that most Englishmen are Philistines and will cling "to the old-fashioned ideas of social order and decency"; after calling for a boycott of "immoral" novels, he asks that the "much-abused but most necessary official, the Licenser of Plays, . . . harden his heart and do his duty."[5] It was such attacks on art that caused Shaw to declare himself "a specialist in immoral and heretical plays"; if it is Harry Quilter's and Arthur Waugh's morality which art is supposed to uphold, then art is not, Shaw insists, and must not be moral.

The Victorian moralist was particularly hostile to the fin-de-siècle aesthetes because, by declaring morality and art separate, the aesthetes challenged his power to criticize or condemn art. Both Swinburne's "Notes on Poems and Reviews" and James's "The Art of Fiction" rest on the assumptions that (1) art is by definition independent of morality; (2) chastity is not the same thing as prudery; and (3) art is not for children and thus should not be limited to what seems suitable to them. Moore introduces further grounds for objection to the moralist's intervention, arguing in *Literature at Nurse* that (1) the censorship is not consistent, for it has not succeeded in removing all smut from the bookshelves; (2) it is in human nature to like dirty stories, and suppression of them leads to greater, not to less, perversion; (3) the romantic novel is more seductive than the naturalistic novel.[6] These arguments anticipate some of Shaw's objections to censorship: Shaw, too, cites evidence of immoral literature which has been passed by the censor, believes that repression causes perversion and obsession, and maintains that romantic (i.e., sentimental) art idolizes sensuousness.[7]

But Shaw does not base his plea for toleration on psychological and aesthetic grounds; he instead argues that, without artistic freedom, society will stagnate, that the artist must be allowed to undermine existing values before new ones can replace the outmoded ones. He urges this point at length in "The Rejected Statement" to the Joint Select Committee and repeats it often—in a note to *Androcles and the Lion,* where he parallels the Roman persecution of the Christians and all attempts to stifle iconoclasm

(p. 145) ; in the preface to *Saint Joan,* where he says that society requires "a large liberty to shock conventional people, and a well-informed sense of the value of originality, individuality, and eccentricity" (p. 40) ; and in the preface to *On the Rocks,* where Jesus tells Pilate that "without sedition and blasphemy the world would stand still and the Kingdom of God never be a stage nearer" (p. 183).

In a review of Charles E. D. Ward's *A Leader of Men,* a dramatization of the Parnell–Mrs. O'Shea affair, Shaw maintains that Ward was forced by his fear of the censor to abandon the tragic and moral possibilities of the theme. Shaw wanted Ward to dramatize the affair so as to illustrate the urgent need for changing disastrous marriage laws; instead, "the lady and her lover live happily ever after, the husband being slaughtered by Providence like a Chicago pig for their convenience" (*OTN,* 1: 39). Shaw here accuses the censor of discouraging realistic treatment of an important subject and therefore contributing to the prevalent wickedness of the stage; and he later accused him of trying to pervert *The Shewing Up of Blanco Posnet* by insisting "that all the passages which implicated God in the history of Blanco Posnet must be omitted in representation. All the coarseness, the profligacy, the prostitution, the violence, the drinking-bar humor into which the light shines in the play are licensed, but the light itself is extinguished" (Preface, *Blanco Posnet,* p. 425).

In addition to the theoretical reasons for avoiding censorship, Shaw offers a number of practical objections: (1) no one can possibly read all the plays written in England; (2) even if he could, he could not see all the performances of each play, and the effect of lines can be altered by their delivery or the gestures accompanying them; (3) once a play is licensed by the Lord Chamberlain, a local constable is helpless in trying to stop an obscene performance because the play has been sanctioned by an officer of the king; and (4) big business, having invested money in it, will oppose its closing. Another practical objection is that the police cannot "do the work of the Pope," nor can the Lord Chamberlain.[8] Shaw points out that "the Lord Chamberlain's reader is not selected by examination either in literature or morals," yet "he is the Tsar of the theatres" (*OTN,* 1: 48). For his efforts in protecting the English from "their assumed love of filth," the censor receives the following epitaph from Shaw: "He was a walking compendium of vulgar insular prejudice, who, after wallowing all his life in the cheapest theatrical sentiment (he was a confirmed playgoer), had at last brought himself to a pitch of incompetence which, outside the circle of those unfortunate persons who have had to try and reason with him personally, can only be measured by reading his evidence before the Commission of 1892, and the various letters of his which are just now finding their way into print" (*OTN*, 1: 49). The censor simply forbids "everything that is not customary," and "nothing is customary except vulgarity."[9] Consequently, good drama is retarded, and salacious plays are often given licenses.

Shaw offers two solutions to the problem of the production of offensive plays: boycott them, or issue local licenses to the theaters, so that the manager is obliged to keep an orderly house or be closed. The first idea is developed in Shaw's review of "The Living Pictures," an exhibition which brought the wrath of the National Vigilance Association and its secretary, William Alexander Coote, down on the Palace Theatre in 1895. Shaw finds nothing indecent in the "Living Pictures," but he does find something wrong with Coote's sensitivity to them. He explains that "a certain number of people . . . are morbidly sensitive to sexual impressions, and quite insensible to artistic ones"; because these people are abnormally sensitive to the sight of the human body, life offers to them constant temptations to sin. The only solution is not to close the Palace Theatre but to keep such people away from it (*OTN*, 1: 80–86). The other solution to the problem of offensive drama prevents the theater from becoming a bawdy-house by local control of the theater. Because to Shaw the theater is the church, he objects to lawless or obscene behavior in it. He agrees with Coote's demand "that the community . . . suppress indecent exhibitions," but he deplores the "attempt to make nudity or semi-nudity the criterion of indecency"—a point recalling Swinburne's distinction between chastity and prudery. Shaw is very careful to distinguish between law, which must be enforced, and opinion, which must not be forced on others.

The numerous pleas for artistic freedom from Shaw and the

aesthetes suggests the extent of public hostility toward their art. The major reason for this hostility was the increasing distance between the masses and the artist. Morris had found a "sad truth" in the fact that the public knows nothing of art, "that there is no popular art to-day, no art which represents the feelings and aspirations of the people at large."[10] But, whereas Morris hoped to make art a part of everyone's daily life, the fin-de-siècle aesthetes insisted that art has no place in most men's lives. Ruskin and Morris had hated bourgeois commercialism and the degradation of labor; but the fin-de-siècle aesthetes, influenced by the French decadence, hated the vulgar masses of mankind and wished to withdraw from an ugly, materialistic world.

Finally, imitating Whistler's and Pater's aloofness from an aesthetically ignorant public, some fin-de-siècle aesthetes argued that the barrier between the artist and the public was essential to art. George Moore asserted flatly that art which becomes popular is doomed: "Think of the fate of an author who puts forward a new idea tomorrow in a book, in a play, in a poem. The new idea is seized upon, it becomes common property, it is dragged through newspaper articles, magazine articles, through books, it is repeated in clubs, drawing rooms; it is bandied about the corners of streets; in a week it is wearisome, in a month it is an abomination."[11] And Symons declared that respectability and popularity ruined Millais, who "deliberately abandoned a career which, with labour, might have made him the greatest painter of his age, in order to become, with ease, the richest and most popular."[12]

Shaw, of course, indicts conventional morality and middle-class respectability as decisively as Moore, Symons, or Beardsley did. His early work, Shaw says, shows "the revolt of the Life Force against ready-made morality in the nineteenth century" (Preface, IK, p. xix), and his subsequent art fulfills the same aim of exposing and condemning moral pretensions.[13] Shaw also distrusts the great mass of men, who, in his opinion, have no taste for art and no talent for government. Furthermore, like the fin-de-siècle aesthetes, he considers the genius, including the artist-genius, different in kind from other men; the genius feels more and understands more than the ordinary man. He makes his own laws and behaves according to his own code.

59

But Shaw and the fin-de-siècle aesthetes react differently to the unsympathetic and aesthetically ignorant public. The aesthetes typically withdrew from public life and in their lives and their art expressed indifference to bourgeois values; as Shaw told Stephen Winsten, "They were afraid of ugliness and they turned to a visionary world where nothing was ugly."[14] On the other hand, Shaw wanted a close rapport between artist and audience, for how else can art alter manners and morals? Whereas Symons and Moore believed that popularity ruins a work of art, Shaw welcomed popularity for his plays, knowing that a preacher has to have a congregation if his sermon is to take effect.

However, when Shaw set about educating the public to his point of view, it was not at the expense of catering to the public demand for entertainment. He insisted that drama exists not to please the public but to edify it. "Even if the public really knew what it likes and what it dislikes—a consummation of wisdom which it is as far from as any child—the true master-dramatist would still give it, not what it likes, but what is good for it" (*OTN*, 1: 267–68). Shaw followed this principle in writing his plays in his own manner and with his own message, in spite of complaints from critics about his dramatic form and radical opinions. Furthermore, he was convinced that even great artists had failed when they refused to follow this principle. He calls Shakespeare's "pot boilers" (*As You Like It, Much Ado about Nothing*) a result of the public preference for his "splendid commonplaces" (*A Comedy of Errors, A Midsummer Night's Dream, Hamlet*) over his original drama (*All's Well That Ends Well, Measure for Measure*).[15] And he calls the "happy" ending to *Great Expectations* Dicken's violation of the Cromwellian and Shavian rule of "not what they want, but what is good for them" (*OTN*, 1: 94). Shaw thus shares Pater's or James's or Symons's aristocratic hauteur toward the artistically and morally inadequate public, but he prefers reform of the public to withdrawal from it.

Shocking the public is one of the techniques which Shaw found most effective in awakening it. In "Shocking as a Fine Art" Holbrook Jackson divides devotees of the art into two types—individual (Wilde, Beardsley, Symons, Beerbohm) and social (Shaw, Grant Allen); he says that both types arose from "the same demand for more freedom, more experience, more sensation, more life."[16] Again, the difference between Shaw and the fin-de-siècle aesthetes in the art of shocking was the crucial one: the aesthetes practiced the art for its own sake; Shaw used it for therapeutic purposes. He says, "It is necessary to shock people violently to make them think seriously about religion."[17] He did not have to look far for "shocking" material; it was visible all around him. Because of his abnormally "normal" vision, Shaw states, "All I had to do was to open my normal eyes, and with my utmost literary skill put the case exactly as it struck me, or describe the thing exactly as I saw it, to be applauded as the most humorously extravagant paradoxer in London" (Preface, *Plays Unpleasant*, p. vii). As society defines morality, Shaw was a deviate; as Shaw defines it, almost everybody else is.

In summary, we can see points of agreement between Shaw and the fin-de-siècle aesthetes in their antibourgeois and antidemocratic prejudices and in their desire to shock the public. However, unlike the fin-de-siècle aesthetes, Shaw did not withdraw from the people, but sought to effect through his "normal" art a change in society and, ultimately, a change in the nature of humankind. Common enemies such as Harry Quilter, Arthur Waugh, and other upholders of Victorian morality led him and the aesthetes to similar demands for artistic freedom. Shaw's demands arose from a conviction that, if man is to progress, he must have freedom to reject old systems and formulate new ones. Whereas the aesthetes were objecting to restrictive theories and rules in art and were denying that morality was an issue, Shaw was objecting to labelling art "immoral" and insisting that, if the artist is to express an ever-changing religion, he must be free to offend the public and its censor.

Chapter VII

THE FORM AND THE CONTENT
OF ART

HAW DESCRIBED the genius as a man divinely inspired to carry on the work of the Life Force by "building up an intellectual consciousness of [Nature's] own instinctive purpose" (Epistle Dedicatory, *M&S*, p. xx). This description applies not only to the man of action but to the artist-genius as well, who, according to the preface to *Plays Pleasant* (p. viii), reflects the purpose of the Life Force "in the magic glass of his artwork." It is no surprise, then, to find Shaw referring to himself as a divinely inspired writer: "I am not governed by principles; I am inspired, how or why I cannot explain, because I do not know; but inspiration it must be; for it comes to me without any reference to my own ends or interest."[1] His explanation to the Abbess of Stanbrook of how he came to write *The Black Girl in Search of God,* to which the Abbess strongly objected, is that God commanded him to write it and then to publish it.[2] That this explanation was not facetious is evident in Shaw's statement to his biographer, Archibald Henderson, that there was "something behind the creation of a play all the time, of which I was not conscious, though it turns out to be the real motive of the whole creation."[3]

Yet Shaw is closer to the aesthetes' belief in a carefully wrought art than his theory of divine inspiration and his Ruskin-influenced comments on the ease of artistic productivity would suggest. Though he believed that "the person who writes slowly and with great deliberation does not necessarily write better than one who writes in great heat," he also said, "In my plays there is not a word I have not brooded over until it expressed the exact meaning."[4] An explanation of this apparent contradiction is suggested in one of Shaw's letters to Mrs. Patrick Campbell, in which he says, "I never have to think of how to say anything in prose; the words come with the thought: *I often have to argue a thing carefully to get it right;* but when I have found the right thing to say it says itself instantly" (italics added).[5] It would seem that the careful, deliberative stage comes for Shaw in the thinking rather than in the executing stage. One recalls Dante Gabriel Rossetti's method of composition, which was to lie on the couch before beginning a work until he had thought it through; Rossetti explained that he would mentally "cartoon" the work "beforehand, by a process intensely conscious but patient and silent."[6] Shaw was speaking of a similar process when, in a journalistic debate with the playwright Terence Rattigan he said, "The difference between his practice and mine is that I reason out every sentence I write to the utmost of my capacity before I commit it to print, whereas he slams down everything that comes into his head without reasoning about it at all."[7] For Shaw the idea may originate with inspiration and be recorded with ease, but between the conception and the finished work is a conscious and deliberative stage.

Shaw even espouses the fin-de-siècle aesthetes' conviction that *ars est celare artem.* Just as Whistler argues that art appears effortless because the artist has labored to remove all evidence of effort, Shaw says that his writing is very difficult because he makes "solid disquisitions on the heaviest subjects, from political economy to classical music, come out as if they were the airiest *jeux d'esprit.*"[8] This idea receives its most detailed expression in Shaw's comments on acting. He believed that an actress first has to learn to speak— to avoid voice strain, bad diction, and corrupt vowels; then she must perfect the technique of appearing not to be acting. At first she picks a number of "points" to make smoothly; then she increases the number of points until, if she is great, "she is always making points." Using the actress Eleanora Duse as an example, Shaw notes that she integrates "the points into a continuous whole, at which stage the actress appears to make no points at all, and to proceed in the most unstudied and 'natural' way" (*OTN*, 1: 147).

Just as Shaw's insistence on divine inspiration and "natural" composition requires qualification and redefinition of terms, so too his defense of ideas over plot in drama requires careful examination. When Shaw said that he was "a dramatic poet, not a plot-monger,"[9] he made a distinction essential to understanding his attitude toward dramatic form. As Shaw uses it, *plot* does not mean the arrangement of incidents into a meaningful pattern of cause and effect; it means instead a mechanical formula, like that used in those "clumsy booby traps," the French well-made plays. Shaw's dramatic criticism of the 1890s aimed to demolish these plays, which Shaw says lack not only meaningful action, believable characters, and important themes but also skillful construction and effective staging. He condemned their awkward exposition, contrived scenes, and improbable endings and recommended instead a dramatic form which grows out of the interrelationship of character, idea, and incident.

Like Henry James, who conceived of the novel as "a living thing, all one and continuous, like any other organism,"[10] Shaw uses an organic metaphor to suggest the dramatic form he wishes to see in place of the formula plot. He criticizes the secondhand ideas "dove-tailed into a coherent structure instead of developing into one another by any life of their own" in J. Comyns Carr's *King Arthur* and the lack of "dramatic soil" for the growth of incidents in *Cheer, Boys, Cheer!* (*OTN*, 1: 16, 206). Conversely, he praises Henry Arthur Jones's plays because they "grow: they are not cut out of bits of paper and stuck together" (*OTN*, 2: 14). His account of the origin of *Widowers' Houses* also illustrates his hostility to mechanical plotting. William Archer was to provide the scenario for Shaw's dialogue, but Shaw "used up" all of Archer's plot by the second act and "wanted some more to go on with"; Archer refused to continue the collaboration. According to Shaw, they disagreed about the merits of a well-made play over a play which "will construct itself, like a flowering plant, far more wonderfully than its author can consciously construct it" (*Portraits*, pp. 21–22).

Though rejecting "plot" as a valid way of constructing drama, Shaw never suggests that dramatic form is unimportant. Instead, he says that one of the purposes of the dramatist is "to shew the connexion between things that seem apart and unrelated in the haphazard order of events in real life."[11] He distinguishes between gathering information and truth-telling, between making an exact record of events, as newspaper items and photographs do, and making sense of them, as art does.

> When a man writes a drama or a book or preaches a sermon or employs any other method of art, what he really does is to take the events of life out of the accidental, irrelevant, chaotic way in which they happen, and to rearrange them in such a way as to reveal their essential and spiritual relations to oneanother. Leaving out all that is irrelevant, he has to connect the significant facts by chains of reasoning, and also to make, as it were, bridges of feeling between them by a sort of ladder, get the whole thing in a connected form into your head, and give you a spiritual, political, social, or religious consciousness.[12]

Shaw could therefore endorse Whistler's assertion that the artist must "pick, and choose, and group with science" the elements of nature; but, Shaw would add, this selectivity and organization is no end in itself. Such phrases as "to reveal their essential and spiritual relations to oneanother" or "give you a spiritual, political, social, or religious consciousness" are foreign to Whistler and the fin-de-siècle aesthetes.

A frequent theme of both Shaw and the aesthetes concerning the relationship between artistic form and content is the idea of music as "the type of all the arts." Pater used an analogy between the arts and music to refer to the perfect integration of form and matter; Whistler used it to describe the subordination of subject to form; Wilde and Symons used it to suggest either the mystery at the heart of all art or simply the sonorous effect of poetry; and all used it as a means of emphasizing the importance of form.[13] Similarly, in "The Religion of the Pianoforte," Shaw said, "The greatest of the great among poets, from Aeschylus to Wagner, have been poet-musicians." In "Literature and Art" he wrote that a literary man with a message "becomes a master of rhetoric that affects you like music. . . . It acts on your senses and imagination in some strange way that, although you do not altogether under-stand the content of it, yet you feel that it is a great ringing message to you, a penetrating message that goes home."[14] Thus, he emphasized Shakespeare's ability to create verbal music, and he said that his own plays "are essentially poetic dramas and should be sung." Answering a critic's comment on his kinship to Congreve and Sheridan, he says, "There is more of Il Trovatore and Don Giovanni in my style than of The Mourning Bride and The School for Scandal."[15]

A comparison of Shaw's and the aesthetes' commentary on music reveals precisely their differences: Shaw demands subject and meaning in music, condemning Mendelssohn, Offenbach, and Italian opera on the basis of this demand and praising Bach, Wagner, Berlioz, Liszt, Beethoven, and Richard Strauss. In *The Sanity of Art* and *The Perfect Wagnerite* he distinguishes between composers of decorative and dramatic music. The former, like Academy painters and writers of well-made plays, follow "laws of pattern designing" or, like exponents of art for art's sake, create "a graceful, symmetrical sound-pattern that exists solely for the sake of its own grace and symmetry" (*SA*, p. 295). On the other hand, Wagner, freed by Mozart and Beethoven from the necessity of prescribed patterns, is purely dramatic; his ideas are essential and are woven "into a rich musical fabric" (*Wagnerite*, pp. 264–69). Though Shaw clearly prefers dramatic art, he does not condemn all decorative art. The playwright, for example, is free to use "all the rhetorical and lyrical arts of the orator, the preacher, the pleader, and the rhapsodist" (*Quintessence*, p. 146). Moreover, there are two kinds of decorative art: (1) art for its own sake, last exemplified in its pure form in the music of the thirteenth, fourteenth, or fifteenth centuries, much of which "is very beautiful, and hugely superior to the stuff our music publishers turn out today"; and (2) academic art, which failed to recognize the need for new forms when music ceased to be pattern and became poem or story (*SA*, pp. 295–300). Therefore, when Shaw says that the greatest artists, such as Shakespeare, Shelley, and Mozart, are masters of both decorative and dramatic music, he means that they combined "pure form" and idea. His objections are to academism, the attempt to make laws requiring all art to be decorative.

These objections amount to an insistence that artistic form be suited to the artist's purpose and matter; Wagner found a new form to suit his dramatic purpose, just as Shaw was creating a new form of drama to suit *his* purpose. This form has been called "a static drama of the intelligence" and "slices of life on the stage";[16] it had, like some of the aesthetes' art, a nonanecdotal quality. Shaw described the new form in this way: "A first-rate play seems nowadays [1906] to have no situation, just as Wagner's music seemed to our grandfathers to have no melody, because it was all melody from beginning to end. The best plays consist of a single situation, lasting several hours."[17] And he instructed an actors' conference on the production of a Shaw play, "Don't be afraid of being static. I am not leading up to a murder but to a thought."[18] A drama which is all situation and which intends to produce thought by discussion involves a redefinition of action and of incident, just as James's fiction required a redefinition of incident or Whistler's painting a redefinition of "subject." Shaw is sympathetic, for example, to Whistler's attempt to force people to look at his painting as artistic form rather than as anecdote. Whistler knew, Shaw says, "that if he left a woman's face discernible the British Philistine would simply look to see whether she was a pretty girl or not, or whether she represented some of his pet characters in fiction, and pass on without having seen any of the qualities of artistic execution which made the drawing valuable" (*SA*, p. 292). As Whistler obliterated details in order to emphasize line and color in painting, Shaw obliterates "plot" in order to concentrate on the essence of drama, that is, the integration of fable and idea.

Finally, Shaw's well-known statements on the importance of ideas in art, including even music, his praise of Ibsen and Wagner for their philosophy and his criticism of Shakespeare for his lack of it need to be balanced against his comments on the primarily emotional effect of art. In a *Saturday Review* article Shaw maintains that the appeal to human "instincts and passions" constitutes the most valid claim to immortality that art has. He explains that a play ages in this manner: first, "its manners and fashions will begin to date"; then its reputation may return if its ideas are powerful enough to save it from oblivion; next, its morals will begin to date. "Yet if it deals so powerfully with the instincts and passions of humanity as to survive this also, it will again regain its place, this time as an antique classic, especially if it tells a capital story" (*OTN*, 2: 167). Here he attributes the permanent value of a classic play to its universal qualities; later, in the Epistle Dedicatory to *Man and Superman,* he says that a play's permanence is determined by its style and form. In a remarkable defense of form over idea, he says, "Disprove his [the artist's] assertion after it is made, yet its style remains. Darwin has no more destroyed the style of Job nor of Handel than Martin Luther destroyed the style of Giotto. All the assertions get disproved sooner or later; and so we find the world full of a magnificent debris of artistic fossils, with the matter-of-fact credibility gone clean out of them, but the form still splendid" (p. xxxv). This belief is identical to Wilde's or Symons's or Yeats's faith in the transitory nature of everything but art. However, Shaw goes one step farther in his belief in impermanence and change; he says that eventually the art form itself will lose its appeal when human sensibilities evolve to a higher plane of existence, as they have in Shaw's utopia in part 5 of *Back to Methuselah.*

Shaw's comment on the permanence of style occurs, ironically, in the same passage in which he condemns art for art's sake. In this passage he also dismisses as mechanical any style which is not a direct result of an idea or a conviction.

> I know that there are men who, having nothing to say and nothing to write, are nevertheless so in love with oratory and with literature that they delight in repeating as much as they can understand of what others have said or written aforetime. I know that the leisurely tricks which their want of conviction leaves them free to play with the diluted and misapprehended message supply them with a pleasant parlor game which they call style. I can pity their dotage and even sympathize with their fancy. But a true original style is never achieved for its own sake: a man may pay from a shilling to a guinea, according to his means, to see, hear, or read another man's act of genius; but he will not pay with his whole life and soul to become a mere virtuoso in literature, exhibiting an accomplishment which will not even make money for him, like fiddle playing. Effectiveness of assertion is the Alpha and Omega of style. He who has nothing to assert has no style and can have none: he who has something to assert will go as far in power of style as its momentousness and his conviction will carry him. (Pp. xxxiv–xxxv)

Here "style . . . for its own sake" has the same ambiguity as Shaw's description of decorative music: it is, first of all, the imitation of the old masters, the academic art which Shaw and his Pre-Raphaelite brothers condemned; secondly, it is playing with language, "a pleasant parlor game," which Shaw finds abhorrent but which Pater says "satisfies a real instinct in our minds—the fancy so many of us have for an exquisite and curious skill in the use of words."[19]

Shaw's opposition to "style . . . for its own sake" finds expression in his attack on the "insane and hideous rhetoric" of Elizabethan writers (*OTN*, 1: 130). Whereas Pater finds a "delightful side" to the "dainty language and curious expression" of *Love's Labour's Lost,* Shaw says that Shakespeare was at his worst when he was influenced by "the miserable rhetoric and silly logical conceits which were the foible of the Elizabethans" (*OTN,* 1: 203). Shaw parodied Elizabethan language in *The Admirable Bashville,* a dramatization of his novel *Cashel Byron's Profession* (*T&T,* p. 85). This play is, Shaw says, "in the primitive Elizabethan style"; it is a mélange of quotations from Elizabethan plays inserted in a blank verse deliberately overwrought and filled with archaisms— a style that could serve as a burlesque of "that foppery of words, of choice diction" described in *Marius the Epicurean,* filled with "archaisms and curious felicities, . . . quaint terms and images picked fresh from the early dramatists, and lifelike phrases of some lost poet preserved by an old grammarian, racy morsels of the vernacular and studied prettinesses."[20]

Appropriately, *The Admirable Bashville* is one of the few pieces of art for art's sake (i.e., art that "has nothing to assert") in Shaw's canon; he took advantage of a practical necessity—the need to protect *Cashel Byron's Profession* from dramatic piracies—to create "a literary joke." And, also appropriately, it emphasizes his contempt for playing with language and form and following mechanical rules:

> I observed the established laws of stage popularity and probability. I simplified the character of the heroine, and summed up her sweetness in the one sacred word: Love. I gave consistency to the heroism of Cashel. I paid to Morality, in the final scene, the tribute of poetic justice. I restored to Patriotism its usual place on the stage, and gracefully acknowledged The Throne as the fountain of social honor. I paid particular attention to the construction of the play, which will be

found equal in this respect to the best contemporary models. (*T&T*, pp. 85–86)

The play illustrates his theory that, without anything to assert (he was simply protecting his copyright), an artist lacks a style; he follows a formula and creates neither an effective form nor meaningful content.

In place of what he considers an artificial style, Shaw demands in idiomatic, vernacular style. Though he could advise Golding-Bright, the young critic of *Advice to a Young Critic*, "to admit, with absolute respect, the right of every man to his own style,"[21] his stylistic preferences are clear. One of his criticisms of his own novel *Immaturity* is that the style has "propriety" and "correctness," but that it lacks idiom; he adds parenthetically, "Later on I came to seek idiom as being the most highly vitalized form of language" (Preface, *Immaturity*, p. xxxix). In his dramatic criticism he finds fault with plays which substitute "literary" for idiomatic speech, as, for example, the dramatization of Hall Caine's *The Manxman*, which Shaw says reveals that "the Manx race are without a vernacular, and only communicate with one another by extracts from Cassell's National Library, the Chandos Classics, and the like" (*OTN*, 1: 251).

Though the aesthetes and Shaw disagree about the effectiveness of a "dainty" or "delicate" style created out of the artist's sense of play, a style belonging to what Max Beerbohm called "the 'precious' school of writers,"[22] the aesthetes would agree that a style arising out of the imperfect combination of subject and form is to be condemned. Shaw's belief that a great stylist must have "something to assert" is perfectly compatible with Pater's "Style" or his "School of Giorgione," in which effective style and form are defined as the artistic fusion of matter and form, or with James's "The Art of Fiction," where James says that "there is surely no 'school'—Mr. Besant speaks of a school—which urges that a novel should be all treatment and no subject. There must assuredly be something to treat; every school is intimately conscious of that. . . . In proportion as the work is successful the idea permeates and penetrates it, informs and animates it, so that every word and every punctuation point contribute directly to the expression."[23] Shaw's emphasis on ideas does not divide him and the aesthetes as much as it might at first seem, for Shaw says that "after all, the main thing in determining the artistic quality of a book is not the opinions it propagates, but the fact that the writer has opinions" (Epistle Dedicatory, *M&S*, pp. xxxiii–xxxiv). This suggestion that ideas are primarily important because they produce "artistic quality" is from an artist's, not a propagandist's, point of view.

Where Shaw and the aesthetes differ is not so much on the theory of style as on personal preferences in style. Whereas Pater, Symons, Wilde, and Yeats prefer the lyric impulse and the perfectly wrought form of jewel-like little masterpieces, Shaw prefers the more expansive style that prose allows.[24] Yeats's hatred of the "very clever young journalists" who, admiring Ibsen, "hated music and style" and the Ibsenite playwrights whose "expression is as common as the newspapers where they first learned to write"[25] is unfair to Shaw. Because Shaw seldom ignored an opportunity to attack art for art's sake, style, and even art itself has often obscured the fact that, like the aesthetes, he is a highly conscious literary artist. As Richard Burton correctly points out in his chapter on Shaw, "The Theatre Craftsman," the unusual form of Shaw's drama should not be mistaken for formlessness: "Right or wrong as to the results, [Shaw] knows the rules of the game, consciously alters or ignores them, chooses to do what he does, and takes the risks."[26]

Chapter VIII

ART AND REALITY

NE OF SHAW'S most persistent ideas is that he is a realistic dramatist, taking "all my dramatic material either from real life at first hand, or from authentic documents."[1] Shaw's realism was, on one level, as we have seen, a part of the Pre-Raphaelite return to nature—a rejection of academic rules and an insistence that the artist record accurately what he sees. But on another level it was as removed from the everyday, familiar world as the work of the most detached fin-de-siècle aesthete.

On occasion the fin-de-siècle aesthetes also appealed to a realistic standard like that of the Pre-Raphaelites. For example, Whistler asked his critics to judge his paintings by observing reality rather than other paintings; he argued that, if the critics of his color and tone would look at the people rather than at the other paintings in the gallery, they would see "how 'quiet' in colour [the people] are! how 'grey!' how 'low in tone.' "[2] And Aubrey Beardsley affirmed the realism of his first cover for *The Yellow Book*—a drawing of a lady playing the piano, with an open field as background—by appealing to the historical fact that Gluck played the piano and composed several works in a field, with a bottle of champagne at each side; "I tremble to think," Beardsley observes, "what critics would say had I introduced those bottles of champagne."[3] Shaw offers the same appeal to extraordinary but actual events in defending *Arms and the Man* from what critics took to be the improbable nature of Bluntschli's behavior. After citing numerous doscuments verifying the terror, caution, and hunger of brave men in battle, Shaw says, "I have stuck to the routine of war, as described by real warriors, and avoided such farcical [real] incidents as Sir William Gordon defending his battery by throwing stones, or General Porter's story of the two generals who, though brave and capable men, always got sick under fire."[4]

But unlike Shaw—and Whistler and Beardsley in the instances cited—the fin-de-siècle aesthetes usually avoided applying the term *realism* to their work because of its associations with either representationalism or naturalism, to which they objected on the grounds that both catered to vulgar tastes and eschewed style. For example, Wilde's "The Decay of Lying" attacks "realistic" (i.e., naturalistic and representational) art because it is uninteresting, improbable, and vulgar; Zola, Wilde says, tells truthfully what he sees but is wrong artistically because he is dull; and Charles Reade, after creating one beautiful book, began "raging and roaring over the abuses of contemporary life like a common pamphleteer or a sensational journalist."[5] Although Shaw (or, for that matter, Wilde) was capable of "raging and roaring" over contemporary abuses, his concept of realistic art is more like that of Wilde than that of Zola. Shaw denied that he had "ever been what you call a representationist or realist. I was always in the classic tradition, recognizing that stage characters must be endowed by the author with a conscious self-knowledge and power of expression, and . . . a freedom from inhibitions, which in real life would make them monsters of genius. It is the power to do this that differentiates me (or Shakespear) from a gramophone and a camera."[6] More often than not, Shaw's realism refers to more than perception of the familiar world. In *The Quintessence of Ibsenism* he warns that his realism is not to be associated with that of Zola and De Maupassant, but with that of Plato. His realism is not simply accurate reproduction of empirical reality, but an attempt to represent the essence behind the illusory sensible world—to use Shaw's terminology, "to realize the future possibilities by tearing the mask and the thing masked asunder." The mask to Shaw is idealism, a much confused term because people use it to describe both (1) illusion and (2) the attempt to destroy illusion. Shaw uses *idealism* in the first sense and gives the name *realism* to the second. Unlike the idealist (or romanticist, a term Shaw also contrasts with "realist"), the Shavian realist, combining a utopian and practical imagination, has "the power to imagine things as they are without actually sensing them."

To Shaw the realist illuminates the reality existing behind the shadows of the apparent world—the reality not visible to most people. Thus he considered Rodin a realistic sculptor because he was able to see behind the mask of reputation and sculpt the "real" man. With "accurate vision" and "incorruptible veracity," Rodin created busts "of real men, not of the reputations of celebrated persons" (*Portraits*, pp. 227–31). This Platonic view is compatible with Wilde's concept of the liar-artist, who does not attempt to copy nature but creates an imaginary world, an "untrue" and "unreal" world superior to the ordinary one. The primary difference is in the terminology, not the idea: the "real" vision of the artist Shaw describes is similar to the "unreal" vision of Wilde's artist.

In fact, Wilde's attack on realism and his insistence that art deal with the unreal and the unfamiliar implies not so much the need for abandoning realism as for redefining what is real. The background for such an extension of the province of art was provided by Ruskin and the Pre-Raphaelites, who believed that the artist must be true to his own observation of nature; Ruskin had introduced a relativistic note when he said that the art produced will be as various as the artists' visions. And Pater's philosophy had clearly placed reality in the mind of the individual artist, whose own sensations and reactions are the materials of art. Such an individualistic, subjective world constitutes "reality" for the fin-de-siècle aesthetes: it is implicit in Wilde's assertion in "The Decay of Lying" that art does not copy, but creates life; it is the basis for James's "fine central intelligence"; it is the basis for Symons's praise of the French symbolists for being able to suggest by symbol the reality of the spiritual world, apprehended only mystically; and it is the basis of Yeats's defense of "personal utterance," the lyric impulse, over propagandistic or "realistic" (i.e., journalistic, propagandistic) art.

So too Shaw's theory calls for an artist who is interested primarily in creating a world which represents his inner vision. When the musician-hero of *Love among the Artists* explains that "there is an art which is inspired by a passion for beauty, but only in men who can never associate beauty with a lie" (p. 330), the hero, who speaks for Shaw, is not so far from the position of Wilde's "The Decay of Lying" as one might at first assume. To Shaw the artist is a truth teller, but the nature of that truth and the reality it describes involves a rejection of much that ordinary people see, so that to them it seems to be a distortion, an exaggeration, a lie. Shaw believes that literary people and dramatic critics are especially conditioned to conventional ideas of reality: "Hence Captain Bluntschli, who thinks of a battlefield as a very busy and very dangerous place, is incredible to the critic who thinks of it only as a theatre in which to enjoy the luxurious excitements of patriotism, victory, and bloodshed without risk or retribution."[7]

Of course, Shaw's art is indeed a lie in that, being art and not life, it involves a reshaping of experiential reality. Shaw readily admits, with Whistler and Wilde, that the artist must create, not copy, life: "Holding a mirror up to nature . . . is not a correct definition of a playwright's art. A mirror reflects what is before it. Hold it up to any street at noonday and it shews a crowd of people and vehicles and tells you nothing about them. A photograph of them has no meaning. . . . The playwright must interpret the passing show by parables."[8] He also differentiates between accurate portrait-painting and fictional characterization. In a review of his novels, he concedes that the heroine of *Cashel Byron's Profession* "is super-human all through" and "that her inside is full of wheels and springs"; but he says that fiction does not require "flesh and blood": "The business of a novelist is largely to provide working models of improved types of humanity."[9] Although he often used living models for numerous characters in his work—e.g., Cecil Lawson (Cyril Scott), Sidney Webb (Bluntschli), Jenny Patterson (Julia Craven), William Morris (Apollodorus), Ellen Terry (Lady Cicely), Edward Aveling (Dubedat)—he freely altered his models. Thus when Mrs. Patrick Campbell objected to Orinthia in *The Apple Cart*, he wrote: "Orinthia is not a portrait: she is a study for which you sat as a model in bits only. . . . I am an artist and as such utterly unscrupulous when I find my model."[10] And, when he used historical figures—Burgoyne, Caesar,

Joan—he says that, though he followed historical reality, of necessity he altered it to conform to the limitations of stage representation. In *Saint Joan* he departed from history "to condense into three and a half hours a series of events which in their historical happening were spread over four times as many months" and "to make its figures more intelligible to themselves than they would be in real life"; therefore, Cauchon, Lemaître, and Warwick are represented as saying "the things they actually would have said if they had known what they were really doing" (Preface, *Joan,* pp. 47, 51).

Shaw's alteration of real people to "improved types of humanity" suggests an agreement with Wilde's contention that art is better than life. In "The Decay of Lying" Wilde argues that art is, because of its perfection of form, more interesting than life, and even more probable: "It is style that makes us believe a thing—nothing but style." Shaw suggests that art is more interesting than life when, in the preface to *In Good King Charles' Golden Days,* he says, "When we turn from the sordid facts of Charles' reign, and from his Solomonic polygamy, to what might have happened to him but did not the situation becomes interesting and fresh" (p. 153).

At times Shaw even maintains as Wilde does that "life imitates art far more than Art imitates life." In a much parodied overstatement Wilde says that, when the liar-artist returns to a society now vulgarized and bored by facts and truth tellers, he will be welcomed by Art, and life will "try to reproduce, in her own simple and untutored way, some of the marvels of which he talks." As proof, Wilde points to the "aesthetic" lady in a salon trying to look like a lady in Rossetti's art or to the recent change in climate, the "wonderful brown fogs" and "lovely silver mists," a direct result of impressionist painting.[11] So, too, Shaw says, "I have noticed that when a certain type of feature appears in painting and is admired as beautiful, it presently becomes common in nature; so that the Beatrices and Francescas in the picture galleries of one generation . . . come to life as the parlor-maids and waitresses of the next" (Preface, *Three Plays,* p. xix). He says that his aristocrats in *Cashel Byron's Profession* are more priggish than real ones because, when he wrote the novel, he had not yet discovered that "what he supposed to be the real world does not exist, and that men and women are made by their own fancies in the image of the imaginary creatures in his youthful fictions, only much stupider" (p. v). Unlike Wilde, Shaw usually finds most attempts to emulate art reprehensible because the art people choose to imitate is unreal, i.e., idealistic, romantic. He attacks the tendency to found institutions on "fictitious morals and fictitious good conduct" (Preface, *Plays Pleasant*, p. xvi) and condemns the literary men and drama critics who base their ideas on "stage morality and stage human nature" and thus become "idiotically confident of the reality of [their] own unreal knowledge."[12] The trouble is that fictional behavior and attitudes are unworthy of imitation: romantic literature causes man to be needlessly jealous, bellicose, vindictive, superstitious. As proof of this Shaw observes, "Ten years of cheap reading have changed the English from the most stolid nation in Europe to the most theatrical and hysterical." Therefore he would purge England of all romantic art and substitute a realistic art, depicting "real life," which is inconsistent, unjust, and "unthinkable," but also "credible, stimulating, suggestive, various, free from creeds and systems—in short, it is real."[13]

Shaw's final position is that reality does not have to be opposed to art; reality may reside in art, as in the work of Shaw, Ibsen, or Wagner. In a statement clearly asserting the reality of art, Shaw says, "I turned a person, now an M. P., into something real by incorporating him as a character in *The Doctor's Dilemma.* . . . No person is real until he has been transmitted into a work of art."[14] On another occasion Shaw said that the greatest art is a form of self-realization in which the artist himself becomes "completely real." Using the actor Coquelin as his example, Shaw says that the great actor needs roles that reveal a part of his nature to us, and "his best part will be that which shews all sides of him and realizes him wholly to us and to himself. . . . In it he becomes for the first time completely real: he has achieved the aspiration of the hero of Ibsen's fantastic play and become himself at last. This is not acting: it is the final escape from acting, the ineffable release from the conventional mask which must be resumed as the artist passes behind the wing, washes off the paint, and goes down into the false lights and simulated interests and passions of the street."[15]

This reality is the kind of truth to which Shaw's musician-hero who "can never associate beauty with a lie" refers: it is a truth which goes beyond the world of appearance and beyond even the artistic world in which technical mastery enables the artist to produce the illusion of reality. The actress in *Love among the Artists*, Madge Brailsford, has mastered her craft so well that she appears completely natural on the stage; but, as someone observes, she is "stagey in private," and, even when she is most serious, when she is confessing her love for Owen Jack, she is merely acting a role, looking at Jack "with an expression of earnest sympathy which had cost her much study to perfect" (p. 322). Her private staginess brings on the lecture by Jack on the difference between an art inspired by truth and an art inspired by sham:

> We are not a pair, you and I. I know how to respect myself: do you learn to know yourself. We two are artists, as you are aware. Well, there is an art that is inspired by nothing but a passion for shamming; and that is yours, so far. There is an art which is inspired by a passion for beauty, but only in men who can never associate beauty with a lie. That is my art. Master that and you will be able to make true love. At present you only know how to make scenes, which is too common an accomplishment to interest me. You see you have not quite finished your lessons yet. Goodbye. (P. 330)

Shaw would, then, have the artist penetrate to the inner truth behind not only the lie of romantic art but also the lie of everyday life. Although, like the Pre-Raphaelites, he says that he bases his art on observed phenomena and although he claims to deal with the familiar, not the unusual or artificial, he aspires to a realism that captures the essence rather than the sensation of occurrences, that deals with the spirit, rather than the material elements of life, that portrays the inner being rather than the facade. His realism is therefore not that of the naturalist; nor does it depict the conventional world and its values. It is the reshaped, motivated, articulated reality which may be more interesting, and certainly is more meaningful, than life. Like Wilde, Shaw maintains that life imitates art; his regret is that the art imitated is too often a shabby one. Shaw's art offers to supply a reality worthy of imitation.

PART III

THE AESTHETE AND THE SHAVIAN ARTIST

Chapter IX

THE NATURE OF THE AESTHETE-ARTIST

UST AS A COMPARISON of the art theories of the aesthetes and Shaw emphasizes an aspect of Shaw which until recent years had been neglected—the idea of Shaw as artist rather than as philosopher or social critic—a comparison of the image of the artist in the works of the fin-de-siècle aesthetes and Shaw similarly emphasizes the importance Shaw gives to the artist's role. The fact that Shaw expects the artist to prophesy and interpret the next stage of creative evolution would suggest a great difference between the amoral, hypersensitive aesthete-artist and the Shavian artist; nevertheless, Shaw's portraits of artists of whom he approves—Marchbanks, Apollodorus, or, with qualifications, Dubedat—contain some characteristics of the aesthete-artist. Conversely, the artists of whom Shaw disapproves—Hawkshaw in *Immaturity*, Adrian Herbert in *Love among the Artists*, or Octavius in *Man and Superman*—are failures primarily because they are dilettantes, not because they are aesthetes.

In characterizing the aesthete-artist, a distinction must first be made between the artist who wishes to make an art of a highly conscious, aware, and intense life (Pater's Marius and Wilde's Dorian Gray are obvious examples) and an artist in the usual sense, a man dedicated to creating art forms. *Aesthete*, as I define the term, may refer to either kind of artist, by *aesthete-artist* I mean the latter kind. Examples of the aesthete-artist in late nineteenth-century fiction are Apuleius and Flavian in *Marius the*

81

Epicurean; the young man in George Moore's *Confessions of a Young Man;* the novelists and painters in Henry James's "artist" stories; Anton in Dowson's "Souvenirs of an Egoist"; Dick Lightmark and Oswyn in Arthur Moore's and Ernest Dowson's *A Comedy of Masks* (1893) ; and the speaker of Symons's "A Prelude to Life." In these portraits as well as in the fin-de-siècle aesthetes' critical commentary, the artist is an alien to society and either rebels against it or withdraws from it. Believing that personal morality has nothing to do with artistic excellence, he is not of necessity virtuous and may possibly be evil. He is sensitive to ugliness, often to the point of hypersensitivity. Because he consciously tries to salvage out of shapeless and meaningless life an artistic form, he usually acts a role or poses, as a means of asserting the power of artifice over nature. Above all, as a creator of what may be the real thing, he asserts his superiority to society and demands freedom from its restrictions.

In *Confessions of a Young Man* George Moore defends the concept of the alienated artist: "In the past the artist has always been an outcast; it is only latterly he has become domesticated, and judging by results, it is clear that if Bohemianism is not a necessity it is at least an adjuvant. For if long locks and general dissoluteness were not an aid and a way to pure thought, why have they been so long his characteristics?"[1] The idea of the artist as Bohemian is not, of course, one which originated at the end of the nineteenth century; the sense of alienation of the fin-de-siècle aesthete is part of the same impulse that created the Byronic hero, with his scorn for, and withdrawal from, society, or Murger's Bohemian artists in *La Vie de Bohème* (1845). But the romantic sense of isolation was so pronounced for the fin-de-siècle aesthete-artist that he sometimes felt, as Moore suggests, that alienation is a prerequisite for artistic productivity.

In reaction to an artistically ignorant, indifferent, and hostile society, the aesthete-artist either rebelled or withdrew. Artistic rebellion received sanction from both the moral and fin-de-siècle aesthetes; it is at the heart of the Pre-Raphaelite movement and is possibly the major motivation of the fin-de-siècle aesthetes. More than one critic considers revolt against the materialism of Victorian England the primary character of the fin-de-siècle period;

for example, A. J. Farmer (*Le Mouvement esthétique et "décadent" en Angleterre*) says that Pater's aestheticism, Moore's naturalism, Wilde's decadence, and Symons's impressionism are all united in their ideal of emancipation from the out-of-date dogmas of Victorianism.[2] Even the lives of the fin-de-siécle aesthetes dramatized their rebellion. Wilde's costume of the 1880s advertized not only his devotion to beauty but also his rebellion against convention; it is to this rebellious impulse that Ford Madox Ford refers when he says, "When Oscar Wilde wandered down Bond Street in a mediaeval costume, bearing in his hand a flower, he was doing something not merely ridiculous. It was militant."[3]

The alternative to active rebellion against an artistically illiterate public was withdrawal from it. The prototype of such withdrawal is Huysmans's decadent hero, Des Esseintes, who completely withdraws from the sordid vulgarity of ordinary life. Pater's heroes—Winckelmann, Marius, Sebastian van Storck, for example—are also characteristically detached spectators of, rather than participants in, life, in accord with Pater's belief that the aesthetic life demands freedom from involvement. Max Beerbohm satirized this freedom when he said that he came to Oxford as an undergraduate, like Marius to Rome, aspiring to "unswitch myself from my surroundings, to guard my soul from contact with the unlovely things that compassed it about."[4]

Just as the fin-de-siècle aesthetes saw the artist as separate from society, so also they considered his work separate from his personal life. They agreed with Baudelaire's contention that whether or not a poet has a pure and "correcte" life may be of concern to his confessor or the courts—but not to his art. Swinburne made such a separation of morality and art when he said that the priest and the poet have always been enemies and that "what is called the artistic faculty [is not] by any means the same thing as a general capacity for doing good work." Whistler objected to a critic's praise of "a colourless old gentlemen of the academy," who, though virtuous, "as the painter of poor pictures . . . is damned for ever." Wilde even defended an infamous poisoner on aesthetic grounds: "The fact of a man being a poisoner is nothing against his prose. The domestic virtues are not the true basis of art."[5] In Dowson's and Moore's *A Comedy of Masks,* the painter Oswyn exemplifies this theory: an advocate of art for art's sake, Oswyn is personally disreputable but artistically sound: "His life might be disgraceful, indescribable: his art lay apart from it; and when he took up a brush an enthusiasm, a devotion to art, almost religious, steadied his hand."[6]

The artist whose work is not to be judged by moral standards was often considered not amoral but evil. Pater contributes to the image of the artist tinged with corruption in his portrait of Flavian in *Marius the Epicurean*: he "believed only in himself, in the brilliant, and mainly sensuous gifts, he had, or meant to acquire"; he embodies "the spirit of unbelief"; and he seems to Marius "an epitome of the whole pagan world, the depth of its corruption, and its perfection of form."[7] George Moore sees himself as a pagan artist, converted by Gautier to a worship of the flesh. And Wilde's New Hedonism is derived directly from Pater; Dorian Gray, with his youthful beauty and corruption of soul, is the literary descendant of Pater's Flavian, Denys, or Apollo in Picardy.

Sometimes the sensuousness of the aesthete-artist amounts to a hypersensitivity, such as that parodied in *The New Republic,* where Mr. Rose confesses that when he goes into the vulgar city he often takes "a scrap of some artistic crétonne with me in my pocket as a kind of aesthetic smelling salts."[8] The artist in Symons's "A Prelude to Life" is almost equally sensitive, admitting that the thought of dirtying his hands or his clothes or of cleaning his boots disgusted him.[9] Such delicacy is also a characteristic of numerous fictional artists in living, such as Moore's protagonist of "The Lovers of Orelay," whose amorous adventure is almost ruined because of ugly quarters and unaesthetic nightclothes; or John Norton in Moore's *A Mere Accident,* whose hatred of Thornby Place focuses on Mrs. Norton's note to the servants concerning the use of soda on the woodwork; or Dorian Gray, whose love for Sibyl Vane fades because of her bad acting. The idea of the unashamedly sensuous and possibly hypersensitive artist derives, again, from the image of the decadent, especially Huysmans's Des Esseintes, who is pained by a maid's wringing out wet clothes, who is agonized "to hear a piece of stuff torn in two, to rub his fingers over a lump of chalk, to stroke the surface of watered silk,"[10] and who is finally forced for his health's sake to return to Paris and mediocrity as an antidote to his life of sensual refinement.

Another fact of the aesthete-artist's character derived from the decadence is his aversion to nature and preference for artifice, symbolized in satire by Hichens's green carnation and symbolized in the works of the fin-de-siècle aesthetes by the city, cosmetics, and bought love. Symons's "Word on Behalf of Patchouli" is a major critical expression of the revolt from nature; in this essay Symons defends his personal preference for the artificial, asking the critics, "Well, why not Patchouli? Is there any 'reason in nature' why we should write exclusively about the natural blush, if the delicately acquired blush of rouge has any attraction for us?"[11] This preference for artificiality accounts for the aesthetes' defense of self-conscious, deliberate creation over instinctive, "natural" creativity and their belief in the superiority of art to nature. They conceived of the artist as not an observer and copier of nature but as a manipulator and hence the master of nature—an artificer. Some, like Whistler, preferred to use a living lily as a model, and some, like Symons, preferred an artificial one. But they agreed that the artistically gilded lily, whether the model was living or fake, is better, because it is more beautiful, than the one in the garden.

On the personal level, the preference for the artistic over the natural was often expressed in a tendency to pose, to act a role. Again *The Green Carnation* helps to define by its exaggeration: Reggie believes that "everything is a pose nowadays, especially genius."[12] The book satirizes the attitudinizing of Wilde, for whom, Symons says, "Human life has always been something acted on the stage; a comedy in which he may also disdainfully take part, as in a carnival, under any mask."[13] Even when Wilde seems most serious, when he is discussing the nature of art, he protects himself from the possible charge of sincerely advocating a position, of advancing a thesis, by casting the essay in the form of a dialogue, assuming personae, or by parodying his own position. For example, "The Decay of Lying" is a paper prepared for the *Retrospective Review*, published by the Tired Hedonists Club, and read by Vivian and Cyril (the names of Wilde's children); "The Critic as Artist" is a dialogue between Gilbert and Ernest, who are amusing parodies of aesthetes, employing eccentric and extravagant speech. The statement "give [a man] a mask, and he will tell you the truth" enables one to interpret Vivian's or Gilbert's—or even Wilde's—views, but there is always a question of how much credence to give to a persona, especially one who insists "that lying, the telling of beautiful untrue things, is the proper aim of Art."[14] Worthy of note in connection with the mask motif is the fact that other aesthetes, Symons and Yeats, have books entitled *Dramatis Personae*. Furthermore, Beardsley's drawings often portray masked figures, and Dowson's *A Comedy of Masks* finds value in the masks of indifference or amused detachment in that they enable one to live in an otherwise unbearable world. The use of personae or the mask to achieve artistic detachment is a characteristic of the artist central not only to Wilde's theory but to Yeats's theory as well. Yeats says that "one constantly notices in very active natures a tendency to pose, or if the pose has become a second self a preoccupation with the effect they are producing"; the artist, he maintains, must imagine himself a second self, which is his link "with another age, historical or imaginary, where alone he finds images that rouse his energy."[15]

The aesthete's posing might vary in purpose from the affectation and attitudinizing parodied in *Patience* to the occultism of Yeats, but it was, in fact, a way of dramatizing the primacy of art over life, and of the artist over all other men. According to the fin-de-siècle aesthetes' theory, the artist-artificer's creativity makes him superior to society, for he deals with the permanent in existence and provides the perfection of form to fill the moments in a life in constant flux.

Chapter X

THE PORTRAIT OF THE ARTIST
IN SHAW'S NOVELS

ANY SHAW CRITICS feel that Shaw's portraits of artists in his novels and plays belittle the artist's role. For example, in the most extensive critical analysis of Shaw's artist figures, "The Image of the Artist in the Plays of Bernard Shaw," Judith B. Spink says that "the various fictional forms which Shaw gives to the artist have . . . conspicuously less of heroic stature and more of biting satire, than one has any reason to expect from so inveterate an artist." She believes that the artists in Shaw's plays manifest "more of the fool and knave than of the sane and honest man," and she attributes this to Shaw's concern for social as well as artistic goals.[1] Other critics find Shaw's artist figures unimpressive: W. H. Auden says that "the occupational type which [Shaw] cannot draw is his own, the artist"; and J. I. M. Stewart says that Shaw is "almost uniformly unconvincing in the presentation of artists of any sort . . . perhaps because he never very effectively made up his mind about the nature of artistic creation."[2] In the following chapters I hope to show that, in spite of Shaw's tendency to use preachers, soldiers, dentists, pirates, businessmen, outlaws, kings—almost any occupational type rather than artists—as representatives of Shavian ideas, when artists worthy of the name appear in Shaw's work, they are sympathetically represented, realistically drawn, and clearly conceived.

In Shaw's first novel, *Immaturity* (1879), the male protagonists are a young clerk, Robert Smith, to whom the title of the novel refers, and a mature artist, Cyril Scott. Two of the four parts of the novel (one and four) are primarily devoted to Smith; two (two and three), to Scott. Smith is clearly autobiographical, a portrait of the young Shaw, but he receives a great deal of gentle satire for his snobbishness, his rather fastidious habits, his fondness for big words, and his innocence. Scott is the romantic hero in that he woos and wins the realistic seamstress-heroine; furthermore, he has served his apprenticeship in art and is now beginning to receive a well-deserved recognition for his artistic achievement. Critics note the autobiographical element in the portrait of Smith,[3] but none comment on the likelihood that Scott is the young novelist's projection of the mature artist he plans to become; and in this sense it is autobiographical. The fact that Shaw's socialism and his Life Force religion made him become a considerably different artist from Scott may obscure the implicit autobiography, but in 1879 the financially, socially, and artistically secure Scott was no doubt a Shavian ideal. Of all the artists depicted in the novel, Scott is the only one treated sympathetically, and even he receives some satirical treatment for his quick temper and tender sensibility. *Immaturity* is, however, autobiographical only in that Shaw fragments his character in the portraits of the young, sober Smith and the artistically secure Scott, as well as in the portraits of Musgrave the Radical and Harriet Russell, the outspoken, independent Philistine.

Immaturity contains the germ of the *Candida* triangle: the practical, businesslike man with a somewhat pedantic turn; the temperamental artist; and the woman fully in control of both. And in *Immaturity,* as in *Candida,* Shaw's attitude toward art is revealed in his portrait of the artist. Cyril Scott is based on Cecil Lawson (1851–82), a landscape painter whose painting "The Hop Gardens of England," exhibited at the Royal Academy in 1876, had brought him critical attention and some acclaim.[4] Shaw says that Lawson was "very much 'in the movement' at the old Grosvenor Gallery" (Preface, *Immaturity,* p. xli); accordingly, Scott is "an aesthetic pet" of the Grosvenor crowd. Like his prototype, Scott has both Pre-Raphaelite and impressionist leanings. The name of his best-known painting, "Fretted with Golden Fires," suggests Pre-Raphaelite affinities, and his dress reflects that love of "gray frieze" which according to Ford Madox Ford distinguishes Pre-Raphaelite dress: Scott "was dressed in a short loose coat of light grey, which he wore unbuttoned. His hat was shaped in the Swiss fashion, and made of felt of the same color as his clothes."[5] Other details than Scott's "certain affectations in dress and manner" suggest a Pre-Raphaelite artist: Scott's most generous critic admits that he is "a clever fellow who might do good work if he only knew how to draw" (the very charge Shaw brought against Rossetti); Scott "withers," as Shaw says Lawson did, "beneath sarcasm, a sort of attack to which his school was peculiarly exposed"; but his earnestness (like Hunt's or Rossetti's) made him "unable to retort in kind" (p. 131). Like the Pre-Raphaelites, Scott advocates a return to nature, saying of the artist Porson's sketch: "It is an honor to be selected as lay figure by Porson. . . . It may suggest to him the advisability of studying nature at last" (p. 188). He also insists that "the nearest unfashionable square" in London is as suitable a subject for the artist "as the bay of Naples, or a sunset at Damascus" (p. 274). Like the impressionists, Scott is noted for painting foggy landscapes. And like both the Pre-Raphaelites and impressionists, he scorns amateurism in art, believing that "it takes a man all his life, working as hard as he can, to get any sort of power to paint."[6] Scott's combination of Pre-Raphaelite fidelity to nature and devotion to his craft with impressionistic technique and Shavian directness and frankness suggests that he is a composite of the characteristics of the avant-garde artist of the late 1870s, as well as a type of the artist of all ages, a role emphasized by Hawkshaw's greeting to "Raphael Rembrandt Titian Turner Scott."

Scott's temperament is that which Shaw uses in virtually every portrait of an artist in his later works. Scott is, above all, willing to defy convention in his dress, his manners, and his marriage. Nevertheless, he is a social favorite, the first of Shaw's unconventional artists who, like Owen Jack and Trefusis in the novels or Dubedat and Higgins in the plays, are well-loved in spite of their antisocial inclinations. Another characteristic which Scott shares with later Shaw artists is extreme petulance and a kind of childish stubbornness, which causes Scott, like Jack and Higgins in similar situations, to exclaim in the midst of an unreasonable and angry argument, "I am not aware that my temper is a bad one" (*Immaturity*, p. 211).

Just as Scott is Shaw's portrait of a genuine artist such as Lawson, Rossetti, or the future Shaw, minor characters in *Immaturity* illustrate Shaw's concept of what an artist is not. Part 2, "Aesthetics," offers a wide range of artistic types to contrast unfavorably with Scott. The visitors to Halket Grosvenor's house, with its "painted, pannelled, padded, tapestried, blue, green, and gold rooms; with peacocks, flamingoes, jays, and other gorgeous birds depicted on the walls" (p. 104), are familiar to readers of *Punch* in the late 1870s and early 1880s: "There were artists with long hair, haggard cheeks, and silky moustaches, eagerly talking to women; and artists with stumpy beards and neglected appearance talking to one another. There were young ladies, funny, but pleasant to look upon, dressed in sacks, blankets, or dresses apparently let fall from the sky upon them, slipping off their shoulders, and decorated with large bows stuck on all to one side. There are fashionable girls tottering on high heels, and squeezed out of human shape to shew off the skill of their dressmakers" (*Immaturity*, p. 107). Among the types briefly introduced are the Ruskinlike "Analysis of Genius man," who discourses on "Far Removedness in art"; a long-haired musician, who plays his composition, "a Scandinavian Rhapsody in the form of a study for the loose wrist"; numerous "amateur" singers; a poet "with large glassy eyes, in which intelligence was overpowered by languor," who "caresses" the piano, "seeking for harmonies"; a music academician who tells the poet he was "experimenting with Italian sixths, and resolving them, for the most part, improperly"; the lady novelist, who hates Beethoven and wants music to provide "a delicious narcotic" for "the weary mind"; "a young, clean-shaven, pale clergyman, whose attenuated figure stood out from the background of stained window with an effect which, to judge by his bearing, he was not unconscious of"; and a radical, who argues with the pale clergyman's theology and praises Michelangelo's art because it is truly religious. Significantly, Shaw gives to the radical some of his own views, and uses him later to attack music critics, defend Wagner, and praise the realistic heroine. The aesthetic lady from *Punch* also appears: when Isabella Woodward could not hide her weariness with rouge, "she put on a lace-trimmed white muslin dress with hanging sleeves, and caused her maid to procure a lily, which she placed in her

90

bosom. In this attire she descended to the hall with slow steps, and a tristful expression" (p. 186).

Besides Scott, the only artist fully characterized in the novel is Hawkshaw, the "author of Wheat Sheaves, Hamlet, or a Second Book of Revelations, and other travail." He is introduced by Grosvenor as "a consummate master of the French forms," but his poetry is, Shaw says, often "little more than rhythmical lists of garden-produce." Like Swinburne, one of the editors of the "Mermaid Series" of English dramatists, Hawkshaw is an editor of Elizabethan dramatists; he has made a reading of *Hamlet* for "the Gymnasium theatre," and he has translated a Greek tragedy, which is set to the music of Mendelssohn and performed. To recall Shaw's criticism of Elizabethan dramatists, of "redone" Shakespeare at the Lyceum, and of Mendelssohn's music is commentary enough on his attitude toward Hawkshaw's artistic abilities.[7] Hawkshaw associates atheism with aestheticism, explaining that "no man who goes in for being aesthetic ever does believe anything nowadays" (p. 270) ; he finds his inspiration in a brandy bottle, and he wins fame and fortune for "A Song of Bent Branch and Broken Laurel," a song of disappointed love, the real occasion of which is Isabella Woodward's demand that he return the jewels he has extorted from her. A few lines of his description of Harriet and Scott will illustrate his stilted, obscure, and circumlocutory style.

> She is the very sublime of sordid. Now Cyril, though not free from the brutality of the craftsman, derives his inspiration from the true fount of idealism, the antique myth. His sympathy with nature in her veiled aspect, when all her outlines are dim, and impression takes the place of perception, is apparent in the eternal fog, mist, and storm with which he transmutes canvas into nature and thought. In such a mind, the collision with everything most foreign to it, combined and clothed with a certain measure of beauty and a subtle portion of grace, must necessarily produce a bewilderment amounting almost to spell. The mirage is dazzling. (P. 257)

He is also made to say, like *Punch's* aesthetes, "You do everything so consummately, Miss Russell" (p. 276). Harriet accuses him of caring more for the form than the content of his speech, saying to him, "You derive far more pleasure from your own skill in composing pretty phrases than from any gratification which they are likely to afford me" (p. 278), and Scott damns him as an artist when he tells Harriet that Hawkshaw "studies to conciliate society" and "turns out cheap wares by priming himself up now and then for a desperate fit of working" (pp. 284–85). In short, Hawkshaw is an incipient thief, a sycophant, and an artistic fraud. But Shaw finds some merit even in Hawkshaw (whose name is, after all, half "Shaw") : Hawkshaw is not a snob, and thus he honestly evaluates and accepts Harriet; he is best man at Scott and Harriet's wedding; he has a better sense of humor than Scott and can laugh at his own absurdity; and he does not pretend to be more than what he is, like Gilbert's Bunthorne, "an aesthetic sham."

Another artist in the novel who has lost all artistic principles is Vesey, "a landscape painter, who had cultivated a knack of painting ruins and moonlight until he had become celebrated for his views of Melrose and Muckross, of which he painted as many each year as the dealers would buy. His works were all alike, and were recognized without reference to a catalogue by frequenters of the galleries, to their self-satisfaction, and the advancement of his reputation" (p. 195). Vesey is one of the artistic impostors whom Shaw condemns in *The Sanity of Art* for abusing the public's tolerance of impressionistic art by presenting "real absurdities" (*Essays*, p. 292). Vesey is further worthy of note because he introduces a theme that was to become basic to Shaw's concept of the artist, i.e., the incompatibility of artist and woman. Vesey describes his own disastrous marriage and warns Scott of the dangers of combining marriage and art.

Nevertheless, Scott does marry, and he marries a woman who is not sympathetic to his art. In her first conversation with Scott, Harriet Russell makes clear her love of Raphael and her dislike for Scott's "Fretted with Golden Fires," which she considers affected. Scott objects, basing his argument solidly on Pre-Raphaelite theory: " 'Affected' means nothing. Is it like nature? If it differs from the blue and white skies you are accustomed to in pictures, is it because it is more truthful or less so?" To this Harriet "resolutely" answers, "The more study it cost, the more ridiculous it is. . . . It is not pleasing. Besides, what is the use of talking about nature? A painter cannot copy nature with a box full of gaudy clays made into mud with oil."[8] Harriet's Philistine nature is revealed to the aesthetic initiate when shortly afterwards she declares that she considers W. P. Frith's "The Railway Station" a "splendid picture"; Scott's comment on this is that Frith "found in a railway station a very suitable field for the exercise of his genius."[9] Harriet acts as a corrective to Scott's "artistic" temperament; she criticizes his lack of humor and maintains that an artist's "sensitiveness" is merely the name he gives his impatience. In spite of her Philistinism, Harriet, like Candida, expresses part of Shaw's values, in that she is sensible, practical, independent, and a natural boss. She impresses the outspoken radical, Musgrave, as a woman with "more sense in her bustle than all the other women here have in their bonnets" (p. 311); Lady Geraldine, another commonsense spokesman and a confessed Philistine, also finds Harriet charming.

Smith, the ostensible hero of *Immaturity,* has little to say about art. But he knows enough about art to praise the modern Pre-Raphaelites over medieval artists, and he confesses to Isabella Woodward that he is an amateur poet. He even makes up a notebook of his poems for her, including his "Lines to a Southern Passion Flower"; this poem, "an unusually florid apostrophe in heroic couplets," written for a music-hall dancer whom Smith once admired, is, he discovers, better than his other poems because of its "having been written warmly about a woman, instead of coldly about an abstraction."[10] Except for his attempts at poetry, for which he is apologetic, Smith is a man of business—an early version of the man of affairs who nevertheless knows something of art, a character type represented in the later novels by Edward Conolly, Cashel Byron, and Sidney Trefusis.

I have discussed *Immaturity* at some length for two reasons: it is preoccupied with matters of art, focusing on an artist as one of the heroes; and it was written at the height of the Pre-Raphaelite phase of the aesthetic movement. The date of the Whistler-Ruskin trial is 1878; in that year the second series of Swinburne's *Poems and Ballads* was published, and young Oscar Wilde won the Newdigate prize at Oxford for his *Ravenna.* In 1879 Meredith's *The Egoist,* James's *Daisy Miller* and *The Madonna of the Future and Other Tales,* and George Moore's *Flowers of Passion* were published. Popular aestheticism, influenced by thirty years of Pre-Raphaelite exhibits and especially influenced by the success of

Morris and Company, was receiving widespread advertisement in the pages of *Punch*. In this artistic milieu, it is no surprise that Shaw's *Immaturity* contains a section called "Aesthetics." The novel does not, notably, attack all aesthetes. Shaw's portrait of Cyril Scott, who is, like Cecil Lawson, "very much 'in the movement,' " reveals Shaw's sympathies with the sincere, earnest, hardworking artist; and Scott's few comments on art hint at a theory of art very much like Shaw's, especially in his fidelity to nature and his craftsman's pride. The aesthetes whom Shaw despises are the hangers-on and the dilettantes of the sort attacked in *Punch;* they are the ones to whom Shaw undoubtedly refers in *Pygmalion* when, in describing Mrs. Higgins's portrait, he says that the Rossettian dress was a fashion "which, when caricatured by people who did not understand, led to the absurdities of popular estheticism in the eighteen-seventies" (*Pygmalion*, p. 244). The parade of people at Halket Grosvenor's house, and Grosvenor himself, are the "people who did not understand" Rossetti's or Morris's intentions.

Shaw's second novel, *The Irrational Knot* (1888), opens with a satirical glance at an aristocratic attempt to bring art to the people. The "Parnassus Society," sponsored by the Countess of Carbury, is giving a musical concert for the working men at Wandsworth. The program, performed by ladies and gentlemen, is inartistic; and the working men are bored by all except Marmaduke Lind's "negro melody" with banjo accompaniment. It should be noted that Shaw is not here satirizing Morris's aspirations: the Countess's concert is an aristocratic gesture to inferiors; it does not feature art, but amateurism of the worst kind. The working-class audience is, Shaw suggests, understandably bored.

At this concert the hero—a practical man of genius, Edward Conolly—meets his future wife, the aristocratic Marian Lind. Although Conolly is not an artist, he has had an aesthetic education superior to that of English aristocrats, who know only what is fashionable, not what is good, in art. He is thus able to distinguish amateurs from professionals and is unable to tolerate any but the best in art; in fact, his superiority to his aristocratic wife in aesthetic matters is one of the reasons his marriage fails. Before he has heard Marian sing, he discerns that she is "a commonplace amateur"; and, after their marriage, his sensitive musical ear disturbs Marian so much that she refuses to sing in his presence.

Conolly's primary interests, however, are in the mechanical and business spheres; the artists of the novel are an actress, a lady novelist, and a Newdigate poet. The actress is Conolly's sister, Susanna, who shares the family genius and is, her lover says, "the cleverest woman in London." She is versatile, intelligent, and independent. Like Conolly, she is indifferent to convention. She has "a horror of marriage" and refuses to marry Marmaduke Lind, though she is willing to live with him. She achieves fame as Lalage Virtue, a music hall entertainer, but her career is wrecked by alcoholism. According to Conolly, her ruin is the result of her enslavement and debauchment by society, which "by the power of the purse, set her to nautch-girl's work, and forbade her the higher work that was equally within her power" (p. 332). This analysis, however, comes as somewhat of a surprise in this novel, which focuses on personal marital problems rather than on socioeconomic ones.

The lady novelist, Elinor McQuinch, is a Shavian spokesman in the novel. Her repressive childhood has not squelched her "stubborn, rebellious, and passionate" nature; her indifference to convention is expressed in her appearance, her admiration of Susanna Conolly's independence and talent, her resolution never to marry, and her desire to earn her own living. She is frank, outspoken, and iconoclastic. She tells Conolly, "I am always stabbing people. I suppose I like it" (p. 120); and she tells Marian, "My disposition is such that when I see that a jug is cracked, I feel more inclined to smash and have done with it than to mend it and handle it tenderly ever after." By the end of the novel, she has begun her career with a novel, *The Waters of Marah*, which has received favorable reviews, but about which no other information is given.

The aesthete-artist in *The Irrational Knot* is the pompous Sholto Douglas, who, like Oscar Wilde, has won the Newdigate prize at Oxford. His canon, including a "Note on Three Pictures in Last Year's *Salon*," some sonnets, and an unfinished drama, indicates that he is incapable of producing a major work of art. He professes an "insensibility to the admiration of the crowd" (p. 121); denounces, as Ruskin did, the "mechanical contrivances" which are "crowding and crushing the beauty out of our lives, and making commerce the only god"; and idealizes Athenian life (p. 134). He is pompous and sober, and he worships Marian Lind. His account of his love for Marian illustrates his pedantic and confused style, which also, Marian points out, "dreadfully" mixes metaphors.

> I think I walked through life at that time like a somnambulist; for I have since seen that I must have been piling mistake upon mistake until out of a chaos of meaningless words and smiles I had woven a Paphian love temple. At the first menace of disappointment—a thing as new and horrible to me as death—I fled the country. I came back with only the ruins of the doomed temple. You were not content to destroy a ruin: the feat was too easy to be glorious. So you rebuilt it in one hour to the very dome, and lighted its altars with more than their former radiance. Then, as though it were but a house of cards— as indeed it was nothing else—you gave it one delicate touch and razed it to its foundations. Yet I am afraid those altar lamps were not wholly extinguished. They smoulder beneath the ruins still. (Pp. 227–28)

Sholto's style is like Hawkshaw's, but his professed seriousness of artistic purpose and his long-suffering love for Marian anticipate the portrait of Adrian Herbert in *Love among the Artists*. Unlike a genuine Shavian artist, Sholto easily abandons all his lofty artistic ideals for love.

The necessity for the artist to be free from domestic entanglements is a major theme of *Love among the Artists* (1881). After Owen Jack proposes marriage to Mary Sutherland and is refused, he exclaims, "I have committed my last folly. . . . Henceforth I shall devote myself to the only mistress I am fitted for, Music." He tells Mary that she is right to refuse him, for "I have no business in the domestic world"; later he says, with a sense of the narrow escape he has had, "*I* hanker for a *wife! . . . I* grovel after *money!* What dog's appetites have this worldly crew infected me with! No matter: I am free: I am myself again. Back to thy holy garret, oh my soul!" (pp. 201–3). When the actress Madge Brailsford declares her love for him, he explains that he creates romance from everything and expresses his passion in his music, that "my art is enough for me, more than I have time and energy for occasionally." To her question, "And so your heart is dead?" he answers, "No: it is marriage that kills the heart and keeps it dead. Better starve the heart than overfeed it. Better still to feed it only on fine food, like music" (pp. 328–29). The marriage of Aurélie Szczympliça and Adrian Herbert illustrates the correctness of Jack's advice; Adrian is ruined as an artist because his love for Aurélie supersedes his artistic ambition. He says, "When I think of Aurélie, there is an end of my work" (p. 300). On the other hand, Aurélie knows that her art must come first and, at one point, asks, "What madness possessed me, an artist, to marry? Did I not know that it is ever the end of an artist's career?" (p. 287). However, she stays married and is not ruined, because she continues to put her music first. She tells Adrian, "I cannot love. I can feel it in the music—in the romance—in the poetry; but in real life—it is impossible. . . . I must content myself with the music. It is but a shadow. Perhaps it is as real as love is, after all" (p. 314). *Love among the Artists* answers, then, the question about marriage which Cyril Scott asks Vesey in *Immaturity*. In spite of Vesey's advice to the contrary, Scott does marry, but he is the last artist in Shaw's work to concern himself "with the small beer of domestic comfort." *Love among the Artists* contains Shaw's first full statement of the *Candida* secret: the need of the artist to be free from domestic cares so that he can explore and express the vision of "Tristan's holy night."[11]

The artists in *Love among the Artists* have other traits that identify Shaw's genuine artists. Like Cyril Scott, all are temperamental, impatient, and at times unreasonable. They also all defy or ignore convention, thereby asserting a superiority that their genius gives them. Aurélie justifies her rudeness to Adrian's mother with this explanation: "I am an artist, and queens have given me their hands frankly. Your mother holds that an English lady is above all queens. I hold that an artist is above all ladies" (p. 251). This sense of dignity which art bestows on the artist explains as well Jack's indifference to decorum in dress and manners or Madge's transformation from a proper English girl to an impressive, independent woman.

The three artists are all professional: they work hard; they do not romanticize or glamourize their roles; they willingly accept pay for their work, though they do not work because of the pay. Echoing Cyril Scott, Jack calls himself "a master of my profession" who has, in spite of public indifference, "never composed one page of music bad enough for publication or performance" (p. 95). He ridicules the notion that a man must look like Mozart and must love music in order to be a composer: "I do not look like a writer of serenades. . . . I am no enthusiast: I leave that to the ladies. Did you ever hear of an enthusiastically honest man, or an enthusiastic shoemaker? Never; and you are not likely to hear of an enthusiastic composer—at least, not after he is dead" (p. 96). His advice to Madge, whom he tutors in elocution, is three-fold: master the craft of acting; "no grabbing at money, or opportunities, or effects" (p. 102); and, finally, abandon the art inspired by "a passion for shamming" for an art "inspired by a passion for beauty" (p. 330).

Aurélie Szczympliça has this "passion for beauty." She has both technical skill and what she calls her "fine touch," the touch of genius which finally distinguishes the artist from the nonartist. Ironically, Herbert, the nonartist, explains the truth "that earnestness of intention, and faith in the higher mission of art, are impotent to add an inch to my artistic capacity" (p. 295). Living with Aurélie has convinced him that "faith and earnestness are of no use in [art]: mere brute skill carries everything before it"; he has come to believe that the artist's mission is simply to produce and sell art. He takes Aurélie as "a case in point. Even the Times does not deny that *she* is a perfect artist. Yet if you spoke of her being a moral teacher with a great gift and a great truth, she would not understand you, although she has some distorted fancy about her touch on the piano being a moral faculty" (p. 296). In his cynicism, Adrian is only half right: Shaw would agree that "there are only two sorts of painters, dexterous ones and maladroit ones" (p. 296); but he would not agree that the sole motive of the dexterous ones is commercial, nor does he believe that art is but a matter of "brute skill." Though Aurélie tells an admirer that she has "the soul commercial within me" and though she looks on her art as "an artist's business," she is not motivated by desire for gain but a desire to reveal her "fine touch." Adrian mistakes Jack's and Madge's and Madame Szczympliça's refusal to romanticize their art for cynical commercialism; and he confuses a willingness to accept deserved pay with artistic prostitution. He also fails to understand Madame Szczympliça's "moral" force, for he confuses good intentions and a worship of art with the elevating effect of great art.

Adrian Herbert is Shaw's most detailed portrait of an aesthete-artist. At the beginning of the novel he is painting a Pre-Raphaelite subject, "The Lady of Shalott," in which, he says, he is "aiming at the seizure of a poetic moment" (p. 13). Adrian's work also evidences "the prodigious expenditure of elbow grease" that Shaw found in Holman Hunt's painting. Mary tells Adrian, as Ruskin told Rossetti, "Your sketches have too much work in them" (p. 82); and later, Adrian agrees: "I strove to make up for my shortcomings by being laborious, whereas I now perceive that mere laboriousness does not and cannot amend any shortcoming in art except the want of itself" (p. 295). Though Adrian's Arthurian subject, his earnestness, and his labor suggest a Pre-Raphaelite artist, in reality he is one of those "who did not understand" Pre-Raphaelitism; his work is a failure when compared to genuine Pre-Raphaelite painting. Charlie Sutherland is disturbed by the lady's "deuce of a scraggy collar-bone" and the unrealistic landscape seen through the high window; even Mary, who has been imagining "the river bank, the golden grain, the dazzling sun, the gorgeous loom, and armor of Sir Lancelot," is disappointed in the painting (pp. 12–14). One has only to recall Shaw's description of Hunt's "Isabella and her Basil Pot," in which the "magnificently vigorous woman" and the "joyousness of her abounding strength" belie the catalogue description of the painting as an "expression of her grief," or his praise of Millais's rich color,[12] to know that Adrian's "Lady of Shalott," who has "a certain sadness and weakness about her that is very pathetic," does not measure up. Furthermore, Adrian's aestheticism is but a pose: he willingly abandons art for love. He is what Jack and Madge and Aurélie despise in art—"a duffer," "a humbug" (pp. 148, 149). Adrian's mother accurately states that "he will never paint. I am not what is called an aesthete; and pictures that are generally understood to be the perfection of modern art invariably bore me, because I do not understand them. But I do understand Adrian's daubs; and I know they are invariably weak and bad" (p. 23). However, before his marriage Adrian achieved a kind of success because, Jack says, he is "neither too good for the Academy people nor too bad for the public" (p. 189).

Adrian has an admirer and, for a time, a disciple, in Mary Sutherland; but she has too much common sense to continue to be "an aesthetic daughter of the Man with the Muck Rake" (p. 22). She tells Adrian, "As to Art, I am not exactly getting tired of it; but I find that I cannot live on Art alone; and I am beginning to doubt whether I might not spend my time better than in painting, at which I am sure I shall never do much good. If Art were a game of pure skill, I should persevere; but it is like whist, chance and skill mixed. . . . In future I may sketch to amuse myself and to keep mementos of the places with which I have pleasant associations, but not to elevate my tastes and perfect my morals" (p. 84). During the course of the novel, Mary has a chance to marry Adrian, the duffer, and Jack, the artist, and refuses both for a Philistine, John Hoskyn.

Hoskyn likes Landseer's paintings and all the paintings that Mary hates. Nevertheless, he is better able than Mary or Adrian to recognize and appreciate Owen Jack's art because he relies on his senses and expresses his honest opinion, whereas Mary and Adrian have their tastes prejudiced by formal training. Hoskyn and Lady Geraldine, the sensible dowager who also appears in *Immaturity*, present the healthily Philistine point of view, offering satiric comments on even Shavian art, as when Lady Geraldine asks Jack, who has just spoken his mind to her, "Is this the newest species of artistic affectation, pray? It used to be priggishness, or loutishness, or exquisite sensibility. But now it seems to be outspoken common sense; and instead of being a relief, it is the most insufferable affectation of all" (*LAA*, p. 179).

The subsequent careers of the characters in *Love among the Artists* are discussed in chapters five and six of *Cashel Byron's Profession* (1882), devoted to Mrs. (Mary Sutherland) Hoskyn's evening. Mrs. Hoskyn is said to be happy with her Philistine husband; Madame Szczympliça receives more praise for her "enchanted" playing; and Adrian Herbert is once again attacked, this time by Lydia Carew, who says that his pictures "suggest that he reads everything and sees nothing" (the same criticism Shaw offered against Swinburne), and by Cashel, who realistically appraises Adrian's painting and finds it lacking.

Shaw's last novel, *An Unsocial Socialist* (1883), contains another aesthete-artist, by this time a well-defined character type in Shaw's work. Chichester Erskine is the "author of a tragedy entitled The Patriot Martyrs, dedicated with enthusiastic devotion to the Spirit of Liberty and half a dozen famous upholders of that principle, and denouncing in forcible language the tyranny of the late Tsar of Russia, Bomba of Naples, and Napoleon the Third" (p. 150). Trefusis, the hero of the novel, says that Erskine is "a devoted champion of liberty in blank verse, and dedicates his works to Mazzini, etc." The allusion to Swinburne and Songs before Sunrise and to Wilde's Vera, or the Nihilists is unmistakable. There is also possibly an allusion to William Michael Rossetti's Democratic Sonnets in the king-killing argument, in which Erskine says, "I admire a man that kills a king," and Trefusis, anticipating The Apple Cart, argues that "a king nowadays is only a dummy put up to draw your fire off the real oppressors of society" and deserving of sympathy rather than assassination (p. 199). One of the Democratic Sonnets, "Tyrannicide," begins, "We cannot argue of Tyrannicide. / An instinct in the world avows it just."[13] But Erskine is not, as Scott was not, a purely personal portrait; he has more than topical relevance. He satirizes a type of artist and is a composite of many poets' traits. Like Holman Hunt, he has "made sketches in Palestine." Like Hawkshaw, he drinks for inspiration, and like Sholto Douglas and Adrian Herbert, he says, "I hate business and men of business; and as to social questions, I have only one article of belief, which is, that the sole refiner of human nature is fine art" (p. 165).

His friend, who accompanies him to Palestine and to European art galleries and who is himself the owner of an art collection, is Sir Charles Brandon, a rich dilettante.

> He was a little worn, in spite of his youth, but he was tall and agreeable, had a winning way of taking a kind and soothing view of the misfortunes of others, could tell a story well, liked music and could play and sing a little, loved the arts of design and could sketch a little in watercolors, read every magazine from London or Paris that criticized pictures, had travelled a little, fished a little, shot a little, botanized a little, wandered restlessly in the footsteps of women, and dissipated his energies through all the small channels that his wealth opened and his talents made easy to him. He had no large knowledge of any subject, though he had looked into many just far enough to

replace absolute unconsciousness of them with measurable ignorance. Never having enjoyed the sense of achievement, he was troubled with unsatisfied aspirations that filled him with melancholy and convinced him that he was a born artist. (P. 141)

In the novel Erskine and Sir Charles are harmless, but absurd; Trefusis persuades both of them to sign his socialist petition by appealing to their snobbery and pride, convinced that their "hesitation is the uncertainty that comes from ignorance" not from ungenerous, cowardly, or prejudiced motives.

The hero of *An Unsocial Socialist*, Sidney Trefusis, is sometimes assumed to represent Shaw's repudiation of art. Certainly Trefusis offends the aesthetic sensibilities of other characters in the novel: Erskine is disappointed to find Trefusis absorbed in reading a Blue Book rather than *The Patriot Martyrs;* to Sir Charles's horror, Trefusis demonstrates how his pistol practice has wrecked the statues and walls of his Graeco-Roman eighteenth-century English manor house. Trefusis also condemns the modern novel. He tells Agatha that a novel is "a lying story of two people who never existed, and who would have acted differently if they had existed."[14] Trefusis's "Letter to the Author" (the appendix to *An Unsocial Socialist*) lectures the author on the folly of writing novels, which are limited by the morality of their female readers and are "only the tail of Shakespear," who with his "poetry of despair" was "the first literary result of the foundation of our industrial system upon the profits of piracy and slave-trading" (p. 259). Trefusis does, undeniably, repudiate certain kinds of art: specifically, a poetic drama expressing the republican sentiments of a writer whose social conscience does not prompt him to sign Brown's socialist petition; the pseudo-Greek and Roman statuary of an eighteenth-century manor; the nineteenth-century novel; and, by implication, all "poetry of despair." Except for his objection to the novel form, Trefusis does not express a change in Shaw's attitude toward art. As I have indicated above, in all the novels Shaw hates incompetence and sham in art, and he expects art to tell the truth at least insofar as it expresses the vision of the artist and is not a mere imitation of artistic custom or fashion. In *An Unsocial Socialist* the change is in his attitude toward the novel form, at least as he knew it, not toward art.

As a matter of fact, Trefusis is himself a special kind of artist. He says that "the only art that interests me is photography" (p. 159), but his photography is not an impartial reproduction of scenes from life. Like the naturalist, Trefusis photographs the sordid life of the poor, but, unlike the naturalist, he does not attempt objective reporting of the facts. He juxtaposes pictures of the hideous environment of the oppressed with pictures of the luxurious lives of the rich, including their servants' quarters and their stables; accompanying the pictures are comparative figures on incomes, rents, profits, etc. Trefusis, then, organizes his photographs so that they illustrate a thesis, and then he uses them for propagandistic purposes. He shows them to Sir Charles and Erskine in the hope of converting the two to socialism, explaining, "You have seen in my album something you had not seen an hour ago, and you are consequently not quite the same man you were an hour ago. My pictures stick in the mind longer than your scratchy etchings, or the leaden things in which you fancy you see tender harmonies in grey" (p. 207). Trefusis thus separates himself from painters such as Whistler, who paint "tender harmonies" and believe that subject matter and morality are irrelevant in art. Trefusis uses his art of photography in the same way that Shaw later uses his dramatic art: to awaken, to shock, to persuade. It has a message; and, when accompanied by Trefusis's lecture on "Socialism or Smash," it is not a "poetry of despair" but of hope. Trefusis's hope for the future includes a Morrisian vision of beauty as a vital part of everyone's daily life.

An Unsocial Socialist does not, then, reject art. It rejects hackwork, as the other novels do; it rejects novel writing and is significantly, the last novel Shaw completed. It adds to Shaw's concept of the artist the idea that he must work for the reform of society either directly through his art, as Trefusis does, or as a prerequisite for genuine art, as Donovan Brown, the Pre-Raphaelite socialist-artist in the novel, does. In Shaw's last novel, the socialism is new, but the hero is not. As a realistic artist with something vital to express, Trefusis contrasts with the dilettantes, Sir Charles and Erskine, just as in preceding novels the genuine artists—Scott, Jack, Madame Szczympliça—contrast with the ineffectual Hawkshaw and Adrian Herbert. Trefusis's practical side has also been anticipated in the earlier novels, each of which has its businesslike, record-keeping, outspoken practical man. Even *Love among the Artists* introduces the sensible, honest, realistic John Hoskyn, who, though a minor character, is the romantic hero of the novel in that he wins the heroine and they live happily ever after. These practical men appear to be hostile to art, but in actuality they are merely hostile to effete art. Young Smith in *Immaturity* knows enough about art to deliver a lecture on it; Conolly in *The Irrational Knot* knows a great deal about everything, including art; Hoskyn, in spite of his Philistinism, appreciates Madame Szczympliça's and Owen Jack's art. Trefusis is the culmination of Shaw's fictional heroes: he embodies the independence and forcefulness of the artist-hero and the business sense of the practical hero; but in place of the earlier artists' devotion to art and the practical men's interest in business and work is Trefusis's devotion to social reform.

With Trefusis as the artist figure in Shaw's last novel, it should come as no surprise that Shaw's next creative work, excluding his critical essays and a fragmentary novel, are two of his most overtly propagandistic plays, *Widowers' Houses* (1885–92) and *Mrs. Warren's Profession* (1893–94), both, like Trefusis's photography, exposing and explicating social evils. After these "Bluebook plays," as Shaw called them,[15] Shaw changed the focus of his drama; though his plays never lost all social orientation, they became broadened in scope as Shaw's religion of the Life Force absorbed (without replacing) his Fabian socialism. Accordingly, in *Candida* and his later plays, the artist figure is no longer the socialist reformer but the poet-prophet, a literary descendant of the artists in Shaw's novels before *An Unsocial Socialist*. Praed, Octavius, and Apollodorus are dramatic variations of the aesthete-artist found in the novels. Likewise Dubedat, Shakespear (in *The Dark Lady of the Sonnets*), Henry Higgins, presumably the mature Marchbanks, and certainly the mature Shaw are variations of the type of artist genius found in the novels.

In the novels Shaw contrasts the aesthete with the expressor of Shavian values: Hawkshaw (aesthete) with Scott (artist), Harriet (Philistine), and Smith (man of affairs); Sholto Douglas (aesthete) with Conolly (man of affairs); Adrian Herbert (aesthete) with Owen Jack (artist) and Hoskyn (Philistine); Chichester

Erskine (aesthete) with Trefusis (artist and man of affairs). However, in order to make the contrast favorable to the Shavian spokesman, Shaw gives to the aesthete a set of characteristics which apply more to a hero of popular sentimental drama than to Dante Gabriel Rossetti or Oscar Wilde or Aubrey Beardsley. For example, the aesthete in Shaw is extremely conventional; far from being an outcast from society, he has the approbation of society and is shocked at any breach of propriety. Linked with his social conformity is his aesthetic conventionality, so that he has less real aesthetic sensitivity than the Philistine, who at least can form an independent opinion about art. Though Shaw's aesthete talks about the sanctity and power of art, he will sacrifice his art either for social approval or woman's love. Of the characteristics of the aesthete-artist, Shaw's aesthete has only the trait of affectation, and he is even capable of dropping the pose of aestheticism. Ironically, Shaw's portraits of true artists draw on numerous characteristics of the genuine aesthete-artist: the Shavian artist is not concerned with conventional morality and, until Trefusis, with any morality except the morality that attends the effective expression of an artistic idea (such as Madame Szczympliça's "moral faculty," her "fine touch"); the Shavian artist is an alien to society, his very genius making him different from, and superior to, ordinary men; he is sensitive, at times impatient and angry at the world's indifference; and, though he does not romantically confuse suffering and creativity, he is devoted to his art, willing to sacrifice worldly happiness for it.

Chapter XI

THE AESTHETE-ARTIST IN SHAW'S EARLY PLAYS

ECAUSE OF HIS CONVICTION that the artist is an iconographer of a living religion, Shaw devoted his creative energies to writing about the religion and its men and women of action; the fact that few artists appear in his plays is in itself a comment on his idea of an artist's function. After *Candida,* which with its preface contains Shaw's definition of the artist's role, Shaw's major concern is for artistically depicting creative evolution, not for talking about art and artists. It is as though he had spent his literary apprenticeship looking for a clarification of his role, and, having found it, he states it once for the record in *An Unsocial Socialist,* modifies it in *Candida,* then goes about his real business as one of the men of genius "selected by Nature to carry on the work of building up an intellectual consciousness of her own instinctive purpose" (Epistle Dedicatory, *M&S,* p. xx). When artists do appear in Shaw's plays, they are merely variations of the character types developed in the novels. The artist-figure in the early plays— Praed *(Mrs. Warren's Profession)*, Apollodorus *(Caesar and Cleopatra)*, Marchbanks *(Candida)* and Henry Apjohn *(How He Lied to Her Husband)* before their final conversion, and Octavius *(Man and Superman)*—is best understood as Shaw's refinement of the conventionally courteous and honorable, the socially acceptable, the love-worshipping aesthete-artist of the novels.

Praed, the architect in *Mrs. Warren's Profession,* preaches "The Gospel of Art" and believes that art can reveal romance and beauty

—"a wonderful world"—to Vivie. Like the avant-garde artists of the 1890s, Shaw as well as the aesthetes, Praed advocates rebellion against conventional authority, telling Vivie, "I am a born anarchist." He wants "real" interpersonal relationships, and repudiates "gallantry copied out of novels" because it is "vulgar and affected" (pp. 179–80). Nevertheless, Praed is as proper as Shaw's earlier aesthete-artists; Shaw calls him an upholder of "conventionally unconventional" behavior and upbraids the critics who take him for "the sole sensible person on the stage" (Preface, *Mrs. Warren*, p. 164). Praed is refined and chivalrous; and, though he professes to admire "modern young ladies," he is unprepared for Vivie's Philistine practicality. When Vivie tells him that she tried for fourth wrangler at Oxford only because her mother paid her to do it and that she would not do it again for the same amount, Praed, who believes that such honors bestow "culture," is "damped." In spite of contrary evidence, Praed continues to believe that the world is beauty and romance and, at the end of the play, proposes that Vivie go with him to Italy, where she "will cry with delight at living in such a beautiful world." Even when Vivie reveals to him Mrs. Warren's profession, he is only momentarily upset; he recovers instantly to pay Vivie a "sentimental compliment." According to the play, his Gospel of Art is as bad as Mrs. Warren's "Gospel of Getting On," for, as Vivie tells him, "if there are really only those two gospels in the world, we had better all kill ourselves; for the same taint is in both, through and through" (p. 236). Praed is of no value to society because he is not genuinely realistic and rebellious; we know nothing of his art, but, given his world view, it would be based on the illusion that this is the most beautiful of all possible worlds.

The poet of *Candida* contrasts sharply with the self-deceived Praed. Marchbanks is Shaw's portrait of the aesthete-artist being shaken out of his faith in love and honor and being changed into a tough-minded, realistic, independent man, the kind of artist who, like Owen Jack, "can never associate beauty with a lie." Though Marchbanks has many of the external characteristics and some of the attitudes of the aesthete-artist such as Sholto Douglas or Adrian Herbert, he does not pay mere lip-service to art, his sensitivity is no pose, and he tries to rid himself of illusions. Critics have likened

Marchbanks to Shelley, to Lord Alfred Douglas, to William Morris, to Shaw himself.[1] Shaw claimed that "De Quincey's account of his adolescence in his *Confessions*" furnished the germ of *Candida*.[2] All of these are partially correct, for Marchbanks is a composite of several poets and of many poetic traits; he is "the Poet, who must enlighten the world as to its goal, and must teach men to think and feel nobly."[3]

The appearance and mannerisms of Marchbanks emphasize his kinship to De Quincey's youth, whose "constitutional infirmity of mind ran but too determinately towards . . . dreamy abstraction from life and its realities."[4] Marchbanks "is a strange, shy youth of eighteen, slight, effeminate, with a delicate childish voice, and a hunted tormented expression and shrinking manner"; he is irresolute, timid, intense, nervous—"so uncommon as to be almost unearthly" (*Candida*, p. 91). The idea of an older woman influencing the dreamy youth Shaw may have taken also from De Quincey's *Confessions*: De Quincey's hero has a benefactress, Lady Carbery, who is ten years older than he and who, like Candida of Eugene, thinks "highly of my powers and attainments." And De Quincey's hero also idolizes "a lovely lady" in a picture which he keeps over his mantelpiece at school; the lady's face is "radiant with divine tranquillity" and she acts as "a special benefactress to me . . . by means of her sweet Madonna countenance."[5] Marchbanks, it will be recalled, has chosen for the Morell hearth Titian's Madonna "because he fancied some spiritual resemblance" between Candida and the lady.

Marchbanks also has affinities with the "boy poet" of the decadence (Lord Alfred Douglas and Aubrey Beardsley come to mind), a type satirized in *Punch* for publicizing his "erotic affairs." Marchbank's pain in society seems a deliberate allusion to the hypersensitivity of the decadent aesthete. He is nervous and ill at ease in everyday social situations, as the stage directions in his first scene state. He behaves "nervously," "anxiously," "apprehensively," "irresolutely," "miserably," "with an expression of hopeless suffering"; he worries about what to pay the cabman, and he is "terrified" at the prospect of sitting on a public platform. His "poetic horror" at the idea of Candida's filling the lamps, scrubbing, and peeling onions approaches the pain that Des Esseintes in Huysmans's *A Rebours* feels on hearing a maid wringing out wet clothes or hearing cloth torn in two, except for this important difference: Marchbanks is pained by an idea (of the woman he loves performing menial tasks), and the decadent is pained by an aesthetically offended physical sense. But, like Des Esseintes, Marchbanks shrinks from the brutal and coarse; he explains to Morell that he does not tremble at the idea of being a poet but at the want of poetry in others; and Morell's threatened violence makes Marchbanks almost hysterical.

But Marchbanks is more than a Shavian version of De Quincey's youth or of the decadent aesthete. His character has most in common with Shaw's earlier portraits of serious artists, who, as we have seen, share numerous characteristics of the genuine aesthetes. Marchbanks's miserable and lonely childhood has caused him to feel alienated from the world. He also hates, as the aesthetes do, society's reverence for "goodness": as he explains to Prossy, fear and shame keep people from loving and understanding each other; when she objects to his boldness, he says, "Nothing thats worth saying is proper" (*Candida*, pp. 103–5). He confesses to Candida that "doing wrong" makes him happy, but he means by "wrong" natural behavior that is considered wrong by society, a wrongdoing that in Shaw's view is the only means of destroying illusions. Like Shaw's other genuine artists, Marchbanks is not afraid of defying conventional morality. Also, like Shaw's other artist-protagonists, he does not talk about whether or not his art is moral; it is simply his way of life.

The same sensitivity that makes him uneasy in mundane conversation, inept in business affairs, awed by machines, and terrified of violence gives him an ability to understand and to stir human feelings. After a few minutes of talking with Prossy, he understands not only that she is in love but whom she loves; and Prossy's "feelings are keenly stirred" by his talk (p. 104). After Candida's unconscious cruelty to Morell, Marchbanks can "feel his [Morell's] pain in my own heart" (p. 118). When Candida is asked to choose between the two men, Marchbanks understands her anger and interprets it for Morell; and, when she states her choice, he "divines her meaning at once" (pp. 137–38).

Marchbanks is able to summon extraordinary courage to express what he feels to be important, such as Prossy's unrequited love or his love for Candida. In his first battle with Morell over Candida, his cringing manner changes, and he speaks "vehemently" and "ruthlessly." He is "unimpressed and remorseless" at Morell's oratory. When he speaks "wildly" and "impetuously," he goads Morell to the threat of physical violence, at which Marchbanks shrinks, "cowers," and "screams passionately." But he is not deterred from his intention to "force [the truth] into the light." He continues "with petulant vehemence," "with renewed vehemence," and finally "with lyric rapture" his onslaught on Morell's complacency. This scene foreshadows Marchbanks's triumph in the final battle for Candida, when he proves the stronger of the two. In the final scene, when Candida recalls how lonely and unhappy his life has been, he points out that there were compensations: "I had my books. I had Nature. And at last I met you"; and, finally, it is Marchbanks who has "the ring of a man's voice" in his speech, while Morell kneels to accept Candida's blessing "with boyish ingenuousness" (pp. 139–40).

Marchbanks's growth to independence, his artistic coming of age, is the significant event in *Candida*. The conflict of the play can be seen as a struggle between a child and a man, between the weak and the strong. Ironically, the eighteen-year-old boy becomes "as old as the world"; the physically strong, socially and morally sure clergyman proves "the weaker of the two." The play builds to a climactic scene in which Marchbanks, through Candida's insistence that he drop all attitudes, including a "gallant attitude, or a wicked attitude, or even a poetic attitude," comes to realize the perfection of love: "In plain prose, I loved her so exquisitely that I wanted nothing more than the happiness of being in such love" (p. 129). But this recognition is not enough for the poet; it merely makes him sentimental and noble, willing to sacrifice himself for love of Candida. Candida (and Shaw, as his dramatic criticism makes clear) has only "infinite contempt for this puerility" and says, "Much good your dying would do me!" (p. 131). She perceives that his education is incomplete, that he must learn a final lesson. And when he learns "to live without happiness," he becomes wiser than his teacher.[6] At the end of the play Candida is no more able than Morell to comprehend the "open secret" in the poet's heart. Marchbanks thus changes from the poetic knight to the neophyte poet; or, to adapt the terms of the preface to *Plays Pleasant* to Marchbanks's growth, he changes from the Pre-Raphaelite at his best[7] to a poet struggling to develop into something higher.

Because critics sometimes forget that Marchbanks is a young poet, and thus no more (and no less) like Shaw the mature artist than the priggish clerk Smith in *Immaturity* is like his creator, and because they cannot always avoid judging a character according to values outside the play, Marchbanks is one of the most maligned of Shaw's characters. One critic calls him "an aesthetic prig, unhealthy and unbalanced"; another correctly calls him "the popular version of the artistic temperament," but incorrectly considers him an unpleasant and dangerous figure, who is insensitive to others' feelings—"ruthlessly selfish" and filled with "desperate courage," callousness, maliciousness, and cynicism: "It would not be hard to make out a case for Marchbanks as the villain of the piece."[8] Such readings of Marchbanks's character, as I have indicated above, rely too heavily on the appearance and mannerisms of the youth and not enough on the glimpses of character revealed in his forthright and bold speech. Like the genuine artists in Shaw's novels, Marchbanks refuses to be bound by convention; he is a sensitive outcast from society. Though he admits that "all the words I know [except 'Candida'] belong to some attitude or other" (p. 125) and though he is capable of playing a role, as when he heroically plays "the Good Man" in Morell's absence, he is also capable of dropping the pose in the interest of truth-telling. And finally, as do all of Shaw's other artist-protagonists except Cyril Scott, he rejects love for art, thus becoming more like the genuine aesthete-artist than he is at the beginning of the play when he has the appearance of the stereotyped aesthete but not the dedication to art alone.

Marchbanks does not talk about the moral function of art; on the other hand, neither does he profess a faith in art for art's sake. The character associated with art for art's sake is Morell, with his "mere rhetoric." What Morell considers "the gift of finding words for divine truth" Marchbanks calls "the gift of the gab." In their first confrontation, Marchbanks begs Morell to "put aside all that

111

cant," but Morell, according to the stage directions, "continues steadily with great artistic beauty of delivery" (pp. 97–98). Candida echoes Marchbanks's criticism when she tells her husband that people come to his church because "you preach so splendidly that it's as good as a play for them." The women are all in love with him, she says, "And you are in love with preaching because you do it so beautifully" (pp. 114–15). She calls his sermons "mere phrases." And, like Praed in *Mrs. Warren's Profession,* Morell is the "conventionally unconventional" character in the play (p. 118). With superb irony, Shaw gives the semihysterical and effete aesthete-artist the realist's strength and the artist's independence; to the masterful, moral, successful socialist preacher he gives romantic illusions and a penchant for art for its own sake. However, Morell is not made reprehensible; he has his share of human folly and is satirized for it, but he also has redeeming qualities in his real courage, his social conscience, and his final humble acceptance of the truth.

In *Caesar and Cleopatra* Shaw creates a believer in art for art's sake in Apollodorus, who introduces himself as "a worshipper of beauty" and "a votary of art." Though Apollodorus, the patrician carpet merchant and aesthete, is partly modeled on William Morris (above, pp. 10–11), he is not a faithful portrait of Morris. In the first place, Apollodorus is historical, appearing in Plutarch's *Life of Caesar* in the account of "the first occasion . . . that made Caesar to love [Cleopatra]": "She, only taking Apollodorus Sicilian of all her friends, took a little boat, and went away with him in it in the night, and came and landed hard by the foot of the castle. Then having no other mean to come into the court without being known, she laid herself down upon a mattress or flockbed, which Apollodorus her friend tied and bound up together like a bundle with a great leather thong, and so took her upon his back and brought her thus hampered in this fardle unto Caesar in at the castle gate."[9] In the second place, Apollodorus's appearance is not like Morris's; the stage direction describes Apollodorus as "a dashing young man of about 24, handsome and debonair, dressed with deliberate aestheticism in the most delicate purples and dove greys, with ornaments of bronze, oxydized silver and stones of jade and agate. His sword, designed as carefully as a medieval cross, has a blued blade showing through an openwork scabbard of purple leather and filigree" (*C&C*, p. 137). This description in no way suggests the hearty, bearded Morris, characteristically dressed in rough serge, who is said to have resembled a ship's captain more than an aesthete.[10] Furthermore, Morris became so active in arts and crafts and political movements that in the 1880s and 1890s he was often used as a contrast to the aesthetes; and Shaw was especially cognizant of Morris's change to a socialist-reformer-"saint." The allusions to Morris are in the nature of a private joke, a personal reminiscence which is both a tribute to, and a gentle satire on, his old friend.[11]

Apollodorus is so much the aesthete that he applies an aesthetic test to all things, even to the gods. He praises Caesar's proposal that Cleopatra "come with me and track the flood to its cradle" because "Caesar is no longer merely the conquering soldier, but the creative poet-artist" (p. 175). When Caesar says that "as dogs we are like to perish now in the streets," Apollodorus says, "What you say has an Olympian ring in it: it must be right; for it is fine art" (p. 182). Speaking of the Egyptian gods, he says, "The only one that was worth looking at was Apis: a miracle of gold and ivory work" (p. 187). In these three statements Shaw gives to Apollodorus all the attitudes of Shaw's artist, i.e., the romantic man of feeling, the kind of artist Shaw became only under ether, the artist condemned in the preface to *Three Plays for Puritans* and literally damned in *Man and Superman*. Apollodorus praises Caesar's speeches of love and of despair, and he perceives not the religion represented by the Egyptian icons but only the artistry of their form. Like the aesthete-artist in Shaw's novels, Apollodorus is not only a devotee of art but a devotee of woman; he sings of the pangs of love and serves as Cleopatra's "perfect knight," her polite and gallant "servant."

As in *An Unsocial Socialist*, Shaw contrasts this aesthete-artist with the man of affairs, who is also an artist of sorts. Caesar occupies himself with the Roman arts of peace and war, government and civilization, which, he tells Apollodorus, are of greater value than "a few ornaments." Nevertheless, Caesar does recognize merit in Apollodorus's art, in that it offers amusement to men, courtship to the ladies, and welcome relief from a life of action. Caesar pays tribute to Apollodorus after Rufio has scornfully called Apollodorus a "popinjay":

> The popinjay is an amusing dog—tells a story; sings a song; and saves us the trouble of flattering the Queen. What does she care for old politicians and camp-fed bears like us? No: Apollodorus is good company, Rufio, good company.
>
> RUFIO. Well, he can swim a bit and fence a bit: he might be worse, if he only knew how to hold his tongue.
>
> CAESAR. The gods forbid he should ever learn! Oh, this military life! this tedious, brutal life of action! That is the worst of us Romans: we are mere doers and drudgers: a swarm of bees turned into men. Give me a good talker—one with wit and imagination enough to live without continually doing something! (P. 167)

Caesar is echoing Wilde's defense in "The Critic as Artist" of the contemplative, artistic man over the man of action; Wilde had said, "Action . . . is always easy. . . . It is the last resource of those who know not how to dream . . . the one person who has more illusions than the dreamer is the man of action." The play suggests that life without art is incomplete. Even Caesar becomes an artistic man on occasion, dressing gorgeously, waxing poetic, and wooing Cleopatra (in the banquet scene, act 4), just as Apollodorus on occasion fights in Caesar's campaigns. At the end of the play, Caesar leaves the government of Egypt to Rufio, but he leaves the art of Egypt in Apollodorus's charge, admonishing him to "remember: Rome loves art and will encourage it ungrudgingly" (p. 190).

Caesar's patronage of art comes from an appreciation of both the limitations and the value of art. This is not so of the ordinary Englishman, represented in the character of Britannus, whose attitude toward art reverts to that of the "amateur aesthetes" of *Punch*, those for whom art was a fad, not a serious profession. Britannus considers Apollodorus "a vagabond" until Caesar explains, "Apollodorus is a famous patrician amateur"; at this the "disconcerted" Britannus apologizes to Apollodorus, while explaining to Caesar, "I understood him to say that he was a professional" (p. 151). Shaw's use of the terms *amateur* and *professional* in this specialized sense testifies to the powerful impression the aesthetic controversy of the 1880s had made on him, for by 1898 these terms would have had an old-fashioned ring, recalling the *Punch* attacks on the pseudo-aesthetes in the early 1880s.[12]

Shaw also alludes to amateurs in *Man and Superman;* Don Juan says that "Hell is full of musical amateurs" (p. 95). Shaw's heaven, it should be noted, has no "artistic people," though it is filled with artists, for example, Rembrandt, Mozart, and Nietzsche. Shaw again uses *artist* in two senses: (1) the fashionable, conventional worshipper of beauty and love, and (2) the artist-philosopher. Because Shaw's portraits of artists in the early plays are variations of the former type, his reverence for art tends to be forgotten unless one reminds himself that each play has two artists: the artist figure (Praed, Marchbanks, Apollodorus) and the artist at work in the play (Shaw). Another case in point is *Man and Superman*, where Octavius is "the Artist" of the play, but where the genuine artist is the creator of *Man and Superman*.

In the Epistle Dedicatory Shaw describes the artist as a genius with "all the unscrupulousness and all the 'self-sacrifice' (the two things are the same) of Woman. He will risk the stake and the cross; starve, when necessary, in a garret all his life; study women and live on their work and care as Darwin studied worms and lived upon sheep; work his nerves into rags without payment, a sublime altruist in his disregard of himself, an atrocious egotist in his disregard of others. Here Woman meets a purpose as impersonal, as irresistible as her own; and the clash is sometimes tragic" (p. xx). The artist is "abnormal," "a madman" in the world's view, for his genius nature sets him apart from ordinary men; furthermore, because his preoccupation with art alone frees him "from the otherwise universal dominion of the tyranny of sex," his notions of woman, love, and sex are unreliable—his very freedom from the tyranny makes him prone "to romantic nonsense, erotic ecstasy, or the stern asceticism of satiety" (pp. xx–xxii). This theory of the abnormality of the artist's vision because of his single-minded dedication to art is a restatement of Oscar Wilde's idea that artists are of necessity "lacking in wholeness and completeness in nature" because of their "concentration of vision and intensity of purpose" and their preoccupation with formal beauty.[13] Shaw repeats the idea when Tanner advises Octavius about his role as artist: "You have a purpose as absorbing and as unscrupulous as a woman's purpose"; the artist uses women, Tanner says, as materials for his art and as inspiration for it; he is

> a bad husband . . . a child-robber, a blood-sucker, a hypocrite, and a cheat. Perish the race and wither a thousand women if only the sacrifice of them enable him to act Hamlet better, to paint a finer picture, to write a deeper poem, a greater play, a profounder philosophy! For mark you, Tavy, the artist's work is to shew us ourselves as we really are. Our minds are nothing but this knowledge of ourselves; and he who adds a jot to such knowledge creates new mind as surely as any woman creates new men. In the rage of that creation he is as ruthless as the woman, as dangerous to her as she to him, and as horribly fascinating. Of all human struggles there is none so treacherous and remorseless as the struggle between the artist man and the mother woman. Which shall use up the other? that is the issue between them. (Pp. 23–24)

Octavius, of course, is the reverse of this description: far from being unscrupulous, he is chivalrous and gallant; instead of being an "abnormal" member of society, he is the embodiment of conventional attitudes and opinions; instead of pursuing art with a single-minded passion, he pursues Ann Whitefield and is heartbroken at her rejection of him. The description of Octavius on his first appearance in the play emphasizes his good looks, his elegant attire, his "engaging sincerity," "modern serviceableness," and "amiable nature"; one has only to recall the anarchic manners and dress of Owen Jack or Marchbanks to know that this is not the portrait of a Shavian artist, but of the romantic hero of a conventional play, a resemblance noted by Shaw: "He must, one thinks, be the jeune premier; for it is not in reason to suppose that a second such attractive male figure should appear in one story" (p. 4). Tavy's opinions match his proper appearance: he considers Violet's disgrace "a frightful thing"; he admires Hector's noble rejection of his inheritance, and is in turn admired by Hector, who "gets on best with romantic Christians of the amoristic sect"; and he refuses to believe that the revolutionary Tanner and the avaricious Ann are serious. He tells Tanner that he makes it "a fixed rule not to mind anything you say. You come out with perfectly revolting things sometimes" (p. 24). To Ann's question about Tavy's future wife, "Suppose she were to tell fibs, and lay snares for men?" he blindly answers, "Do you think I could marry such a woman—I, who have known and loved you?" (p. 154).

Octavius has only one characteristic in common with the artist-philosopher of Shaw's preface: he has a distorted notion of women, and he remains free "from the otherwise universal dominion of the tyranny of sex." But his freedom is not from choice, as is the artist-philosopher's, but from Ann's refusal to have him. Ann tells him that he is "very foolish about women," that, unless he wishes to be disillusioned, he "must keep away from them, and only dream about them" (p. 153). Ann and Tanner call Octavius's artistic temper "an old maid's temperament"—"barren."

Octavius belongs with the worshippers of Love and Beauty in hell, where, as Juan explains, "Our souls being entirely damned, we cultivate our hearts" (p. 88). Octavius demonstrates his kinship to the man of "heart" in hell when he promises never to cease loving Ann, using the Statue's words: "And when I am eighty, one white hair of the woman I love will make me tremble more than the thickest gold tress from the most beautiful young head."[14] And Octavius's world view is appropriate to hell, which Juan calls "a perpetual romance, a universal melodrama," resembling "the first act of a fashionable play, before the complications begin" (pp. 100, 125–26).

Octavius is, then, a dramatization of "the Artist" described in act 3 by Don Juan: "Then came the romantic man, the Artist, with his love songs and his paintings and his poems; and with him I had great delight for many years, and some profit; for I cultivated my senses for his sake; and his songs taught me to hear better, his paintings to see better, and his poems to feel more deeply. But he led me at last into the worship of Woman" (p. 111). His explanation of why the artist idolizes love repeats Shaw's prefatory remarks and Tanner's speech to Octavius: "Now my friend the romantic man was often too poor or too timid to approach those women who were beautiful or refined enough to seem to realize his ideal; and so he went to his grave believing in his dream" (p. 111). But Juan approached women with infamous success, thus coming to know that woman falls somewhat short of the artistic ideal: "That is just why I turned my back on the romantic man with the artist nature, as he called his infatuation. I thanked him for teaching me to use my eyes and ears; but I told him that his beauty worshipping and happiness hunting and woman idealizing was not worth a dump as a philosophy of life; so he called me Philistine and went his way" (p. 113). Like Juan's artist friend, Octavius idolizes women and love. Ann is to him, in Shaw's words,

> an enchantingly beautiful woman, in whose presence the world becomes transfigured, and the puny limits of individual consciousness are suddenly made infinite by a mystic memory of the whole life of the race to its beginnings in the east, or even back to the paradise from which it fell. She is to him the reality of romance, the inner good sense of nonsense, the unveiling of his eyes, the freeing of his soul, the abolition of time, place, and circumstance, the etherealization of his blood into rapturous rivers of the very water of life itself, the revelation of all the mysteries and the sanctification of all the dogmas. (Pp. 15–16)

This view of Ann, Shaw says, is not "in any way ridiculous or discreditable"; and the poetic quality of the description of Ann suggests that Shaw too was capable of viewing woman with this reverence. But Octavius's estimate of Ann is, the play demonstrates, blind to reality. He looks to her for "fulfilment" and "inspiration," and, though Tanner tries to persuade him that marriage to her would give him neither, Octavius remains faithful to his ideal.

Octavius also evidences all the sentiment that Shaw associates with the artist in hell. He "cries unaffectedly" over the death of Mr. Whitefield; tears come to his eyes when Ann torments him; and he is "sobbing softly" after Ann tells him that she cannot marry him. He is compared to "the bird that presses its breast against the sharp thorn to make itself sing" (p. 153), an allusion to Wilde's story of "The Nightingale and the Rose," where the poor bird sacrifices its life for the sake of true love.[15] The contrast between Shaw's two kinds of artists—one with the hellish, the other with heavenly, temperament—is sharply drawn when Octavius tells Tanner that he would like to write a play with Ann as its heroine (p. 22). Given Octavius's illusions about Ann, it would be a romantic play in which the heroine is obedient, kind, and loving, one worthy to be worshipped. In implicit contrast to Octavius's projected play is Shaw's play with Ann as heroine. Interestingly, Shaw's view of the heroine encompasses both Octavius's worship and Tanner's scepticism.

It is tempting to take Tanner as Shaw's spokesman in *Man and Superman*, especially when Shaw says that he "felt about marriage very much as Jack Tanner does in *Man and Superman*."[16] On important issues—on sex, marriage, parent-child relationships, property, etc.—Tanner voices Shaw's views. But he is no more a representative of Shaw than is the Christian socialist preacher Morell, who is Tanner's dramatic ancestor. *Man and Superman* is a reworking, with interesting variations, of the triangle in *Candida*. If *Candida*, which focuses on Shaw's artistic persona, and *Man and Superman*, which focuses on his prophetic persona, are viewed as companion pieces, one finds that Shaw finds validity in both the artistic and active life, a statement also implicit in the Caesar-Apollodorus friendship. Tanner, like Morell, has a social conscience and "the gift of the gab"; but he has Marchbanks's scorn for happiness and final realization that "life is nobler than that." On the other hand, Octavius has Marchbanks's freedom from sexual involvement, but Morell's conventional view of women. Whereas in *Candida* the moralist is the weaker of the two men, in *Man and Superman* the artist is the weaker. But, because Candida chooses the weaker and Ann Whitefield chooses the stronger man, the outcome of the two plays is essentially the same: the moralist-preacher marries; the artist remains uninvolved; and the woman satisfies her mothering instinct. However, Marchbanks is permitted to lose his illusions about domestic life, and Octavius retains his; thus they will be considerably different artists. If in his maturity Marchbanks chose to write a play with Candida as heroine, the woman would not, after his glimpse of Candida's strength and control, be like Octavius's vision of Ann; it would be presumably like Shaw's portrayal of the mother-woman, a vision of her as both romantic enchantress and realistic boss.

A love triangle is also the situation of *How He Lied to Her Husband* (1904), a one-act play which Shaw wrote to fill out the bill in Arnold Daly's New York production of *The Man of Destiny*. In a brief introduction to *How He Lied*, Shaw says that the play illustrates "what can be done with even the most hackneyed stage framework by filling it in with an observed touch of actual humanity instead of with doctrinaire romanticism" (p. 181). In this play the poet, Henry Apjohn, is a familiar Shavian type—an elegant young man who writes poems, fights well, and idolizes a woman. In the original version of the play, Shaw linked Apjohn's idolatry to a romantic misinterpretation of *Candida,* which had been the hit of the 1903–4 theater season in New York. Aurora Bompas, the heroine, is "a very ordinary South Kensington female of about 37, hopelessly inferior in physical and spiritual distinction to the beautiful youth" (pp. 183–84); she imagines that she is Candida (to whom she is also inferior on both counts). Apjohn, identifying with Marchbanks, courts Mrs. Bompas and writes love poems to her. When the playlet begins, the poems are missing and have probably been taken by the sister-in-law, who incidentally objects to the "immoral" Candida. Aurora's distress at the idea of her husband's reading the poems and the husband's pride at having a wife worthy of such adoration destroys Henry's illusions about women, love, and Shaw's *Candida.* When Apjohn exits he not only quotes Eugene's farewell but tears up his tickets to *Candida.*

Shaw omitted the *Candida* discussion in the Standard Edition of the play, presumably because he did not want the playlet regarded as a key to, or a satire of, *Candida* and because it is a topical allusion which is for an age, not for all time. The effect of the *Candida* discussion is not, as many critics of Daly's performances assumed, to satirize *Candida* but to satirize one more romantic notion of the playgoer. Just as Shaw hated the all-for-love motive in the popular drama, he also hated the idolizing of Candida, whose "figurative shawl," Henderson notes, "as a topic became sadly frayed by the animated discussion of *la revoltée* and *la femme incomprise.*"[17] The portrait of the upset, conventional housewife ridicules the folly of the women who misunderstood Candida by applauding her speech to Morell to "put your trust in my love for you," etc. And the portrait of Apjohn is another statement of the poet's need to free himself from romantic illusions about domestic life and, in the original playlet, about art, specifically Shaw's art in *Candida.*

120

Chapter XII

THE UNSCRUPULOUS ARTIST

IN *The Doctor's Dilemma* (1906), Shaw finally creates an artist who fits the description of the unscrupulous artist-philosopher in the Epistle Dedicatory to *Man and Superman*. Unlike the neophyte poets, Marchbanks and Apjohn, Dubedat is young but sure of his philosophy; unlike the iconoclastic reformers, Morell and Tanner, he is an artist, not a propagandist-preacher; and, unlike the unredeemed artists, Praed, Apollodorus, and Octavius, he is not hindered by romantic illusions about women, love, and marriage. Shaw seems to have drawn Dubedat directly from the description of the artist in *Man and Superman*: Dubedat is without scruples regarding money, women, or friendship; and he will lie, cheat, or steal so that he may devote himself to art, which he pursues with single-minded purpose. To the world he is a scoundrel because he disregards conventional morality; Walpole even suggests that Dubedat is a madman: "There's something abnormal about his brain" (p. 143).

The consensus of the critical assessment of Dubedat is that he is thoroughly reprehensible. Burton says that Dubedat, "whose credo is L'Art pour L'Art" and who is an "Irresponsible Bohemian," was a type abhorred by Shaw. Patrick Braybrooke calls him a "pleasant scoundrel," so realistically portrayed that one might find his type "in any studio down Chelsea way." Edmund Fuller finds no dilemma in the play, for moral men are rarer than geniuses: "The consideration given to Louis Dubedat's case seems to me to be an aspect of turn-of-the century romanticism about the artist." J. I. M. Stewart maintains that the doctors treat Dubedat better than does Shaw. Judith Spink, who considers Tanner's description of an artist who "will let his wife starve" not a description of a Shavian hero but of a compulsive "semi-criminal," calls Dubedat "a plain case of the old-fashioned cad and scoundrel." C. B. Purdom pronounces him "worthless."[1]

Shaw's own attitude toward Dubedat is explicit in at least four sources. In the preface to *The Doctor's Dilemma* (pp. 18–19) he says, "I have represented an artist who is so entirely satisfied with his artistic conscience, even to the point of dying like a saint with its support, that he is utterly selfish and unscrupulous in every other relation without feeling at the smallest disadvantage." Shaw then argues that "hardly any of us have ethical energy enough for more than one really inflexible point of honor," and Dubedat's is his art. He concludes that the artist's private vice may be in the public interest:

> Not only do these talented energetic people retain their self-respect through shameful misconduct: they do not even lose the respect of others, because their talents benefit and interest everybody, whilst their vices affect only a few. An actor, a painter, a composer, an author, may be as selfish as he likes without reproach from the public if only his art is superb; and he cannot fulfil this condition without sufficient effort and sacrifice to make him feel noble and martyred in spite of his selfishness. It may even happen that the selfishness of an artist may be a benefit to the public by enabling him to concentrate himself on their gratification with a recklessness of every other consideration that makes him highly dangerous to those about him. In sacrificing others to himself he is sacrificing them to the public he gratifies; and the public is quite content with that arrangement. The public actually has an interest in the artist's vices.

In his 1907 preface to *The Sanity of Art* (*Essays*, pp. 288–89), Shaw maintains that Nordau might perform a service if he would try to determine "the real stigmata of genius; so that we may know whom to crucify, and whom to put above the law." Shaw notes that in *The Doctor's Dilemma* he deals with the problem of the criminal genius, but that the problem is not easily solved. He does not believe that artistic genius should excuse "reckless" dishonesty and selfishness, but he adds, "On the other hand, we cannot ask the Superman simply to add a higher set of virtues to current re-spectable morals; for he is undoubtedly going to empty a good deal of respectable morality out like so much dirty water, and replace it by new and strange customs, shedding old obligations and accepting new and heavier ones." Shaw then argues that, because the genius is conventional in all matters except for the specific area of his genius ("Your genius is ever 1 part genius and 99 parts Tory"), he usually poses no great challenge to society's toleration; when he does scandalize society, he is usually in conflict not with con-temporary feeling in his own class, but with some institution which is far behind the times. Dubedat's disregard for the property of others and his defiance of marriage laws are both instances of con-flict with what Shaw considered outmoded institutions.

In "Biographers' Blunders Corrected" (*Sketches*, pp. 103–4), Shaw corrects Henry Charles Duffin's analysis of Dubedat. He first repeats his thesis from the preface to *The Doctor's Dilemma*: "No man is scrupulous all round. He has . . . certain points of honor, whilst in matters that do not interest him he is careless and unscrupulous." One of Dubedat's models, Shaw says, "was mor-bidly scrupulous as to his religious and political convictions. . . . But he had absolutely no conscience about money and women; he was a shameless seducer and borrower, not to say a thief." Dube-dat, like his living model, has an "inflexible point of honor": "When Dubedat says on his deathbed that he has fought the good fight, he is quite serious. He means that he has not painted little girls playing with fox terriers to be exhibited and sold at the Royal Academy, instead of doing the best he could in his art. . . . There-fore I cannot endorse your dismissal of Dubedat as a mere cad. He had his faith, and upheld it." Finally, in a conversation with Stephen Winsten, Shaw said of Dubedat: "He's a saint when it comes to art but in matters of men and women and almost every-thing else he's a scoundrel."[2] As Audrey Williamson says, almost timidly, in *Bernard Shaw: Man and Writer*, "The suspicion lin-gers that Shaw liked the blackguard artist" (p. 146).

Dubedat is, admittedly, thoroughly reprehensible by conven-tional standards. He prostitutes his wife by referring to her affec-tion for the man to whom he is appealing for money; he borrows a cigarette case and forgets to return it; he takes money for work which he may not deliver; he lies to extort money or to avoid difficulties; he is willing to cheat his wife of her income; he proposes that Ridgeon blackmail his patients into buying art; and he seduces a girl who believes that he has married her, when in fact both she and Dubedat are already married to other people. In a melodrama any one of these faults would make Dubedat the unquestionable villain of the play.

But in a Shaw play, heroism and villainy is never a simple matter of obedience or disobedience to law or custom. Though Shaw considers Dubedat a scoundrel regarding money and women, Shaw also provides Dubedat with a defense. First is the implicit defense: in a socialist state Dubedat would be able to do his life's work without worrying about an income from private patrons; and in an enlightened state, marriage laws would face the fact of polygamy instead of hypocritically ignoring it.[3] Dubedat's explicit defense for his actions is the simple plea that he must have money in order to live and work; he explains blandly to Ridgeon, to whom he has just proposed swindling Jennifer of her money, "Well, of course I shouldn't suggest it if I didnt want the money" (p. 133). He justifies his deception of Minnie Tinwell because she "has had three weeks of glorious happiness in her poor little life, which is more than most girls in her position get. . . . Ask her whether she'd take it back if she could" (p. 137). His behavior is, like many of Shaw's childlike protagonists', beyond good and evil: "He is as natural as a cat" (p. 116), and natural behavior, according to Shaw, is not to be judged "moral" and "immoral."[4]

Even when judged in terms of conventional morality, Dubedat is not as bad as Ridgeon, who has set for himself the godlike task of deciding "not only whether the man could be saved, but whether he was worth saving" (p. 109). Though this admission is appalling to most people, Shaw, who argued that people who were hopelessly antisocial had to be killed and who later was to write an apology for political killing,[5] might have forgiven Ridgeon this presumption. Ridgeon's dilemma, which, contra Fuller, is a real one in the play, arises from the fact that he is enough like Shaw to say, echoing Shaw's attacks on goodness and respectability, that good people are "infernally disagreeable and mischievous" and to wonder if "the world wouldnt be a better world if everybody behaved as Dubedat does than it is now that everybody behaves as Blenkinsop does."[6] In his final choice, however, Ridgeon loses sight of the moral dilemma, for his motives are confused by his love for the artist's wife. Finally, if Jennifer's comments in the final scene can be believed, Ridgeon's human errors and his playing god are not his worst offenses; Jennifer accuses him of having the calloused attitude of the vivisector, i.e., of regarding men as soulless brutes.

But to say that Dubedat is no worse than his judge is no real defense. His defense is in his absolute faithfulness to his art, to which he is willing to sacrifice everything and everybody but which is his "one really inflexible point of honor." The play reveals little about the nature of Dubedat's art,[7] so that we do not know whether or not the sacrifice was of public benefit. But we do know that Ridgeon, who is an art connoisseur, considers Dubedat's work "the real thing" (p. 110) and states unequivocally that Dubedat is a genius (pp. 118, 147, 165).

Like other genuine artists in Shaw's work, Dubedat shocks society; regards art as a profession, not as a moral obligation; and cares for nothing except his work. He has less of an erratic temperament than Owen Jack or Madame Szczympliça, but more of an unconventional nature than either, for he shocks society not because he has unusual dress, manners, or speech, but because he violates its laws and defies its morality. In all these characteristics, he is more like the fin-de-siècle aesthetes than any of Shaw's other artist figures. However, unlike the aesthetes' artists and Shaw's other artists, Dubedat is married. But his is a special kind of marriage. In the first place, unlike Praed, Apollodorus, or Octavius, he does not talk about the spiritual power of women and love. He is chivalrous enough to tell the doctors that "if youd told me that Jennifer wasnt married, I'd have the gentlemanly feeling and artistic instinct to say that she carried her marriage certificate in her face and in her character," but he says this mainly to shame the doctors by contrasting his "immoral" but gentlemanly character with their morality and readiness to suspect evil. He does not pay elaborate court to Jennifer, unless it is to get money or sympathy from her. On the contrary, Jennifer is his protector and support; she confesses to Ridgeon that she aspired to save a man of genius from "poverty and neglect" and to "bring some charm and happiness into his life"; Dubedat was, she believes, the answer to her prayer. Like Candida, she mothers her husband by defending him from hostile opinion and financial distress; and she considers him "just like a boy" (p. 152) in all but his thoughts and his work. But Dubedat, unlike Morell, is not emotionally dependent on his wife; he is like the artist Tanner describes, a man who "pretends to spare her [his wife] the pangs of child-bearing [Jennifer is childless; so was Charlotte Shaw] so that he may have for himself the tenderness and fostering that belong of right to her children. Since marriage began, the great artist has been known as a bad husband" (*M&S*, p. 23). Dubedat's marriage is, then, not the kind of marriage that Octavius would have had: Dubedat uses woman for his own purpose, which is "to guard me against living too much in the skies" (p. 130), or, in plainer words, to see to mundane affairs.

In assessing Shaw's attitude toward Dubedat, the sources of the portrait are helpful. Shaw is said to have acknowledged Aubrey Beardsley[8] as a model for Dubedat, but, if one is looking for artist models for Dubedat, there is more of Rossetti than of Beardsley in the portrait. Dubedat's amours and his personal charm suggest Rossetti; and his attitude toward his patrons seems a direct allusion to Rossetti, who "rejoiced no less in unscrupulously despoiling these Philistines [his patrons] than in pocketing their gold. To him it was self-evident that the sole justification of a business man's existence was to support artists." One of Rossetti's patrons, Mac-Cracken, in the early 1850s commissioned an oil painting and advanced Rossetti a deposit on this; with this deposit and the money for some water colors alleviating his financial distress, Rossetti "did not for some time trouble even to begin it [the oil]. Nor was it, in fact, ever completed."[9] This detail is strikingly like that dramatized in *The Doctor's Dilemma*, when Dubedat says that the drawings for Maclean (even the name of the patron is similar) "dont matter. Ive got nearly all the money from him in advance" (p. 130). Dubedat's attitude toward women and toward money has nothing in it of Beardsley and a great deal in it of Rossetti.

However, Shaw also acknowledged Edward Aveling as one source for Dubedat.[10] A speech by Shaw makes clear the parallels between the character of Aveling and of Dubedat; Shaw characterizes Aveling as "a scamp" who "was a devoted Socialist, Atheist, and

Darwinian, and an impressive orator, and would probably have died rather than deny his faith. But when money or women were concerned he had no conscience, no scruples, no self-control. His borrowings and seductions were innumerable; and his victims were often poor working folk who were dazzled by his oratory."[11] This description of Aveling was made, of course, after the literary fact of Louis Dubedat, and Shaw might have been unconsciously basing this portrait of Aveling on his portrait of Dubedat. But Hesketh Pearson bears out Shaw's description of Aveling, who "on the same day he would borrow sixpence from the poorest man within his reach on pretence of having forgotten his purse, and three hundred pounds from the richest to free himself from debts that he never paid." When Aveling coached science students, Pearson continues, he often took money in advance and then cancelled the lessons; and, when his wife died, he did not marry Eleanor Marx, with whom he was living, but married another woman. After this, Eleanor committed suicide, and Aveling "took no steps to prevent this convenient solution of his domestic difficulties." Pearson completes his account of Aveling with a defense: "Whatever he did, he did without concealment, without shame, with a *desinvolture* that almost forbade disapprobation. . . . He at last died like an atheist saint, spouting Shelley."[12]

If Aveling is a source for Dubedat, he is not the only source, for Shaw also cited Richard Wagner's story "An End in Paris" as another source.[13] Dubedat's attitude toward art is probably derived from his literary model, the artist protagonist of "An End in Paris," one of Wagner's stories of *A German Musician in Paris: Tales and Articles, 1840 and 1841*. Like Dubedat, Wagner's artist dies proclaiming his faith in art.

I believe in God, Mozart and Beethoven, and likewise their disciples and apostles;—I believe in the Holy Spirit and the truth of the one, indivisible Art;—I believe that this Art proceeds from God, and lives within the hearts of all illumined men;—I believe that he who once has bathed in the sublime delights of this high Art, is consecrate to Her for ever, and never can deny Her;—I believe that through this Art all men are saved, and therefore each may die for Her of hunger; . . . I believe in a last judgment, which will condemn to fearful pains all those who in this world have dared to play the huckster with chaste Art, have violated and dishonoured Her through evilness of heart and ribald lust of senses;—I believe that these will be condemned through all eternity to hear their own vile music. I believe, upon the other hand, that true disciples of high Art will be transfigured in a heavenly fabric of sun-drenched fragrance of sweet sounds, and united for eternity with the divine fount of all Harmony.—May mine be a sentence of grace!— Amen![14]

Dubedat's declaration substitutes the names of painters for the names of musicians; it is considerably briefer than the musician's; but it has essentially the same content.

The artistic character of "R . . . ," Wagner's dying musician, is developed in other stories in the series. In "A Happy Evening" "R . . . " reveals his contempt for an artistically indifferent public, especially for its demand for anecdote in music and its confusion of the distinct aims of music and poetry; he denies that occasional art has any vitality except that the occasion may bring on a mood which will be worthy of artistic treatment; and he says that symphonies do not exist to cheer the heart of man: "They exist for themselves and their own sake, not to flip the circulation of a philistine's blood."[15] Another of the series of stories and articles, "The Artist and Publicity," which purports to be one of "R . . . 's" papers, has a section that is peculiarly appropriate to Dubedat; "R . . . " maintains that the genius is not prompted to create by any practical considerations: "One's daily bread, the maintenance of a family . . . do not operate in the genius. They prompt the journeyman, the handworker; they may even move the man of genius to handiwork, but they cannot spur him to create, nor even to bring his creations to market." When he does bring art "to open market," it is because he hovers between the heaven of his inner joy and the hell of public indifference and he feels strong enough "to play with even Evil." But he is incapable of telling lies: "Truth is his very soul." Therefore he finally finds escape from the world's indifference in proud laughter.[16] *The Doctor's Dilemma* reveals no specific points of Dubedat's aesthetic theory; but the ideas of "R . . . ," many of which are akin to those of the English fin-de-siècle aesthetes, may have gone into the formation of Dubedat as a character. Certainly Shaw took for Dubedat the musician's devotion to art and his indifference to working for the sake of feeding himself or supporting a family; in Dubedat there is also a suggestion of the artist's faith in the incorruptibility of his truth, no matter how much he lies, and of his arrogant laughter at an inferior world.

Shaw also borrows from Wagner Dubedat's allegiance to another artist. Wagner's "R . . . " is a disciple of Beethoven; Dubedat is a disciple of Bernard Shaw. Dubedat's profession of allegiance has been taken to be a warning to "spurious Shavians,"[17] but it is best understood when compared with Wagner's comments on "R . . . 's" discipleship. The narrator of "An End in Paris," a friend of "R . . . ," says that the cult of Beethoven deifies "his name, his renown," but is incapable of judging musical merit. For example, the name of Beethoven, prefixed to an hitherto ignored work, secures that work's recognition; but "if your works are composed in that daring individual spirit which you so much admire in Beethoven, [the members of the Beethoven cult] will find them turgid and indigestible."[18] Similarly, Dubedat's use of Shaw's name is to summon up instant recognition of Dubedat's values; ironically, the doctors are not sure who Bernard Shaw is. And, one might add, though Shaw may not have foreseen this irony, Dubedat's independent application of Shaw's tenets to his own behavior has caused many members of the cult of Shaw to dismiss Dubedat as a worthless scoundrel. Shaw does complicate matters by making Dubedat a liar, cheat, and thief as well as an artistic genius, just as he less disturbingly complicates the portrait of the poet Marchbanks by making him physically weak, almost neurotically sensitive, and foolish about a woman. Though Shaw recognized the rascal in Dubedat, I am convinced that he found him a worthy, even though a misguided, follower of Bernard Shaw. When Dubedat says, "I dont believe in morality, I'm a disciple of Bernard Shaw," he is wrong in considering Shaw's name justification for his blackguardism, but he is right in assuming that Shaw would not approve of the doctors' moralizing. In the play the stupidities of some of the doctors and the cynicism of Ridgeon are worse than the infidelity and thieveries of Dubedat, who at least has a defense if not a justification for both. Dubedat does challenge the doctors' morality; he does look on his art as justification for his life; and he is no amateur or dilettante whose real faith is in the love-panacea.

For these reasons Shaw could say of him, "He had his faith, and upheld it."

Shaw creates another "unscrupulous" artist in the character of Shakespear in *The Dark Lady of the Sonnets* (1910). Like Dubedat, Shaw's Shakespear also has the characteristics of the man of genius described in *Man and Superman*. In Shaw's dramatic criticism, Shakespeare emerges as an artist who sacrificed dramatic ideas to worn-out plots and stage conventions and a man who succumbed to a romantic world view and a philosophy of despair. These and other failings Shaw attributes to Shakespeare's familial pride, for, he explains.

> The man of family . . . will plunge into society without a lesson in table manners, into politics without a lesson in history, into the city without a lesson in business, and into the army without a lesson in honor. . . . In short, the whole range of Shakespear's foibles: the snobbishness, the naughtiness, the contempt for tradesmen and mechanics, the assumption that witty conversation can only mean smutty conversation, the flunkeyism towards social superiors and insolence towards social inferiors, the easy ways with servants: . . . all these are the characteristics of Eton and Harrow.[19]

But in his criticism and his play Shaw also insists on Shakespeare's artistic genius; according to Shaw, Shakespeare compensated for his philosophical deficiency by psychological depth and consummate mastery of style.

In *The Dark Lady of the Sonnets* Shakespear is presented not only as a genuine artist but as an artist like Shaw. In the preface to the play Shaw corrects the sentimental view of Shakespeare presented by Frank Harris in his play about the dark lady: "Frank conceives Shakespear to have been a broken-hearted, melancholy, enormously sentimental person, whereas I am convinced that he was very like myself: in fact, if I had been born in 1556 instead of 1856, I should have taken to blank verse and given Shakespear a harder run for his money than all the other Elizabethans put together" (p. 207). In Shaw's play Shakespear's artistic methods also describe Shaw's methods. For example, Shakespear is represented as capturing the poetry of the vernacular by copying down verbatim good phrases that he hears, taking his language from living examples:

THE BEEFEATER. You judge too much by the Court, Sir. There, indeed, you may say of frailty that its name is woman.

THE MAN [*pulling out his tablets again*] Prithee say that again: that about frailty: the strain of music.

THE BEEFEATER. What strain of music, sir? I'm no musician, God knows.

THE MAN. There is music in your soul: many of your degree have it very notably. [*Writing*] "Frailty: thy name is woman!" [*Repeating it affectionately*] "Thy name is woman."

THE BEEFEATER. Well, sir, it is but four words. Are you a snapper-up of such unconsidered trifles?

THE MAN [*eagerly*] Snapper-up of—[*he gasps*] Oh! Immortal phrase! [*He writes it down*]. (P. 232).

The Beefeater does not appreciate Shakespear's plays any more than the ordinary playgoer appreciates Shaw's; he prefers *The Spanish Tragedy*, with its heroics, its vengeance and blood, and its bombast, to the "new-fangled plays," which are "all talk" (p. 231). And Shakespear, like Shaw, laments the world's preference for "murder, or a plot, or a pretty youth in petticoats, or some naughty tale of wantonness" (p. 242) to his plays dealing with social problems.

Like the artist described in *Man and Superman*—the artist that Octavius is not—Shakespear does not idolize women but uses them unscrupulously as matter for his art. The Dark Lady's complaint that "he will tie you down to anatomize your very soul" and then reveal it to all the world (pp. 239–40) echoes Tanner's description of the artist as "half vivisector, half vampire. He gets into intimate relations with [women] to study them, to strip the mask of convention from them, to surprise their inmost secrets" (*M&S*, p. 23). Shaw's Shakespear is impudent, fickle, and proudly superior to the lady; he explains to the queen that he is "not cruel, madam; but you know the fable of Jupiter and Semele. I could not help my lightnings scorching her" (pp. 240–41). When charged with conceit, he asks, "Can I go about with the modest cough of a minor poet, belittling my inspiration and making the mightiest wonder of your reign a thing of nought?"[20] He has the artistic sureness that distinguishes the great artist from the pseudo-artist in Shaw's previous work; his humor and boldness and arrogance recall Owen

Jack's assertion that "I am in my own way—not a humble way—a man of genius myself" (*LAA*, p. 149).

In short, except for his foolish family pride, Shakespear has all the characteristics of Shaw's genuine artist; he is indifferent to convention and unscrupulous in his use of others for his own purposes; he is misunderstood by the public; and he is devoted to "immortal poesy," which invests the vile world "with a magical garment of words to transfigure us and uplift our souls til earth flowers into a million heavens" (p. 236).

Chapter XIII

THE ARTIST-CREATOR OF LIFE

FTER *The Dark Lady of the Sonnets,* Shaw ceased to portray the artist interested in creating a living art form and offered instead the artist who is interested in creating life itself. In Shaw's theology God is the Life Force, which, operating through its agents, evolves by trial and error toward a higher form of life; and to Shaw God is an artist: "God made the world as an artist and that is why the world must learn from its artists."[1] Therefore, the highest kind of artist is the one who aspires, like God, to create life.

Henry Higgins was Shaw's first attempt to depict this kind of artist. Higgins can be seen as a literary artist only by a play on words: i.e., he works with language and is interested in producing beautiful sounds—sounds worthy of "the language of Shakespear and Milton and the Bible" (p. 209); he refers to himself as a "poet" (p. 230), and Eliza calls him "a born preacher" (p. 288). But his art transcends that of the poet-preacher. He is primarily interested in creating life, in changing Eliza, the "squashed cabbage leaf," into a human being. He does this by first "creating a new speech for her," and then creating a new soul for her, so that she may evolve from "creature" to human being with divine potentialities. He tells his mother that he has been "watching her lips and teeth and her tongue, not to mention her soul, which is the quaintest of the lot" (p. 256); and he tries to explain to Eliza that recognizing the value of the human soul is more important than having manners: "The great secret, Eliza, is not having bad manners or

133

good manners or any other particular sort of manners, but having the same manner for all human souls: in short, behaving as if you were in Heaven, where there are no third-class carriages, and one soul is as good as another" (p. 288). Throughout the experiment Higgins looks on Eliza as a lower form of life, referring to her as a "creature," an "animal," an "insect," a "cat." He does not consider her human until she defies him; then he warns her that "if you dare to set up your little dog's tricks of fetching and carrying slippers against my creation of a Duchess Eliza, I'll slam the door in your silly face" (p. 290). Eliza demonstrates that she is indeed a lower form of life than Higgin's ideal by her snobbery when she plans to cut her old associates, by her vengeful desire to "get a bit of my own back" from all who hurt her, by her slaving for the sake of approval (Higgins calls this trading in affection), and, finally, by her hatred of Higgin's coldness. Not until she asserts her independence from him does he tell her, "By George, Eliza, I said I'd make a woman of you; and I have. I like you like this" (p. 294). He nevertheless continues giving her orders; and he remains, Shaw says in the epilogue to the play, in a godlike relation to her (p. 307). She is, however, transformed by Higgins; both her speech and her soul become more refined under his tutelage.

Like Shaw's God, Higgins is not infallible; he is sure of himself in working with Eliza's speech, but he proceeds experimentally on the difficult job, the creation of life (i.e., soul). To Pickering's objection that Eliza "must understand thoroughly what she's doing" before she consents to the experiment, Higgins says, "Do any of us understand what we are doing? If we did, would we ever do it?" (p. 224). To Eliza's accusation that by changing her he made trouble for her, he answers, "Would the world ever have been made if its maker had been afraid of making trouble? Making life means making trouble" (p. 290). Furthermore, he confesses that he too has profited from the experiment, that he has "learnt something from [Eliza's] idiotic notions" (p. 289).

Though Higgins is a very special kind of artist, his characteristics are those of Shaw's other fictional artists. In temperament he is like Cyril Scott, Owen Jack, or Madame Szczympliça: extremely petulant, easily angered, and unconscious of his irascible nature. Just as Jack impatiently storms at his pupils and then assumes that "perhaps you did not perceive my annoyance, and so took whatever I said too seriously,"[2] so Higgins protests to Eliza, after he has lost his temper twice in rapid succession and is about to lose it again: "You have caused me to lose my temper: a thing that has hardly ever happened to me before" (*Pygmalion*, p. 271). Higgins's feuding with Mrs. Pearce recalls Jack's abuse of Mrs. Simpson, the landlady who looks after him, criticizes his manners, and is consequently the recipient of violent abuse.

Jack is in fact an early version of Professor Higgins,[3] especially in his taking a pupil for tutoring in elocution. His "very exacting" method of instruction anticipates that of Higgins: Madge "often could hardly restrain her tears when he emphasized her defects by angrily mimicking them, which was the most unpleasant, but not the least effective, part of his system of teaching. He was particular, even in his cheerful moods, and all but violent in his angry ones; but he was indefatigable, and spared himself no trouble in forcing her to persevere in overcoming the slovenly habits of colloquial speech. The further she progressed, the less she could satisfy him" (p. 101). As she progresses, Jack gives her no "word of encouragement or approval" (p. 102). Higgins also bullies, yells, mimics, demands perfection, and offers no praise for his student's accomplishments. Jack is considered antisocial because of his petulance, arrogance, and frankness; Higgins is a social failure for the same reasons, e.g., his mother asks him not to attend her at-home, for "you offend all my friends: they stop coming whenever they meet you" (p. 245). Yet both men are ladies' men. The girls whom Jack teaches idolize him, and Madge Brailsford falls in love with him; Mary Sutherland hesitates when he proposes marriage not because she finds him unattractive but because she has never considered marrying him and believes that she cannot endure the strain of marriage with a genius. Higgins is also attractive to women, in spite of his efforts to discourage them. Mrs. Pearce tells Pickering, "Theres more ways than one of turning a girl's head; and nobody can do it better than Mr. Higgins" (p. 220); Eliza says the same thing to Higgins in the final scene: "You can twist the heart in a girl as easy as some could twist her arm to hurt her" (p. 289). But both Jack and Higgins are "confirmed old bachelors"—Jack after Mary's rejection of him and Higgins from childhood.

The reason for Higgins's bachelorhood, Shaw says, is that Higgins's mother provided with her Pre-Raphaelite beauty an ideal of excellence which cannot be reached by other women.[4] Like Candida, Mrs. Higgins looks on Higgins and Pickering as "two children" (p. 275); she calls her son a "good boy" (p. 246) or a "silly boy" (p. 254), and instructs, humors, and scolds him as she would a child. In Mrs. Pearce, Higgins has a Candida-like housekeeper and business manager; therefore, from Eliza he wants only "good fellowship" (p. 289). Thus Higgins, according to Shaw, has the best of womankind; he retains the ideal of woman, as Octavius does, by remaining single; he receives the babying that Candida lavishes on Morell from his mother and Mrs. Pearce; and he remains free of marriage ties, redirecting his sexual energies into intellectual and aesthetic passion. Emotionally, Higgins is closer to the Shavian superman of *Back to Methuselah* than to the previous Shavian artists, for he has rejected the life of the senses for the life of the mind and warns Eliza,

> If you cant stand the coldness of my sort of life, and the strain of it, go back to the gutter. Work til youre more a brute than a human being; and then cuddle and squabble and drink til you fall asleep. Oh, it's a fine life, the life of the gutter. It's real: it's warm: it's violent: you can feel it through the thickest skin: you can taste it and smell it without any training or any work. Not like Science and Literature and Classical Music and Philosophy and Art. You find me cold, unfeeling, selfish, dont you? Very well: be off with you to the sort of people you like. Marry some sentimental hog or other with lots of money, and a thick pair of lips to kiss you with and a thick pair of boots to kick you with. If you cant appreciate what youve got, youd better get what you can appreciate. (P. 292)

Though these sentiments look forward to Shaw's Ancients, Higgins's freedom from sexual ties recalls Jack's return to his "holy garret" or Marchbanks's flight into the night. It also recalls Shaw's description of the struggle between Woman and the man of genius, to which Higgins refers when he says that "women upset everything. When you let them into your life, you find that the woman is driving at one thing and youre driving at another" (p. 228).

Higgins's unscrupulous use of others in his pursuit of linguistic science ("your art," his mother calls it, p. 254) recalls Shaw's concept of the ruthless artist described in *Man and Superman* and dramatized in *The Doctor's Dilemma*. Like Dubedat, Higgins is capable of being charming when he needs something. His technique for "getting round" women is to coax them "as a child coaxes its nurse when it wants to get anything out of her."[5] Mrs. Pearce accuses him of "walking over" people, for "when you get what you call interested in people's accents, you never think or care what may happen to them or you" (p. 225). Eliza also accuses him of walking—rather "running"—over people:

> LIZA. . . . I wont be passed over.
>
> HIGGINS. Then get out of my way; for I wont stop for you. You talk about me as if I were a motor bus.
>
> LIZA. So you are a motor bus: all bounce and go, and no consideration for anyone. (P. 288)

Higgins originally decides to experiment with Eliza because she "doesnt belong to anybody—is no use to anybody but me" (p. 222). And in act 3 he clearly looks on his mother's guests as bearable only as part of his experiment; he says to the Hills, "We want two or three people. You'll do . . ." (p. 248). Higgins's calloused attitude (like Dubedat's cynical use of others) offends everyone, especially Eliza, who tells him, "Youve no feeling heart in you" (p. 223). However, he does "care for life, for humanity," and he cares for Eliza because she is "a part of it" (p. 289).

In *Pygmalion* the artist is interested not in painting pictures but in transforming people, in changing flower girls into duchesses, in trading their animality for spiritual independence. In *As Far As Thought Can Reach,* part 5 of *Back to Methuselah*, Higgins has evolved into "a square-fingered youth [named Pygmalion] with his face laid out in horizontal blocks, and a perpetual smile of eager benevolent interest in everything . . . the smile of a simpleton, and the eager confidence of a fanatical scientist" (p. 220). Pygmalion is a "soulless creature! A scientist! A laboratory person" (p. 220) to the youthful worshippers of love and beauty. He does not consider himself an artist and scorns artists because they lack intellect. He is, however, introduced by the master sculptor Martellus as "an artist who has surpassed both you [Arjillax] and me

137

further than we have surpassed all our competitors" (p. 219). Like Higgins, Pygmalion is not interested in art but in life itself and, in the play, creates a man and woman. Pygmalion has discovered how to change lifeless substance into living consciousness, but he cannot equal nature; thus his "masterpieces of art" are inferior forms of life—that is, they are "prehistoric" humans of the kind found in the twentieth century. They are "of noble appearance, beautifully modelled and splendidly attired," but they are vain, pompous, unthinking, passionate, jealous, lying, and violent. After the woman kills Pygmalion, she and the man cringe from judgment, accuse each other, and finally die in cowardly despair. Their tragedy amuses the Children who have observed it, but the Ancients look on Pygmalion's masterpieces as "loathsome dolls," "abominations," and "laboratory refuse" (pp. 233, 236).

In *As Far As Thought Can Reach* Pygmalion is a child, or else he would not have interest even in the art of creating living dolls. The Ancients will have nothing to do with works of art nor with any other games of childhood—"this dancing and singing and mating" (p. 201). They do not attend the festivals of the arts, and they avoid the Children, who are children because of their interest in art and love, their boredom with philosophy and science, and their horror at the idea of an eternity of contemplation. In other words, the Ancients and the Children are dramatizations of the blessed and the damned described in act 3 of *Man and Superman.* The Ancients have grown out of the desire to play with dolls, even with dolls with "the final perfection of resemblance to life." They have learned that the only valuable use of man's creative energy is to "alter the shape of his own soul," and for this work they do not need art; the Children use art to perceive their souls, but the Ancients "have a direct sense of life" (p. 242). Their only "dolls" are their bodies, which they are striving to shed so that they may become vortices of pure thought.

The Children of *As Far As Thought Can Reach* have evolved farther than most twentieth-century men; they look on the humans created by Pygmalion with detachment and curiosity, then with horror and disgust, and finally with amusement. Their aim is to "enjoy life," to cultivate and refine the senses and feelings by art and love. In the play Ecrasia represents the aesthete, and Acis is the lover. Ecrasia demands that art depict beauty alone, and she equates beauty with prettiness. Therefore, she protests when Arjillax sculpts realistic busts of the Ancients instead of "ideally beautiful nymphs and youths" (p. 215). She believes that art is greater than the artist, that physical beauty is "of supreme importance," and that art, unlike real life, brings happiness (p. 242). Acis is scornful of art, believing that he has "the direct impulse of life" instead of the make-believe approach to life that art offers. He says, "Love is a simple thing and a deep thing: it is an act of life and not an illusion. Art is an illusion" (p. 247). Strephon is another believer in love, who asks Pygmalion, "Why did you not make a woman you could love?" (p. 227). Strephon is heartbroken because The Maiden whom he loves has matured, i.e., she has grown out of the childish "arts and sports and pleasures" and is becoming more like the Ancients.

The transitional stage of life represented by The Maiden is, in Shaw's evolutionary scheme, equivalent to that of Don Juan in *Man and Superman,* or of Henry Higgins in *Pygmalion;* her lover applies the same terms to her that others apply to Juan and Higgins: she is "losing all heart, all feeling" and aspires to a "cold and uncomfortable" life (pp. 203–4). She admits that she once lost her heart to Strephon, but "now I seem to have lost it altogether: bigger things are taking possession of me" (p. 204); she would be bored spending her hundreds or thousands of years of life in dancing, singing, or lovemaking. When Strephon, echoing Eliza Doolittle, accuses The Maiden of not caring for him, her answer is like that of Higgins: "Nonsense! I care for you much more seriously than before; though perhaps not so much for you in particular. I mean I care more for everybody" (p. 205). However, unlike Higgins, The Maiden has lost all interest in human contact. Higgins is eager to have Eliza back for the sake of "good fellowship" as long as she understands that neither is bound to, nor dependent on, the other; The Maiden is less patient and less attached to Strephon: "I do not dislike you; but you bore me when you cannot understand; and I think I shall be happier by myself in the future" (p. 205).

The artists Arjillax and Martellus are also in the transitional stage between childhood and maturity. Arjillax considers a sculptor godlike in his revelation of spirit through form and his natural and inevitable creativity. Echoing Shaw's theory in the prefaces to *Plays Pleasant* and *Three Plays for Puritans,* he says that the artist provides a glimpse of the next stage of evolution and that he must take care to produce models worthy of emulation, since life imitates art: "The statue comes to life always. The statues of today are the men and women of the next incubation. . . . Let no man dare to create in art a thing that he would not have exist in life" (p. 247). As a result of this theory, Arjillax has given up sculpting beautiful figures and now sculpts busts of the Ancients. Martellus, the master sculptor, has also given up modeling "images of loveliness"; but he has progressed farther than Arjillax and given up modelling statues of the Ancients as well, for he has come to believe that "anything alive is better than anything that is only pretending to be alive" (p. 218). Martellus introduces Pygmalion, who has succeeded in producing life.

As Far As Thought Can Reach depicts humanity in all stages of evolution from twentieth-century humanity to humans of an age as far as thought can reach. The twentieth-century humans created by Pygmalion are not worth saving; they are merely a dangerous amusement for the Children and bits of debris to the Ancients. The Children are far more advanced on the Shavian evolutionary scale: they are born in late adolescence and spend only four years in "babyish gambols." In the transitional stage between childhood and maturity are The Maiden, who has developed a social conscience and lost all sensual interests, and the artists, who are themselves at various levels. Arjillax has given up art devoted to beauty alone; Martellus has given up art for life; and Pygmalion has developed the art of creating life. Yet to the Ancients, who devote their energies to the shaping and creating of self, all these are children. On this evolutionary scale Shaw would probably place himself, the iconographer of a living religion and the portrayer of the wisdom of the Ancients, at the stage of Arjillax. Arjillax notably espouses Shavian theories of art, including a preference for realistic rather than pretty studies, a belief in the artist's godlike powers to reveal spirit in form, a desire to provide artistic models worthy of imitation, and a desire to forecast the next stage of evolution. Clearly Shaw had passed the stage of admiring "pretty-pretty confectionery," and he just as clearly had not reached the stage of Martellus, who has smashed all his statues and given up art.

The kinds of artists represented in *Back to Methuselah* demonstrate that, during Shaw's long career, there was very little change in his concept of the artist. In general, all his portraits of artists are of the types appearing in embryonic form in *Immaturity*, Shaw's first novel. Hawkshaw (aesthete and lover) and Cyril Scott (genuine artist) reappear in *Back to Methuselah* as the Children and Arjillax, respectively. The major development in these two types is that the rascality (unscrupulousness) of Hawkshaw eventually becomes a trait of the true artist and that, after Scott, none of Shaw's artists marries for love, and most of them do not marry at all.

The aesthete in Shaw's fiction and drama believes that art has a high moral purpose, but, because he has conventional opinions about art and life, his concept of morality is limited to what is socially acceptable. He is courteous, chivalric, and often eager to fight for the sake of honor; he worships love and idolizes women; and he is a duffer in art. Examples of this type of artist are Sholto Douglas, Adrian Herbert, Chichester Erskine, Praed, and Octavius. Marchbanks and Apjohn before their final recognitions and Apollodorus also have many of these characteristics. The Children in *As Far As Thought Can Reach*, especially Ecrasia and Acis combined, are of this type.

The genuine artist in Shaw's work rejects talk of the high moral purpose of art and devotes himself instead to perfection of his craft. He is not, however, only a craftsman but, at his best, a truthteller as well. He is alienated from society because of his Bohemian appearance, his rude manners, his straightforward speech, his shocking opinions, his sensitivity, or his rascally behavior. He will sacrifice others as ruthlessly as he will sacrifice himself to his art. Examples of this type are Cyril Scott, Susanna Conolly, Nelly McQuinch, Owen Jack, Madame Szczympliça, Madge Brailsford, Dubedat, Shakespear, and Henry Higgins.

A third type of artist depicted by Shaw is the artist-creator of life, who rejects the artifact for life itself. Examples of this type of artist include all the creative geniuses who express the Life Force in their lives and make an art of their profession; Caesar, with his arts of war and of government, is an obvious example. This type of artist is suggested also in *Immaturity*, where, in spite of his youth, Smith is Harriet's instructor in language and the arts, and in *Love among the Artists*, where Jack, not content with having taught Madge to speak, tries to transform her from a sham to a real woman by awakening her to the art of truth telling. Shaw's first full study of such an artist is Higgins, who anticipates Martellus and Pygmalion in *Back to Methuselah*.

Shaw's aesthetes are almost the reverse of the actual aesthete; in fact, in that their faith is usually placed in something other than art, they cannot properly be called aesthetes at all. They are men of sentiment, men of "heart." On the other hand, Shaw's real artists are very much like the actual aesthete: they place their art above their own and others' welfare; though they do not talk about its being all-sustaining, they find that it drains all their passion and energy; they are outcasts from society; and they are temperamental and sensitive, often to the point of hypersensitivity.

As one would expect, Shaw's genuine artists are not identical to the fin-de-siècle aesthetes. For instance, they never consider alienation from society essential to their artistic integrity. Owen Jack, Madame Szczympliça, and Dubedat are willing to make money from their art; all the artists, even the "unsocial socialist," are personally charming and indeed very "social." They, like their creator, would not agree with Moore's, Symons's, or James's contention that popularity ruins a work. They are, however, realistic enough to believe that art seldom achieves popularity. Another point of difference is that the aesthetes' sensitivity tends to be toward the sensuous and the Shavian artists' toward the emotional or spiritual; for example, Marchbanks's sensitivity is for intuiting and interpreting the feelings of others, and his aesthetic squeamishness is mainly caused by coarseness and brutality in others, not by offenses to his senses. Another difference is that Shaw's artists try to avoid posing unless, as Lady Geraldine says, the forthright expression of common sense is itself a pose. At any rate, Owen Jack opposes sham in art; and Candida forces Marchbanks to abandon all his attitudes.

The critical point of difference is that, whereas both the moral and the fin-de-siècle aesthetes place their faith and aspirations in art, Shaw's artists evolve toward a rejection of art and an acceptance of a contemplative, ascetic state. The She-Ancient in *Back to Methuselah* was once an aesthete-artist, and her progress illustrates the evolution of the Shavian artist:

Stage 1 (sensuous beauty): "When I was a child, Ecrasia, I, too, was an artist, like your sculptor friends there, striving to create perfection in things outside myself. I made statues: I painted pictures: I tried to worship them.

Stage 2 (realistic, "unpleasant" art): "I, like Arjillax, found out that my statues of bodily beauty were no longer even beautiful to me; and I pressed on and made statues and pictures of men and women of genius, like those in the old fable of Michael Angelo. Like Martellus, I smashed them when I saw that there was no life in them: that they were so dead that they would not even dissolve as a dead body does.

Stage 3 (life-creation: " . . . It was to myself I turned as to the final reality. Here, and here alone, I could shape and create. . . . For five more years I made myself into all sorts of fantastic monsters.

Stage 4 (creative mind, the utopia not yet achieved): "And suddenly it came into my mind that this monstrous machinery of heads and limbs was no more me than my statues had been me, and that it was only an automation that I had enslaved. . . . The day will come when there will be no people, only thought." (Pp. 243–45)

According to Shaw, all true artists evolve in this manner. Thus he maintains that Ruskin and Morris changed from artists to social critics to prophets and saints (see pp. 4, 7).

Shaw's contemplative heaven finds its nearest parallels in the literature of the aesthetes in Pater's "Sebastian van Storck" (in *Imaginary Portraits*) and Wilde's "The Critic as Artist." In "Sebastian van Storck" the ideal of the *tabula rasa* leads the hero to reject love, riches, and power for a contemplative life. But Sebastian is an entirely different kind of person from Shaw's She-Ancient; Sebastian demands from art "visionary escapes"; he is attracted to Catholicism because of "its unfailing drift towards the concrete" and because of its rich tradition; he has a strong death-wish; and he isolates himself from worldly concerns to hasten "the restoration of equilibrium, the calm surface of the absolute, untroubled mind."[6]

Shaw's Ancient, on the other hand, desires greater creative activity and a greater consciousness of life instead of escape and rest; in contrast to Sebastian's search for the *tabula rasa,* she seeks to become intensely vital mind. Wilde's contemplative man is a dreamer, an artist, and stands in contrast to the active man, not to the sensuous man. Shaw's contemplative man, the Ancient, is a vitalist, a mental "man of action," struggling with reality and escaping from art and all sensuous appeal.

The aesthetes' nearest parallels to Shaw's contemplative ideal emphasize very different values; the aesthete's usual ideal—the creation of sensuous beauty—is even farther removed from that of Shaw's. Morris's heaven in *News from Nowhere* suggests the ideal of the moral aesthetes: it consists of clean, wholesome, creatively active lives in gorgeous surroundings; Symons's ideal, influenced by Pater's *The Renaissance,* suggests that the fin-de-siècle aesthetes' approximation of heaven consists of intense awareness of life's fleeting moments, apprehended by the senses. Neither of these utopian states approaches Shaw's. Thus, though Shaw's late nineteenth- and twentieth-century artists are indebted to, and sometimes modelled on, his aesthetic contemporaries, in their final form (represented by the She-Ancient) the Shavian artists will have evolved to a state not only different from, but unacceptable to, the aesthetes.

One way to illustrate the crucial difference between Shaw and the aesthetes is to compare Shaw's *As Far As Thought Can Reach* to Yeats's "Sailing to Byzantium" (1927), since the two roughly contemporary works have so many motifs in common as to suggest actual indebtedness. Both works cope with the problem of growing old and dying. And both begin with a picture of the world of youth and sensuality. Yeats devotes the first stanza of his poem to the young, fertile, but "dying generations"; Shaw's play begins as an Ancient unconsciously intrudes into the youthful world and says, in effect, that this "is no country for old men" ("Sailing to Byzantium," 1. 1) : "I did not know there was a nursery here, or I should not have turned my face in this direction. . . . It would be painful to me to go back . . . to your babyish gambols: in fact I could not do it if I tried. . . . My children: be content to let us ancients go our ways and enjoy ourselves in our fashion" (*As Far As Thought*

Can Reach, p. 200). Shaw's Children, like Yeats's "young / In one another's arms" (11. 1–2), are "caught in that sensual music" ("Sailing to Byzantium," 1. 7), which Shaw's Ancient describes as "dancing and singing and mating" or "arts and sports and pleasures." In Shaw's depiction of the Children's world, lovemaking, a birth, and death (Pygmalion's and his two twentieth-century humans') parallel Yeats's characterization of the young world: "Whatever is begotten, born, and dies" (1. 6). The Children are horrified at the Ancients' failure to "enjoy life"; they do not like to associate with the Ancients, and they dislike Arjillax's art depicting them; in Yeats's words, they "neglect / Monuments [in Shaw's play, both the Ancients and the busts of Ancients] of unaging intellect" (1. 8).

Shaw's play and Yeats's poem also have similar portraits of the old man. Yeats's "aged man"—"a paltry thing / A tattered coat upon a stick" (11. 9–10)—could describe Shaw's Ancients, with their facial furrows, their baldness, and sexlessness; like Yeats's old man, who will sing of the magnificence of his soul (11. 10–14) "and louder sing / For every tatter in its mortal dress" (11. 11–12), the Ancients spend their lives in ecstatic contemplation of the soul and in spiritual creativity.

In the third stanza of "Sailing to Byzantium," Yeats's prayer to the holy sages also expresses the aspirations of Shaw's Ancients:

> Consume my heart away; sick with desire
> And fastened to a dying animal
> It knows not what it is; and gather me
> Into the artifice of eternity. (11. 21–24)

In Shaw's play, one of the signs of change from childhood to maturity is the loss of heart, the cooling toward the joys of childhood (i.e., of all of human life as twentieth-century man knows it). The Ancients have already lost one part of their humanity; and they hope to lose the last vestige of the "dying animal" and to be gathered "into . . . eternity":

THE HE-ANCIENT. . . . Whilst we are tied to this tyrannous body we are subject to its death, and our destiny is not achieved.
THE NEWLY BORN. What is your destiny?

145

THE HE-ANCIENT. To be immortal.

. . . .

THE SHE-ANCIENT. None of us now believe that all this machinery of flesh and blood is necessary. It dies.

THE HE-ANCIENT. It imprisons us on this petty planet and forbids us to range through the stars.

. . . .

THE SHE-ANCIENT. The body was the slave of the vortex; but the slave has become the master; and we must free ourselves from that tyranny. (Pp. 245–48)

Thus Shaw and the aesthete (here, Yeats) agree that the summer world of youth and love is a "dying" world, and both aspire to transcend it by casting away the body and attending to the soul. Where they differ is on the question of how one should spend eternity, once the transcendent state has been achieved. Shaw's Ancients aspire to become vortices of pure thought; Yeats aspires to achieve immortality through the artifact—"such a form as Grecian goldsmiths make." Yeats's eternity is an "artifice"; Shaw's is contemplation.

A comparison of these two works illustrates once again, then, the essential distinction between the aesthetes and Shaw. The aesthete places his faith in art, in "the holy city of Byzantium"; but Shaw's faith and hope are in life (i.e., mind). Therefore, Shaw's Children are not precisely like Yeats's "dying generations." The Children have almost achieved Yeats's heavenly vision; art is a vital part of their lives; they sing beautifully, dance gracefully, look lovely, and celebrate the arts. But after only four years, they abandon art and all images. In Shaw's utopia Yeats would outgrow his faith in art, as Martellus does, explaining, "In the end the intellectual conscience that tore you away from the fleeting in art to the eternal must tear you away from art altogether."[7]

The conclusion one draws from this comparison is the same as that to be drawn from an examination of Shaw's portraits of artists from Cyril Scott, "the aesthetic pet," to the Ancients, with their desire to rid themselves of the final image, the body: Shaw owes more to the aesthetes than he acknowledged, and probably more than he was aware of; his faith in the power of art approaches an aesthete's faith; his portraits of unscrupulous, alienated, sensitive, and dedicated artists draw on characteristics of the aesthete. But, in the final analysis, Shaw's faith is in values other than art: in the life and mind of humanity. His artists are portraits of the best of present mankind, but, in time, he believes, they will have served their purpose of envisioning and interpreting the new religion, and, perhaps by 31,920 (as far as thought can reach), they can abandon art altogether.

Chapter XIV

SHAW THE ARTIST

HAW'S greatest and most complete portrait of an artist is the character that he created for himself, G. B. S. the platform orator, Corno di Bassetto the music critic, Shaw the music critic, the drama critic, the playwright, and, in his personal life, the philanderer, the socialist, the devil's disciple, etc. Interestingly, this complex character is closer to the fin-de-siècle aesthete than any of Shaw's fictional portraits of artists. For example, few of Shaw's fictional artists consciously pose; but he readily acknowledged his ability to act a role, justifying his pose by proposing, like Henry James, that "humanity is immense, and reality has myriad forms."[1]

> Like all men, I play many parts; and none of them is more or less real than another. To one audience I am the occupier of a house in Adelphi Terrace; to another I am "one of those damned Socialists." A discussion in a club of very young ladies as to whether I could be more appropriately described as an old josser or an old geezer ended in the carrying of an amendment in favor of an old bromide. I am also a soul of infinite worth. I am, in short, not only what I can make of myself, which varies greatly from hour to hour and emergency to no-emergency, but what you can see in me. (*Portraits*, p. 82)

Winsten records Shaw's comment that "one has to dramatize oneself or else remain completely insignificant"; and he notes that Shaw seemed to lose his temper only by premeditation, that every gesture seemed "studied, probably with the help of a mirror."[2]

148

Though Shaw was a self-confessed actor, he did not consider his role playing an affectation or an attitude but a "simple natural phenomenon." In his 1917 review of Dixon Scott's *Men of Letters,* Shaw attacks Scott for "taking the method of nature, which is a dramatic method, for a theatrical pose." Every man, Shaw insists, has to assume a number of masks in order to function in society; and to some men the mask is especially essential: "Every man whose business it is to work directly upon other men, whether as artist, politician, advocate, propagandist, organizer, teacher, or what not, must dramatize himself and play his part" (*Portraits,* p. 235). In a speech of 1889 called "Acting, By One Who Does Not Believe In It," Shaw reveals that he does indeed believe in it, even to the extent of suggesting, like Wilde, that a mask enables a man to tell the truth or, like Yeats, that the mask is a link with the permanent in existence.[3] Shaw says that acting is self-realization, not sham, that a great actor, given a great role, can achieve an expression of his total personality which is more real than life itself. As an example, Coquelin calls himself "a sham—that is, an actor," but he "is less an actor than any other comedian on the stage." In him "individuality is concentrated, fixed, gripped in one exceptionally gifted man"; and, if he were given a part that "shews all sides of him and realizes him wholly to us and to himself," he would become "completely real" as he lost "the conventional mask" that man in everyday affairs has to assume. The argument is very similar to that of Yeats: "Active virtue as distinguished from the passive acceptance of a current code is therefore theatrical, consciously dramatic, the wearing of a mask."[4] The acting of roles, then, Shaw finds inevitable and desirable: inevitable because "all the world's a stage," desirable because a good actor influences others and achieves a realization of self unattainable in ordinary life.

Shaw also found acting a way of coping with an unimaginative world. In the autobiographical preface to *Immaturity* Shaw says that "if the term had been invented then [when he first came to London] I should have been called The Complete Outsider" (p. xliv). He was not, however, an outsider in aesthetic and intellectual matters, so that, with the acquisition of a religion (defined as "a clear comprehension of life in the light of an intelligible theory"), he was able to set "in triumphant operation" his literary and critical abilities. But his religion did not make him any less strange to the mass of mankind; he was still set apart because of his unique spiritual vision, symbolized by his clear and exact vision in a distorted and blind world. His estrangement did not result in withdrawal but in role-playing; Shaw explains,

> The mere rawness [of socially insecure youth] which so soon rubs off was complicated by a deeper strangeness which has made me all my life a sojourner on this planet rather than a native of it. Whether it be that I was born mad or a little too sane, my kingdom was not of this world: I was at home only in the realm of my imagination, and at my ease only with the mighty dead. Therefore I had to become an actor, and create for myself a fantastic personality fit and apt for dealing with men, and adaptable to the various parts I had to play as author, journalist, orator, politician, committee man, man of the world, and so forth. (Preface, *Immaturity*, p. xliii)

Like the fin-de-siècle aesthetes, then, Shaw felt alien to Victorian society and assumed a pose, often a pose like that attributed to Owen Jack in *Love among the Artists*—the pose of "outspoken common sense . . . the most insufferable affectation of all."

Though Shaw considered himself an outsider, he did not think of himself as a Bohemian. Apropos of the visit of a French journalist who was shocked to find "England's most advanced thinker" living in a bourgeois household, Shaw said to Stephen Winsten, "I tried sandals, but they didn't work."[5] Nevertheless, Shaw's dress expressed a Bohemian impulse. In *The Aesthetic Movement in England* Hamilton mentions dress reform as one of the beneficial effects of the aesthetic movement; he sees the trend toward more informal and comfortable attire as an extension of Wilde's protest against Victorian ugliness in men's dress and refers to a book entitled *Art in Costume,* which pleads for "soft, low-crowned hats, jackets, knee-breeches, and stockings"[6]—a precise description of Shaw's fin-de-siècle costume. Max Nordau also associates dress such as Shaw's, specifically Jaeger woolens, with the fin-de-siècle art movements.[7] Later in life, Shaw dressed more conventionally; or, rather, the dress which had struck late Victorian society as unusual became, in the twentieth century, more socially acceptable. However, Shaw retained certain eccentricities of dress; for example, he wore socks which, following the Jaeger system, were fitted for the right and left foot and had toes in them; at Ayot-St.-Lawrence, even after Charlotte's death, he dressed formally for dinner each night; and he was ultrasensitive to white collars against the color of human flesh, and wore grey or colored ones instead.[8]

Shaw did not, however, think of himself as a hypersensitive artist. And he took care to dissociate himself from those whom he considered voluptuaries, i.e., the meateaters, winebibbers, idolaters of women, and worshippers of art. When Clive Bell wrote "The Creed of an Aesthete," expressing astonishment at Shaw's beliefs in *Back to Methuselah* and saying that "the people who really care for beauty do not care for it because it comes from God or leads to anything. They care for it in itself," Shaw called Bell "a fathead and voluptuary" who does not recognize intellect as a passion superior to sense.[9] Shaw also feuded with G. K. Chesterton and Hilaire Belloc, who considered Shaw a Puritan ascetic and whom Shaw considered Roman Catholic voluptuaries. In "The Chesterbelloc: A Lampoon" Shaw asserts that "cowards drink alcohol to quiet their craving for real stimulants: I avoid it to keep my palate keen for them" (*Portraits*, p. 80). However, Shaw's teetotallism (applying to coffee, tea, and tobacco as well as to alcohol) and vegetarianism are just as indicative of hypersensitivity as a sybaritic existence is; as Holbrook Jackson notes, Shaw's personal habits approach the Epicurean ideal of Pater's Marius.[10] As though in support of this, in "The Chesterbelloc" Shaw defines his addiction to work as a voluptuous indulgence. Though he probably would not have liked the comparison, art, music, and philosophy, as well as work, caused him to "be present always at the focus where the greatest number of vital forces unite in their purest energy. . . . To burn always with this hard, gemlike flame, to maintain this ecstasy." In "On Going to Church" he says that beautiful churches are more than adequate substitutes for the stimulation of drugs and drink; in "The Religion of the Pianoforte" he advocates music as a means of making "a nation of skilled voluptuaries"; and in "The Aesthetic Man" (*Everybody's Political What's What*) he traces his education to an aesthetically sensitive childhood. Shaw's Ancients, who have lost all joy in the senses, in art and in love, are enjoying "real stimulants" in thought. The familiar passage above from the conclusion to *The Renaissance* could with perfect appropriateness be put into the mouth of one of the Ancients in *Back to Methuselah;* in fact, an Ancient says to the Youth who deplores the Ancients' "miserable" life, "Infant: one moment of the ecstasy of life as we live it would strike you dead" (p. 202).

Shaw's hypersensitivity is not to art and philosophy alone. He had other sensitive aesthetic reactions as well, the most striking of which was his reaction to the appearance of the printed page. Shaw attributes his concern for beauty of composition to the influence of Morris, saying that "Morris led me to look at the page of a book as a picture, and a book as an ornament."[11] Shaw supervised the publishing and printing of his books, and he was fastidious in his typographical preferences: his primary demand was for "evenness of the block of colour"; he hated "rivers" in the type and admits that he rewrote in proof lines "so widely spaced as to make a grey band across the page"; and he carefully balanced and justified lines and spaced words.[12] An artist who will rewrite for no other reason than to make the page more attractive is no propagator of ideas alone; obviously, Shaw's concern for beauty extended even to the layout of the printed page. The beauty of his pages, like the beauty of his art, does not reside, of course, in prettiness; both the books and the art in them have an austerity suited to their matter. Shaw's typography uses no ornamentation, no flowers, no devices, no rules.

In addition to his sense of alienation, his conscious pose, and his acute sensitivity—all characteristics of the fin-de-siècle aesthete—Shaw also created for himself the persona of an immoral artist. In *Three Plays for Puritans* he defends diabolonianism in the preface and writes a play in which the devil's disciple is a hero. When he told Winsten that a genius must sell himself to the devil,[13] he was reiterating a theory developed early in his career and held throughout his life, that the genius by definition is dangerous to society because he upsets convention, attacks institutions, and disregards morality. His portrait of himself as artist is like the image of the unscrupulous artist described in the Epistle Dedicatory to *Man and Superman.* Repudiating the sentimental fiction that he rose to fame by his virtue, he says that he laid

the foundations of my high fortune by the most ruthless disregard of all the quack duties which lead the peasant lad of fiction to the White House, and harness the real peasant boy to the plough until he is finally swept, as rubbish, into the workhouse. I was an ablebodied and able-minded young man in the strength of my youth; and my family, then heavily embarrassed, needed my help urgently. That I should have chosen to be a burden to them instead was, according to all the conventions of peasant lad fiction, monstrous. Well, without a blush I embraced the monstrosity. I did not throw myself into the struggle for life: I threw my mother into it. I was not a staff to my father's old age: I hung on to his coat tails. . . . Callous as Comus to moral babble, I steadily wrote my five pages a day and made a man of myself (at my mother's expense) instead of a slave. And I protest that I will not suffer James Huneker or any romanticist to pass me off as a peasant boy qualifying for a chapter in Smiles's Self Help, or a good son supporting a helpless mother, instead of a stupendously selfish artist leaning with the full weight of his hungry body on an energetic and capable woman. (Preface, *IK*, pp. xv–xvi)

St. John Ervine considers this story a self-libel invented by Shaw, whose head "was full of romantic nonsense about ruthless artists who refused to let themselves be diverted from their purpose by conventional opinions on morals or public duty or common humanity." Ervine argues that Shaw worked when other boys would have been in school, that Shaw's support cost his mother less than his sisters', that "his room was there" anyway, that he was working very hard at writing, that his mother was using a bequest of £1300 to Shaw from his grandfather, and that, besides, he was not well cared for.[14] But none of these arguments denies the fact that in his mid-twenties Shaw lived on others while he wrote his five novels. And, if his head "was full of romantic nonsense about ruthless artists," it is the "nonsense" on which the Shavian philosophy is based. From his earliest to his latest work Shaw advocates challenging "conventional opinions on morals or public duty or common humanity."

Shaw, then, chose to dramatize himself as the unscrupulous artist who, as Tanner says, "will [among other things] let . . . his mother drudge for his living at seventy, sooner than work at anything but his art" (*M&S*, p. 23). Furthermore, his marriage, like Dubedat's, was, according to Shaw, the result of a woman's desire to bring order to the life of a man of genius; Shaw says that in 1898, when he married, Charlotte had found him ill and living in clutter and dirt and had taken on the task of nursing him back to health and ordering his domestic affairs.[15] The protective woman appears often in Shaw's work; she is Mrs. Simpson in *Love among the Artists,* Jennifer Dubedat in *The Doctor's Dilemma,* Mrs. Pearce and Eliza in *Pygmalion.* Candida is the epitome of this type; in the play Shaw has her choose Morell, but in a letter written twenty-five years after the play and twenty-two years after his own marriage, Shaw says that no doubt later "some enterprising woman married [Marchbanks] and made him dress properly and take regular meals."[16] Shaw's marriage was childless and, according to Shaw, unconsummated, because Charlotte was afraid of having children.[17] But *Man and Superman* offers a different reason: the artist "pretends to spare [his wife] the pangs of child-bearing so that he may have for himself the tenderness and fostering that belong of right to her children" (p. 23). Shaw did not fulfill, of course, all the traits of the artist described by Tanner; he was not "a child-robber, a blood-sucker, a hypocrite, and a cheat" (*M&S,* p. 23); but he did portray himself as a man ruthlessly using others for his own purposes.

Like his fictional artists, Shaw was thoroughly professional in his attitude toward his art, emphasizing the importance of an artist's mastery of technique; he insisted that he was "no mere man of genius, but a conscientious workman as well."[18] He looked on art as his work rather than as his mission, and, with Madame Szczympliça, he could have said, "I have the soul commercial within me" (*Love among the Artists,* p. 337). He not only declined to starve in a garret but he took care to keep a prosaic account of his financial affairs. He maintained that an artist should be a businessman and sell his completed work; he told Winsten, "The moment a painting is complete it becomes merchandise."[19] Like Rossetti, James, and Wilde, he found nothing wrong in desiring financial success. He jealously guarded his copyrights and handled financial transactions with shrewd business acumen. An amusing letter of 1896 to the editor of *The Contemporary Review* illustrates his business sense. The editor had paid Shaw too little for his article, "Socialism for Millionaires," which had appeared in the February, 1896, *Contemporary Review.* Shaw begins, "Bless my soul, you will have to pay me a lot more than that unless you will accept the article as a gratuitous contribution." He then states his usual rate, asserts that "I really do not care a rap about the money," but asks nevertheless for £21 rather than £11.[20] Shaw did not, of course, write for money; he believed that an artist produces art out of an inner necessity, not out of a desire for gain. But he found nothing glamorous in poverty (having been poor) and found much positively evil in it. Accordingly, he practiced what he preached in *Major Barbara* and accumulated wealth, the key to power in a capitalistic society.

It is clear that, although Shaw was not a fin-de-siècle aesthete, nevertheless he had many of the characteristics of one, and his fictional aesthetes are less like the real aesthete than Shaw himself was. Shaw even created some acknowledged examples of art for art's sake, which I have not discussed in the preceding chapters because none of the examples is a major work, and to establish Shaw's connection with the aesthetes I preferred to rely on evidence from the major works. However, Shaw's examples of art for art's sake need to be noted, along with his defense of them. Most of them appear in *Trifles and Tomfooleries* (published 1926), consisting of six short plays, prefaced by a statement that "all playwrights and all actors tomfool sometimes if they can. The practice needs no apology if it amuses them and their audiences harmlessly. Irresponsible laughter is salutary in small quantities. One throws off these things as Beethoven threw off a few bagatelles, and Mozart a few senseless bravura pieces for friends who were violinists. Besides tomfoolery is as classic as tragedy" (p. 81). Shaw assures the reader that these playlets are not "utterly void of wit and wisdom, or their figures characterless; for this kind of work would be unbearable if it added deficiency to folly." Some are occasional pieces such as *The Admirable Bashville*, which was written to protect the dramatic rights of *Cashel Byron's Profession*, and *Passion, Poison, and Petrifaction, or The Fatal Gazogene: A Brief Tragedy for Barns and Booths*, written "at the request of Mr Cyril Maude . . . for the benefit of The Actors' Orphanage." A subtitle explains *Press Cuttings: A Topical Sketch Compiled from the Editorial and Correspondence Columns of the Daily Papers during the Women's War in 1909*. Shaw calls *A Glimpse of Reality: A Tragedietta* (1909) "a trifle" (as distinct from a "tomfoolery"), meaning presumably that it has a serious theme but is not a full and serious treatment of that theme. *The Fascinating Foundling* is subtitled *A Disgrace to the Author; The Music Cure* is called *A Piece of Utter Nonsense*: both are light exercises on the motif of female mastery of the male. Shaw has several admitted "actor's plays": *Great Catherine* (1913), written for Gertrude Kingston; *Annajanska, the Bolshevik Empress* (1917), written for Lillah McCarthy; and *The Six of Calais* (1934), which puzzles critics, Shaw says, because it "has no moral whatever." In the preface to *The Six of Calais* Shaw justifies the absence of a moral on the grounds that "a playwright's direct business is simply to provide the theatre with a play. When I write one with the additional attraction of providing the twentieth century with a up-to-date religion or the like, that luxury is thrown in gratuitously; and the play, simply as a play, is not necessarily either the better or the worse for it" (p. 86). He defines a play as the interpretation of chaotic experience by the author's rearrangement of that experience into a meaningful form: "All the academic definitions of a play are variations of this basic function." These statements are not inconsistent with his comments elsewhere deploring "panacea-mongering" and asserting that the morality of art lies in a truthful representation of a view of life.

In addition to the playlets, Shaw wrote a few short stories with apparently no moral; but, as in the case of the playlets, even his most casual pieces are usually infused with some touches of satire, some typically Shavian ideas and motifs, and unconventional, engaging characters. Two stories worthy of note here because of their absence of Shavian theme and their similitude to the fin-de-siècle "plotless" short story are "The Miraculous Revenge" (in *Time*, March, 1885) a Poelike study of the macabre from the point of view of a mad young man, and "The Serenade" (in *The Magazine of Music*, November, 1885), apparently written for no other reason than to produce a humorously ironic effect.[21] But Shaw's more typical short stories discuss an idea or make a social commentary. And the stories and plays which seem designed for no particular purpose, except to create an effect or to entertain and amuse, make up a very small part of the total literary output of Shaw. They are not, however, radical departures from his more ambitious efforts. They are tomfooleries or trifles because they lack the scope and depth of Shaw's major work; but his major work attests to his role as artist, not as preacher. As he told Winsten, "I am a poet, essentially a poet."[22] His propagandizing in art usually took the form not of preaching but of providing a dramatic metaphor for an aspect of human experience; he was fully aware of the difference between a work of art and a propagandistic tract, and he believed that great work of art endures even when the philosophy it expresses is outdated.

The difficulty in finally assessing Shaw's relationship to the aesthetes is that he took pains to dissociate himself from the "art for art's sake faction" but was closer to it than he admitted, perhaps closer than he realized. Like Whistler, who also denounced aestheticism, Shaw has many of the characteristics of the fin-de-siècle aesthetes; he consciously employs masks as a manner of coping with the world; he feels alienated from the world; he is aesthetically sensitive, at times hypersensitive; he defends immorality and the value of shocking conventional people; and he respects artifice, the craft of art.

His theory of art is the result of a curious ambivalence; he denounced art for art's sake but argued, as an aesthete would, that a work of art exists independent of conventional morality and expresses the artist's individual vision. Art for art's sake he associates with academicism and a decorative impulse arising from following rules of art instead of the writer's inner convictions. The passage repudiating art for art's sake in the Epistle Dedicatory to *Man and Superman* is really an attack on academic art which arises out of a knowledge of art rather than a vision of man; Shaw denies that style is possible without opinions, but he recognizes the fact that, long after the ideas are dated, "the style remains." His defense of didacticism is really on aesthetic grounds: the artist's convictions produce art; without them, art is impossible; hence he has "contempt for *belles lettres*, and for amateurs who become the heroes of the fanciers of literary virtuosity" because, having no convictions, they cannot produce great art.

His concept of didactic art is very different from that of, say, Arthur Waugh, the defender of "Reticence in Literature," or of Harry Quilter, the attacker of "The Gospel of Intensity," or of any other defender of Victorian morality. Shaw insists that art is basically immoral (i.e., iconoclastic) and that its "moral" purpose derives from the artist's integrity in representing his vision. In his attacks on Victorian morality, as well as his attacks on censorship of art, Shaw is clearly allied with the aesthetes, and clearly opposed to the upholders of convention, including the upholders of artistic convention, the rule makers and precedent followers, the copiers of models instead of the forgers of new design.

Shaw shares the fin-de-siècle aesthetes' aristocratic scorn of middle-class values and virtues; and he knows that his "normal" (but unique) vision will by bourgeois standards be judged abnormal, unhealthy, and insane. He also knows that as artist his obligation is not to succumb to the demands of the ordinary man's vision but to find a form to express his own in order to give the ordinary man a glimpse of the future and, hopefully, offer him a model worthy of imitation.

Though his final faith in the power of thought to transcend all sensory appeals, including the sensory appeal of art, keeps him from aestheticism, no aesthete could have placed more emphasis on the place of art in man's life than Shaw did. He believed that the artist's role is "to catch a glint of the unrisen sun," to "shew it to you as a vision in the magic glass of his artwork," or, as the She-Ancient who was once an artist says in *Back to Methuselah*, to provide a "magic mirror . . . to reflect your invisible dreams in visible pictures." Shaw saw himself in this role, and his plays are a testament to the poet-prophet who created them.

Notes

Introduction

1. *Iconoclasts: A Book of Dramatists*, p. 262.
2. "A Cursory Conspectus of G.B.S."(1901), in *George Bernard Shaw: A Critical Survey*, ed. Louis Kronenberger, p. 4.
3. *George Bernard Shaw*, p. 81.
4. *The Eighteen Nineties*, p. 196.
5. In *Platform and Pulpit*, p. 44.
6. "The Religion of the Pianoforte," in *How to Become a Musical Critic*, p. 219.
7. "Bernard Shaw and the Making of the Modern Mind," *CE* 23(April, 1962):522.
8. Wilson, "Bernard Shaw at Eighty," in *The Triple Thinkers*, p. 171; "The Fabian Figaro," in *George Bernard Shaw: A Critical Survey*, ed. Kronenberger, p. 156; Nethercot, "The Schizophrenia of Bernard Shaw," *American Scholar* 21 (Autumn, 1952): 455–67; Bentley, *Bernard Shaw, 1856–1950*, p. 203, respectively. Winifred Smith, "Bernard Shaw and His Critics (1892–1938)," *Poet Lore* 47(Spring, 1941): 76–83, notes that before 1916 Shaw's ideas were considered more impressive than his art, but that that criticism has now been reversed. An early defense of Shaw as artist is Richard Burton, *Bernard Shaw*, p. 236.
9. *Eight Modern Writers*, p. 126, and *Bernard Shaw and the Theater of the Nineties*, p. 27.
10. "The Nineties: Beginning, End, or Transition?" in *Edwardians and Late Victorians*, p. 57.
11. W. S. Gilbert, *Patience; or, Bunthorne's Bride*, in *H.M.S. Pinafore and Six Other Savoy Operas*, p. 177.
12. [Robert Hichens], *The Green Carnation*, p. 196.
13. See especially in *Punch* "Nincompoopiana.—The Mutual Admiration Society," 14 February 1880, p. 66; "An Aesthetic Midday Meal," 17 July 1880, p. 23; "Fleur des Alpes; or, Postlethwaite's Last Love," 25 December 1880, pp. 293–94; "Postlethwaite on 'Refraction,' " 15 January 1881, p. 14; and "Whistler's Wenice; Or, Pastels by Pastelthwaite," 12 February 1881, p. 69.
14. *Punch*, 9 April 1881, p. 161, and 12 February 1881, p. 62.
15. "High-Art Below-Stairs," 26 March 1881, p. 134.
16. "The Poetry of an Aesthete," *Dial* 2(August, 1881): 84.
17. "The Aesthete," in *The Choice of Books and Other Literary Pieces*, p. 291; first published in *Pall Mall Gazette*, May, 1882. Harrison's description of the aesthete closely resembles Gilbert's Bunthorne, the "aesthetic sham," who admits that "my mediaevalism's affectation, / Born of a morbid love of admiration!"
18. *The Gentle Art of Making Enemies*, p. 152; and E. R. and J. Pennell, *The Life of James McNeill Whistler*, 2 vols. (Philadelphia, 1908), 1:182.
19. See especially "Winckelman," *The Renaissance: Studies in Art and Poetry*, in *Works*, 1:177–232; also "Animula Vagula" and "New Cyrenaicism," *Marius the Epicurean*, in *Works*, 2: chaps. 8, 9.
20. *The Gentle Art*, p. 254.
21. "French and English Pictures," *Cornhill Magazine* 40(July, 1879): 104.

22. "Mr. Cimabue Brown on the Defensive," *Belgravia* 45(September, 1881): 286.

23. *Academy,* 12 February 1881, p. 125, and 30 April 1881, p. 327.

24. Buchanan, "The Martyrdom of Madeline," *Academy,* 1 July 1882, pp. 11–12.

25. *Punch,* 10 November 1894, p. 225.

26. Harry Quilter, "The Gospel of Intensity," *Contemporary Review* 67(June, 1895): 763.

27. Chesterton, *George Bernard Shaw,* p. 63.

28. I recognize the inadequacy of the terms *moral aesthetes* and *fin-de-siècle aesthetes;* the two categories are logically unrelated, one focusing on value and the other on chronology. In searching for accurate terms, I originally called one group the "moral" and the other the "amoral" aesthetes; however, the latter term is not precise, because it seems to refer to a personal attribute rather than to an attitude toward art. "The aesthetes who believed in an amoral art," which is accurate, is too unwieldly, and "the 'art for art's sake' aesthetes" carries too many uncontrolled connotations. On the other hand, strictly chronological classing into "early" and "late" (or fin-de-siècle) aesthetes is not precise, for not only would "early" have to include Morris (d. 1896) and exclude Pater (d. 1894), but it does not suggest the real nature of the aesthetes who insisted on the moral effect of art. To call the fin-de-siècle aesthetes the "decadents" introduces more problems than it solves, for the problem of defining the English decadence is as vexed as the problem of defining English aestheticism. I do not intend to deal specifically with decadence except in those instances— for example, Pater, Wilde, Beardsley—where the decadent is also an aesthete.

29. For an account of the sensation caused by the Beardsley poster, see Stanley Weintraub, *Beardsley: A Biography,* pp. 86–88. Shaw's statement occurs in a 1904 letter to Florence Farr, in *Florence Farr, Bernard Shaw, W. B. Yeats: Letters,* p. 39.

Chapter I

1. "Smoke and Genius," *Platform and Pulpit,* pp. 82–85.

2. *Platform and Pulpit,* pp. 130–44. For Ruskin's proposals for economic reform, see especially "The Roots of Honour" *(Unto This Last),* which advocates fixed wages and equality of income as first steps in social reform. Julian B. Kaye *(Bernard Shaw and the Nineteenth-Century Tradition,* pp. 19–22) discusses Ruskin's influence on Shaw's economic and political theory.

3. "Pre-Raphaelitism," *The Works of John Ruskin,* 12:344, 387.

4. "Pre-Raphaelitism," 12:388. Ruskin once rejected a Rossetti picture because it was too labored. Sending the picture back, he explained, "The laboured picture will always be in part an *exercise*—not a result," and told Rossetti, "If you will do me a drawing in three days, I shall be obliged to you; but if you take three months to it, you may put it behind the fire when it is done" *(Ruskin: Rossetti: Preraphaelitism,* ed. W. M. Rossetti, pp. 29–30).

5. These statements occur, respectively, in Henry James, "Mr. Arnold Bennett Thinks Play-Writing Easier than Novel Writing," *Partial Portraits,* p. 52; "School," BBC radio talk, 11 June 1937, in *Platform and Pulpit,* p. 275; and Stephen Winsten, *Days with Bernard Shaw,* p. 42. C. E. M. Joad cites Samuel Butler as the source of this theory of Shaw, but Ruskin seems an equally likely influence *(Shaw,* p. 66).

NOTES

6. *The Works of John Ruskin,* 4: 4, 35–36, 42.

7. See especially "On the Real Nature of Greatness of Style," ibid., 5: 44–69, and "The Relation of Art to Morals," ibid., 20: 73–94.

8. "Art and the People: A Socialist's Protest Against Capitalist Brutality; Addressed to the Working Classes (1883)," *William Morris: Artist, Writer, Socialist,* 2: 402. See also *Hopes and Fears for Art,* vol. 22 of *The Collected Works of William Morris,* especially "The Lesser Arts," p. 26, "The Art of the People," p. 39, et passim.

9. "At a Picture Show, 1883," *William Morris,* 2:409, et passim. The idea appears in virtually all of Morris's essays in *Hopes and Fears for Art.*

10. "Art and the People," *William Morris,* p. 386. See also "The Lesser Arts," *Collected Works of William Morris,* pp. 3–6.

11. "Stalin and Wells: A Comment by Bernard Shaw," *New Statesman and Nation* 8, n.s. (3 November 1934): 614. The most thorough study of Shaw and Morris is E. E. Stokes, Jr., "Shaw and William Morris," *Shaw Bulletin* 1 (Summer, 1953): 16–19.

12. *Platform and Pulpit,* p. 96.

13. "Arts and Crafts," reprinted from *The World* (3 October 1888), in Jack Kalmar, "Shaw on Art," *MD* 2(September, 1959): 155–56.

14. *Platform and Pulpit,* p. 30.

15. See, for example, Charles I. Glicksberg, "Shaw the Novelist," *PrS* 25(Spring, 1951): 9; Judith B. Spink, "The Image of the Artist in the Plays of Bernard Shaw," *Shaw R* 6(September, 1963): 83.

16. Archibald Henderson, *GBS: Man of the Century,* p. 121, notes that Morris avidly followed *An Unsocial Socialist* in *To-Day,* the socialist magazine in which the novel appeared in installments in 1884.

17. For example, Apollodorus does not look or dress like Morris. For a discussion of Apollodorus as character type and for other sources of the portrait, see pp. 112–14.

18. In the preface, p. xx, Shaw says, "When I see that the nineteenth century has crowned the idolatry of Art with the deification of Love, so that every poet is supposed to have pierced to the holy of holies when he has announced that Love is the Supreme, or the Enough, or the All, I feel that Art was safer in the hands of the most fanatical of Cromwell's major generals than it will be if ever it gets into mine."

19. Holman Hunt, at any rate, in *Pre-Raphaelitism and the Pre-Raphaelite Brotherhood,* 1:90–91, says that reading *Modern Painters* led to his and Millais's formulation of the theory that resulted in the P.R.B.

20. *The Works of John Ruskin,* 10:188–95.

21. *The Collected Works of William Morris,* 22:302–9.

22. "The Nature of Gothic," *The Works of John Ruskin,* 10:192–95.

23. "The Lesser Arts," *Collected Works of William Morris,* pp. 22–27.

24. *Selected Non-Dramatic Writings of Bernard Shaw,* pp. 378–90.

Chapter II

1. *Pre-Raphaelitism and the Pre-Raphaelite Brotherhood,* 1:130–31.

2. "In the Picture-Galleries: The Holman Hunt Exhibition," reprinted in "Shaw on Art," pp. 150–52, and "Art Corner," *Our Corner* 7 (1 May 1886): 310–11.

3. "Art Corner," *Our Corner* 7(1 February 1886):124.

4. "In the Picture-Galleries," and "The New Gallery—The Kakemonos in Bond Street," in "Shaw on Art," pp. 152–53; "J. M. Strudwick," *Art Journal* 53(April, 1891):77–101; "Art Corner," *Our Corner*, 1 May 1886, p. 310.

5. *William Morris As I Knew Him*, p. 32.

6. John Seward, pseud. [F. G. Stephens], "The Purpose and Tendency of Early Italian Art," *The Germ*, no. 2 (February, 1850), p. 58. *The Germ* was reprinted by AMS Press, Inc. (New York, 1965); all my references to items in *The Germ* are to this edition.

7. Note to "Pre-Raphaelitism," *The Works of John Ruskin*, 12:357.

8. *Pre-Raphaelitism and the Pre-Raphaelite Brotherhood*, 1:149; 2:96.

9. *The Germ*, no. 4 (May, 1850), p. 170.

10. Rossetti's letter of 1857, quoted in *Autobiographical Notes of the Life of William Bell Scott*, 2: 39, and Morris's rev. of *Poems*, by Dante Gabriel Rossetti, *Academy*, 14 May 1870, p. 199.

11. Ruskin, "Pre-Raphaelitism," *Works of John Ruskin*, p. 359.

12. Shaw attributes to Morris exactly this criticism of Swinburne in *William Morris As I Knew Him*, p. 40: "Of Swinburne . . . [Morris] said that [Swinburne] got everything from books and nothing from nature."

13. *The Germ*, no. 2 (February, 1850), p. 59.

14. In *Shaw on Theatre*, p. 38.

15. In *Ruskin: Rossetti: Preraphaelitism*, p. 21. Brown elsewhere objected to Hunt's "microscopic detail" (*Pre-Raphaelitism and the Pre-Raphaelite Brotherhood*, 1:127).

16. In *Autobiographical Notes of the Life of William Bell Scott*, 1:251.

17. *Blackwood's Edinburgh Magazine* 79(February, 1856):218.

18. "Manchester Exhibition of Art-Treasures: The English School and Its Tendencies," *Blackwood's Edinburgh Magazine* 82(August, 1857):156–76.

19. "The New English Art Club—Monet at the Goupil Gallery," in Kalmar, "Shaw on Art," p. 157. In *The Sanity of Art* (*Essays*, p. 292) Shaw says that Whistler and other impressionists had to exhibit "propagandist samples of workmanship rather than complete works of art" in order to educate the public to look for the artistic qualities rather than subject matter in painting. Whistler, of course, would have disagreed with Shaw's suggestion that his sketches were incomplete and that they were in any sense "propagandist."

20. *The Germ*, nos. 1 and 2, pp. 11, 18, 62–63.

21. *Pre-Raphaelitism and the Pre-Raphaelite Brotherhood*, 1:349; 2:428, 479, 487; see also Hunt, "The Ideals of Art," *New Review* 4(May, 1891): 431.

22. *The Germ*, no. 1, pp. 23–33.

23. Hueffer, *Memories and Impressions*, p. 169. Graham Hough (*The Last Romantics*, p. 40) notes that the P. R. B. was made up of two almost opposite strains, "one a patient naturalism, the other . . . a flight from actuality into archaic romance."

24. Hunt, *Pre-Raphaelitism and the Pre-Raphaelite Brotherhood*, 1:135; also ibid., 1:140, 147, et passim. See also W. M. Rossetti (ed.), *Dante Gabriel Rossetti: His Family Letters*, 1:127, 132; and *Praeraphaelite Diaries and Letters*, pp. 300–302.

25. Preface, *Plays Pleasant*, p. vi. Religion to Shaw does not signify orthodoxy or sectarianism. Shaw's creative evolution encompasses all sincerely held beliefs, including the Christian socialism of Morell, the revolutionary doctrine of John Tanner, the Catholicism of Saint Joan, even the capitalism of Andrew

NOTES

Undershaft. Shaw wrote to his friend, Dame Laurentia McLachlan, the Abbess of Stanbrook, that the Jain religion, because of its great number of fantastic images, comes closest to representing the multifaceted unity of God ("The Nun and the Dramatist, George Bernard Shaw to the Abbess of Stanbrook," *Atlantic Monthly,* 198[August, 1956]: 76).

26. For an extensive debate about Pre-Raphaelite influence on Shaw, see the exchange of letters between Richard Nickson and me in *PMLA* 84(May, 1969): 597–607.

Chapter III

1. *Quintessence, Essays,* p. 139.
2. *Bernard Shaw: Collected Letters, 1874–1897,* 623.
3. Ibid., p. 641. See also Shaw's letter to R. Golding Bright, p. 632: " 'Candida' is the poetry of the Wife & Mother—the Virgin Mother in the true sense."
4. "The Nun and the Dramatist: George Bernard Shaw to the Abbess of Stanbrook," *Atlantic Monthly* 198(July, August, 1956):76.
5. Quoted in *Iconoclasts,* pp. 254–55. For a resume of critical opinions of Candida, see A. H. Nethercot, *Men and Supermen,* pp. 8–9; and Walter N. King, "The Rhetoric of *Candida*," *MD* 2(September, 1959): 71–73.
6. *Wagnerite, Essays,* pp. 213–16. Shaw's description of the conflict in *Candida* duplicated his account of the theme of the Ring, pp. 221–22: "The only faith which any reasonable disciple can gain from The Ring is not in love, but in life itself as a tireless power which is continually driving onward and upward . . . growing from within, by its own inexplicable energy, into ever higher and higher forms of organization, the strengths and the needs of which are continually superseding the institutions which were made to fit our former requirements."
7. "Give me my rug. . . . Now hang my cloak across my arm. . . . Now open the door for me" (pp. 93–94). "Well, dear me, just look at you, going out into the street in that state! . . . Look at his collar! look at his tie! look at his hair! One would think somebody had been throttling you. . . . Here! Stand still. [*She buttons his collar; ties his neckerchief in a bow; and arranges his hair.*] There! Now you look so nice that I think youd better stay to lunch after all, though I told you you musnt" (p. 100).
8. George A. Riding, "The *Candida* Secret," *Spectator* 185(17 November 1950): 506 (also in *A Casebook on "Candida,"* ed. Stephen S. Stanton, p. 169).
9. Letter to Huneker, *Iconoclasts,* p. 255 (also in *Casebook,* p. 165). See also Shaw's letter to *The Kansas City Star,* 6 January 1900, reprinted in *Casebook,* p. 170, in which he says that "the poet begins pursuing happiness with a beloved woman as the object of his life"; but he sees "that such happiness could never fulfill his destiny" and goes "out of this stuffy little nest of happiness and sentiment into the grandeur, the majesty, the holiness" of the night.
10. In view of Shaw's later statement that Jesus was "an artist and a Bohemian in his manner of life" (Preface *Androcles,* p. 23), it is no surprise to find the Christ-figure in *Candida* an artist. Shaw believed that Jesus's divinity was potentially available to every man, especially to the man of genius, who is a genius by right of his recognition of the godhead within him. See esp. "Why Jesus More than Another?" and "The Peculiar Theology of Jesus," preface, *Androcles,* pp. 5–6, 41–42.
11. *The Works of Thomas Carlyle,* ed. H. D. Traill, Centenary Edition, Vol.

163

5 (London, 1897), p. 80. For Shaw's debt to Carlyle, see Kaye, *Bernard Shaw and the Nineteenth Century Tradition*, pp. 9–16.

12. Riding, "The *Candida* Secret," p. 506.

13. *Bernard Shaw: Collected Letters*, p. 506. Shaw is writing to Janet Achurch, for whom he wrote *Candida;* he says that the actress needs to become "religious, so that she may recreate herself and feel no need of stimulants." The parallels to "On Going to Church" are obvious.

Chapter IV

1. "Toward a Theory of Romanticism," *PMLA* 66(March, 1951): 5–23. For the Pre-Raphaelite movement as part of the romantic movement, see Louise Rosenblatt, *L'Idée de l'art pour l'art dans la littérature anglaise pendant la période victorienne*, p. 87. Ruth Z. Temple ("The Ivory Tower as Lighthouse," *Edwardians and Late Victorians*, p. 30), notes that the romantic movement led to "realism, naturalism, impressionism, symbolism." See also Rose Frances Egan, "The Genesis of the Theory of 'Art for Art's Sake' in Germany and in England," *Smith College Studies in Modern Languages*, 2(July, 1921) and 5 (April, 1924).

2. "Prosper Mérimée" (1890), *The Works of Walter Pater*, New Library Edition, 8: 12–13. All my references to the works of Pater are to this edition.

3. Hicks, *Figures of Transition*, p. 253.

4. Tennyson's epilogue to the Queen in the Library Edition (1873) of his poems equates French-influenced art with other evils of the age, i.e., loss of faith, soft and cowardly lives, money-lust, etc. Of art for art's sake Tennyson elsewhere wrote "Art for Art's sake! Hail, truest lord of Hell! / Hail Genius, Master of the Moral Will! / The filthiest of all paintings painted well / Is mightier than the purest painted ill!"

5. Nouvelle Edition (Paris, 1875), pp. 18–19, 21. For an account of "The Beginnings of L'art pour l'art," see John Wilcox, *JAAC* 11(June, 1953): 360–77.

6. *Oeuvres Complètes de Charles Baudelaire*, ed. Jacques Crépet, 15 vols. (Paris, 1923–53), 3: xix–xxi. Baudelaire is paraphrasing Edgar Allen Poe's "The Poetic Principle" (1850). Poe's theory of art came to the English aesthetic movement in French, through Baudelaire.

7. "Charles Baudelaire," in *The Complete Works of Algernon Charles Swinburne*, ed. Sir Edmund Gosse and Thomas James Wise, 13:417. All my references to the works of Swinburne are to this edition.

8. Whistler, *The Gentle Art of Making Enemies*, pp. 136, 116, 126–28.

9. Ibid., pp. 131–57. Cf. Swinburne, "The Poems of Dante Gabriel Rossetti," *Complete Works*, 15:43: "There is no progress and no degeneracy traceable from Aeschylus to Shakespeare, from Athenian sculptors to Venetian painters; . . . the gifts of genius are diverse, but the quality is one."

10. *The Romantic '90s*, p. 74.

11. Arnold, *Culture and Anarchy*, pp. 55, 64.

12. Pater, *Works*, 5:38, 182–84. See Rosenblatt, *L'Idée de l'art pour l'art*, pp. 201–2, for other reasons to distrust this paragraph in "Style." Ruth C. Child, *The Aesthetic of Walter Pater* (New York, 1940), p. 70, speculates that Pater in this paragraph may have abandoned "his usual attitude" in reaction to Flaubert's extreme position on form over matter.

13. Quilter ("The Gospel of Intensity," *Contemporary Review* 67 [June,

1895]: 763) calls Wilde "the living embodiment of the theory of l'art pour l'art." Chesterton (*The Victorian Age in Literature*, p. 218) considers Wilde the "captain" of the aesthetes and decadents; Rosenblatt (*L'Idée de l'art pour l'art*, p. 245) says that Wilde was the most aggressive defender of *l'art pour l'art*; Hicks (*Figures of Transition*, pp. 218–31) deals with Wilde as "The Self-Made Symbol"; William Gaunt (*The Aesthetic Adventure*, p. 125) says that Wilde was aestheticism's "vehicle or advertisement." Wilde said of himself: "I was a man who stood in symbolic relations to the art and culture of my age. . . . I awoke the imagination of my century so that it created myth and legend around me: I summed up all the systems in a phrase, and all existence in an epigram" (*The Letters of Oscar Wilde*, ed. Rupert Hart-Davis [New York, 1963], p. 466).

14. *The Green Carnation*, p. 126.

15. *The Gentle Art*, p. 164.

16. See especially "The Decay of Lying" (1889) and "The Critic as Artist" (1890) in *The Works of Oscar Wilde*, and the preface of *The Picture of Dorian Gray* (1891).

17. Hubert Crackanthorpe, "Reticence in Literature: Some Roundabout Remarks," *The Yellow Book* 2 (July, 1894): 265.

18. Hough, *The Last Romantics*, p. 18.

19. Arthur Symons, "Walter Pater: Some Characteristics," *The Savoy* 8 (December, 1896): 40.

20. Crackanthorpe, "Reticence in Literature," *The Yellow Book* 2(July, 1894): 264–65.

Chapter V

1. Preface, *Blanco Posnet*, pp. 374–75. See also "The Law of Change is the Law of God," preface, *Joan*, pp. 37–38. Shaw was convinced that "great writers are always evil influences" (Winsten, *Days with Bernard Shaw*, p. 173).

2. In *Portraits*, p. 219, and *OTN*, 1:9–11. See also "Oscar Wilde: A Letter to Frank Harris, published by him in his Life of Wilde, 1918," *Portraits*, p. 291. In his conversations with Stephen Winsten recorded in *Shaw's Corner*, pp. 98, 190, Shaw maintains that *The Soul of Man Under Socialism* "anticipated all that I had to say" and says that, in his efforts to free the Chicago anarchists of 1886, Wilde revealed a "great spirit."

3. Nordau, *Degeneration*, p. 27.

4. Ibid., pp. 209, 343.

5. Shaw, *Selected Non-Dramatic Writings*, p. 379.

6. Just as Gautier had praised the beauty of Baudelaire's flowers of evil grown in the soil of decaying civilizations, so Symons, "The Decadent Movement in Literature," *Dramatis Personae*, p. 97, praised the work of the decadents, saying of it, "Healthy we can not call it, and healthy it does not wish to be considered." Critics generally look on Shaw as the epitome of artistic sanity and "normality." Shaw said to Winsten (*Days with Bernard Shaw*, p. 103) that most creative men are defective, but "I am possibly the only sane exception." Maurice Colbourne (*The Real Bernard Shaw*, pp. 66–71) says that the word best describing Shaw is "healthy," that "his essential healthy-mindedness and peculiar buoyancy never allowed him to sink into [the fin-de-siècle writers'] bogs of glorified decay," that "the very mention of his name seems to clear the poisoned air a little," and that *The Sanity of Art* "formally buried the corpse" of art for

art's sake. Though Colbourne somewhat overstates the case, he correctly separates Shaw from the decadents.

7. "The Critic as Artist," in *The Works of Oscar Wilde*, 10:144.

8. Preface to the second edition, in *Studies in Prose and Verse*, p. 284.

9. Quoted in Roland A. Duerksen, "Shelley and Shaw," *PMLA* 78(March, 1963): 117.

10. Ibid. (quoted from Shaw).

11. *Days with Bernard Shaw*, p. 195.

12. *Widowers' Houses*, preface, pp. xvii, xix; appendix 1, p. 112.

13. *Bernard Shaw's Letters to Granville Barker*, p. 77.

14. Shaw, "The Religion of the Pianoforte," *How to Become a Musical Critic*, p. 225.

15. "The Aesthetic Man," *Everybody's Political What's What*, pp. 180–82. In this essay Shaw again insists that "the education that sticks after school is aesthetic education," that "the statesman should . . . rank fine art with, if not above, religion, science, education, and fighting power as a political agency," and that art "has become an instrument of culture, a method of schooling, a form of science, an indispensable adjunct of religion" (pp. 178–200).

Chapter VI

1. *A History of Modern Criticism*, 4:371; see also p. 411.

2. *Partial Portraits*, pp. 404–6.

3. "Reticence in Literature," *The Yellow Book* 1(April, 1894): 205–18. Philip Gilbert Hamerton, "The Yellow Book: A Criticism of Volume I," *The Yellow Book* 2(July, 1894): 181–83, agrees with Waugh. Hamerton isolates Symons's "Stella Maris" as particularly objectionable not only for its "offensive" title but also for its subject: "We know that the younger poets make art independent of morals, and certainly the two have no necessary connection; but why should poetic art be employed to celebrate common fornication?" His admission that art and morality "have no necessary connection" apparently lacks conviction, since he objects not only to "Stella Maris" but to some "grossly sensual stanzas" in Swinburne's "Dolores." The moralists' attitude toward aestheticism changed very little in thirty years; in "Notes on Poems and Reviews" (1866) Swinburne had had to defend "Dolores" from similar hostile criticism.

4. Quilter, "The Gospel of Intensity," *Contemporary Review* 67(June, 1895): 776–81.

5. Hugh E. M. Stutfield, "Tommyrotics," *Blackwood's Edinburgh Magazine* 157(June, 1895): 843–44.

6. *Literature at Nurse* was not available to me; my outline is based on the discussion in Malcolm Brown, *George Moore: A Reconsideration* (Seattle, 1955), pp. 96–98.

7. See especially "The Late Censor," *OTN* 1:50–52; "The Censorship of the Stage in England," *Shaw on Theatre*, p. 74; preface, *Mrs. Warren*, pp. 155–56; preface, *Blanco Posnet*, p. 405; "Censorship as a Police Duty," *Platform and Pulpit*, pp. 198–99; Warren S. Smith, "The Bishop, the Dancer, and Bernard Shaw," *Shaw R* 3(January, 1960): 9; preface, *Three Plays*, p. xx. Fromm, *Bernard Shaw and the Theatre*, pp. 155–66, also discusses "The Censorship" and Shaw.

8. Shaw, "Censorship as a Police Duty," *Platform and Pulpit*, pp. 190–98.

9. Quoted from Shaw in Smith, "The Bishop, the Dancer, and Bernard Shaw," p. 9. There is an echo here of Whistler's "Ten O'Clock" lecture, in which Whistler says that art never exists for the majority, who have only vulgarity in common.

10. Morris, "Art and the People," *William Morris*, p. 391.

11. *Confessions of a Young Man*, in *The Collected Works of George Moore*, 9:456–57.

12. *The Savoy*, no. 6(October, 1896), p. 57.

13. For an extensive discussion of this characteristic of Shaw's art in the early plays, see Charles A. Carpenter, *Bernard Shaw & the Art of Destroying Ideals*.

14. *Days with Bernard Shaw*, p. 219.

15. Preface, *Dark Lady*, pp. 228–30. Shaw dramatizes this idea in *Dark Lady*, p. 242, when Shakespear pleads for a national theater so that playwrights can escape the tyranny of the public, which prefers his "damnable foolishnesses" to his "noble and excellent" plays.

16. *The Eighteen Nineties*, pp. 130–32.

17. Shaw, "The Nun and the Dramatist," *Atlantic Monthly* 198(1956): 74.

Chapter VII

1. Letter to *New York Times*, 2 June 1912, reprinted in *Shaw on Theatre*, p. 116.

2. "The Nun and the Dramatist," *Atlantic Monthly* 198(1956): 70.

3. *Table-Talk of G. B. S.* (New York, 1925), p. 64. Shaw returns to the idea of divine inspiration in preface, *Buoyant Billions*, pp. 3–4, and in preface, *Farfetched Fables*, p. 66. But see Winsten, *Days with Bernard Shaw*, p. 224: "Like Trollope I worked daily at my writing without waiting for inspiration."

4. *Shaw's Corner*, pp. 153–55. See above, pp. 4–5, for Shaw's theory of the effortless nature of artistic creation.

5. *Bernard Shaw and Mrs. Patrick Campbell*, p. 89.

6. *Dante Gabriel Rosetti: His Family Letters*, 1:416–17. Cf. Rossetti's advice, p. 417, to Hall Caine: "Conception, my boy, fundamental brain-work—that is what makes the difference in all art. Work your metal as much as you like but first take care that it is gold and worth working."

7. Reprinted from *New Statesman and Nation* 39(6 May 1950), in *Shaw on Theatre*, p. 289.

8. *Bernard Shaw: Collected Letters*, p. 596. Cf. Whistler, *The Gentle Art*, p. 115: "A picture is finished when all trace of the means used to bring about an end has disappeared." See also Pater, *Marius*, in *Works*, 2:97–98.

9. Quoted from the *Daily Telegraph* in Renée M. Deacon, *Bernard Shaw as Artist-Philosopher*, p. 66.

10. Henry James, "The Art of Fiction," *Partial Portraits*, p. 391.

11. Preface, *Major Barbara*, p. 230. As an example Shaw says that he contrives to let Bill Walker know that Bodger and Undershaft can pay conscience-money when Bill cannot.

12. "Literature and Art," *Platform and Pulpit*, p. 43. See also "The Play of Ideas," in *Shaw on Theatre*, p. 290.

13. Although the idea of music as an expression of perfection is at least as old as the Pythagoreans, the idea probably entered the aesthetic movement

from the French aesthetes. Gautier's poem "Symphonie en Blanc Majeur" is no doubt, as Wilde notes ("The Critic as Artist," pp. 216–17), an influence on Whistler's use of the musical analogy in naming his paintings "Nocturnes" and "Symphonies." Baudelaire's "Notes nouvelles sur Edgar Poe" equates poetry and music; and Verlaine's "Art Poétique" says that verse should soar like music, else it is "mere literature." Pater uses the analogy in "The School of Giorgione," and Wilde echoes it in "The Decay of Lying," "The Critic as Artist," and the preface to *The Picture of Dorian Gray*. Symons (*The Symbolist Movement in Literature*, pp. 87–88, 125) speaks of Verlaine's influence and also refers to "Wagner's ideal, that 'the most complete work of the poet should be that which, in its final achievement, becomes a perfect music.' "

14. "The Religion of the Pianoforte," *How to Become a Musical Critic*, p. 221, and "Literature and Art," *Platform and Pulpit*, p. 45.

15. Winsten, *Days with Bernard Shaw*, p. 27, and *Shaw on Theatre*, p. 186.

16. Holbrook Jackson, *Bernard Shaw*, p. 186; and Joseph McCabe, *George Bernard Shaw*, p. 165.

17. "What Is the Finest Dramatic Situation?" in *Shaw on Theatre*, p. 110.

18. Winsten, *Shaw's Corner*, p. 218. See also "My Way with a Play," *Shaw on Theatre*, p. 269: "I needed no murder: I could get drama enough out of the economics of slum poverty."

19. "Love's Labour's Lost," *Appreciations*, in *Works*, 5:166.

20. Pater, *Works*, 2:56. Pater is describing Apuleius's *Metamorphoses* in this passage, but he describes Euphuism similarly.

21. *Bernard Shaw: Collected Letters*, p. 461.

22. "A Letter to the Editor," *The Yellow Book* 2(July, 1894): 284.

23. P. 400. See also Pater, *Marius*, in *Works*, 1:103: Flavian's "uncompromising demand for a matter, in all art, derived immediately from lively personal intuition" and saved his art "from lapsing into mere artifice." Symons ("What Is Poetry?" *Studies in Prose and Verse*, p. 194) says, "In art, there must be a complete marriage or interpenetration of substance and form."

24. For an analysis of Shaw's style, see Dixon Scott, "The Innocence of Bernard Shaw," reprinted in Kronenberger's *George Bernard Shaw: A Critical Survey*, pp. 72–104; Richard M. Ohmann, *Shaw: The Style and the Man*.

25. *The Autobiography of William Butler Yeats*, pp. 167, 317.

26. *Bernard Shaw: The Man and the Mask*, p. 249.

Chapter VIII

1. "A Dramatic Realist to His Critics," *Shaw on Theatre*, p. 19.

2. *The Gentle Art*, pp. 178–79.

3. Letter "To the Editor of the Pall Mall Budget, April 27, 1894," in *Under the Hill and Other Essays in Prose and Verse*, by Beardsley, 3d ed. (London, 1921), p. 69.

4. "A Dramatic Realist," *Shaw on Theatre*, p. 34.

5. Wilde, *Works*, 10:24.

6. *Shaw on Theatre*, p. 185. John Gassner, "Shaw as a Drama Critic," *Theatre Arts* 36(May, 1951): 28, notes that Shaw's realism is "penetration rather than photography"; Eric Bentley, "The Making of a Dramatist (1892–1903)," *TDR* 5(September, 1960): 11, says that Shaw's realism is a result of showing natural responses in unnatural situations.

NOTES

7. "A Dramatic Realist," *Shaw on Theatre*, p. 35.

8. Letter to Alan S. Downer (21 January 1948), in *The Theatre of Bernard Shaw*, ed. Downer (New York, 1961), p. 16.

9. Shaw, "Mr. Bernard Shaw's Works of Fiction," *Selected Non-Dramatic Writings of Bernard Shaw*, p. 311.

10. *Bernard Shaw and Mrs. Patrick Campbell*, p. 333.

11. "The Decay of Lying," Wilde, *Works*, 10:35, 38, 47.

12. "A Dramatic Realist," *Shaw on Theatre*, pp. 19–20.

13. Preface, *Three Plays*, p. xx; "A Dramatic Realist," *Shaw on Theatre*, p. 20.

14. Winsten, *Days with Bernard Shaw*, p. 187.

15. "Acting, By One Who Does Not Believe In It," *Platform and Pulpit*, p. 16.

Chapter IX

1. Moore, *Collected Works*, 9:419.

2. P. 381, et passim. Richard Le Gallienne ("What's Wrong with the Eighteen-Nineties?" *Bookman* 54[September, 1921]: 3) says that the men of the 1890s "sowed the seed of every kind of freedom of which we are now reaping the whirlwind."

3. Hueffer, *Memories and Impressions*, p. 166.

4. Martin Secker (ed.), *The Eighteen-Nineties: A Period Anthology in Prose and Verse*, pp. 22, 25. This concept of "detachment" is no doubt indebted to Matthew Arnold's "The Function of Criticism at the Present Time" (1865).

5. Swinburne, *Complete Works*, 16:133–36; Whistler, *The Gentle Art*, p. 171; Wilde, *Works*, 10:100.

6. P. 46. Although Dowson here asserts the possibility of personal dissoluteness and artistic purity, the novel demonstrates otherwise, perhaps unintentionally. The exact nature of Oswyn's disreputable behavior is never clear, unless addiction to cigarettes and absinthe and a tendency to deliver lectures on art and tirades against the insipidity of bourgeois taste can be considered "disgraceful, indescribable." Furthermore, Oswyn befriends the hero and heroine. In contrast, Dick Lightmark, the impressionist painter in the novel, like many other villains in Victorian literature, is a betrayer of women and a second-rate artist, who courts success and finally stoops to stealing Oswyn's idea for a painting. Oscar Wilde depicts an artist of a somewhat virtuous bent in Basil Hallward, the ill-fated painter of the portrait of Dorian Gray; Hallward begs Lord Henry Wotton not to sully Dorian's innocence. What these two contradictions between aesthetic theory and artistic practice imply is that there is a great deal of truth in Richard Le Gallienne's thesis that the decadents loved "to pose as mysteriously wicked," but that the 1890s is really a period of innocence (*The Romantic '90s*, p. 165).

7. Pater, *Works*, 2:52–53. A frequent motif in Pater's work is that of the combination of youthful exuberance and beauty with diabolical mischief and evil, as in "Denys L'Auxerrois," *Imaginary Portraits, Works*, 4:45–78, and "Apollo in Picardy," *Miscellaneous Studies, Works*, 8:143–71.

8. W. H. Mallock, *New Republic*, p. 165.

9. *Spiritual Adventures, The Collected Works of Arthur Symons* (London, 1925), 5:18.

10. J. K. Huysmans, *Against the Grain*, Modern Library Paperbacks (New York, n.d.), p. 91.

11. Symons, "Preface to the Second Edition of Silhouettes, Being a Word in Behalf of Patchouli," *Studies in Prose and Verse*, p. 281.

12. [Hichens], p. 3.

13. "An Artist in Attitudes: Oscar Wilde" (1901), *Studies in Prose and Verse*, p. 124.

14. "The Critic as Artist," p. 233, and "The Decay of Lying," p. 63, in *The Works of Oscar Wilde*.

15. Yeats, *Autobiography*, pp. 285, 93.

Chapter X

1. *Shaw R* 6(September, 1963): 82, 87–88.

2. "The Fabian Figaro," *George Bernard Shaw*, ed. Kronenberger, p. 156; Stewart, *Eight Modern Writers*, p. 135.

3. Claude T. Bissell, "The Novels of Bernard Shaw," *UTQ* 17(October, 1947): 39; Glicksberg, "Shaw the Novelist," *Pr S* 25(Spring, 1951): 2; Stanley Weintraub, "Introduction," *An Unfinished Novel by Bernard Shaw* (London, 1958) p. 5; R. F. Dietrich, *Portrait of the Artist as a Young Superman*, p. 71. Dietrich's thorough analysis of Shaw's novels supports at numerous points my analysis of the artist figures, which was published in slightly different form in *ELT* 10 (1967): 130–49.

4. In 1879 Lawson exhibited seven works at the Grosvenor, including " 'Twixt Sun and Moon," "A Morning Mist," "The Haunted Mill," and "Kent" ("The Hop Gardens of England" repainted); in this year he exhibited at the Royal Academy "Sundown," "Old Battersea, Moonlight," and "A Wet Moon." Also of possible relevance to Shaw's novel is the fact that Lawson married in 1879. In addition to Shaw's sketch of Lawson in *Immaturity*, pp. xli–xliii, see the *DNB* entry; "Obituary. Cecil Lawson," *Academy*, 17 June 1882, pp. 439–40; and William Ernest Henley, "Some Landscape Painters," *Views and Reviews: Essays in Appreciation* (London, 1908), 2: 145–46.

5. *Immaturity*, p. 106. See especially Hueffer, "Anarchists and Grey Frieze," *Memories and Impressions*, pp. 133–60. Curiously, his description of Shaw's dress is almost identical to Shaw's description of Scott's; Hueffer says, p. 143: "I think Mr Shaw does not 'dress' at all nowadays, and in the dress affected, at all events by his disciples, the gray homespuns, the soft hats, the comfortable bagginess about the knees, and the air that the pockets have of always being full of apples, the last faint trickle of Pre-Raphaelite influence is to be perceived."

6. *Immaturity*, p. 149. See also p. 285: "Being a master in my trade means being an apprentice for life."

7. Shaw excoriates Renaissance dramatists other than Shakespeare in *OTN*, 1:130–31; 2:181–84; and 3:317–18. Hawkshaw's reading of *Hamlet* is a topical allusion to Sir Henry Irving's 1879 production of *Hamlet* at the Lyceum; see *Punch's* account (11 January 1879, pp. 9–10). For Shaw's comments on the mutilations of Shakespeare at the Lyceum, see especially "Blaming the Bard," *OTN*, 2:195–202; and "Hamlet Revisited," *OTN*, 3:270–74. Shaw considered Mendelssohn's music beautiful, but "subjectless," and therefore dull (*London Music*, p. 248).

8. *Immaturity*, p. 135. Harriet is not echoing the Philistine position only: Ruskin objected to art produced by effort and study; and Millais is reported to have said to W. B. Scott, apropos of an Italian engraving inscribed "From Nature," in which every leaf and every pattern on the girl's dress was rendered

exactly, "That's P. R. B. enough, is it not? . . . It's all nonsense; of course nature's nature, and art's art, isn't it? One could not live doing that!" (*Auto-biographical Notes of William Bell Scott*, 1:278).

9. A *Punch* cartoon (31 May 1879, p. 249) has a "Philistine Father" saying to his artist son, "Why the dickens don't you paint something like Frith's 'Derby Day'—something Everybody can understand, and Somebody buy?" W. P. Frith, a member of the Royal Academy, was a popular painter best known for "The Derby Day" (1858); he was a witness against Whistler at the Whistler-Ruskin trial.

10. *Immaturity*, p. 388. This statement echoes Rossetti's "Hand and Soul" (pp. 26, 31) in which the painter fails when he uses "cold symbolism and ab-tract impersonation" because he "wouldst say coldly to the mind what God hath said to the heart warmly."

11. Quoted from Shaw's letter to the Rugby boys on the *Candida* secret, in George Riding, "The *Candida* Secret," *Spectator* 185(17 November 1950): 506; and Shaw's letter to Huneker, *Iconoclasts*, p. 255. William Irvine (*The Universe of Bernard Shaw*, p. 29, notes the *Candida* theme in this novel, as does Dietrich (*Portrait of the Artist*, p. 123).

12. "In the Picture-Galleries," *MD* 2(September, 1959): 151; "Art Corner," *Our Corner*, February, 1886, p. 123.

13. In *Dante Gabriel Rossetti: His Family Letters*, 2:374.

14. *Unsocial Socialist*, p. 220. Agatha's description of the book she is reading, except the number of volumes, describes *An Unsocial Socialist*: the denouement is near; two people are in love, and Agatha does not know whether they will marry for "this is one of your clever novels. I wish the characters would not talk so much" (p. 221). In this scene Trefusis proposes marriage to Agatha and is accepted.

15. Appendix to *Widower's Houses*, p. 112.

Chapter XI

1. For Marchbanks as Shelley, see especially Duerksen, "Shelley and Shaw," *PMLA* 78(March, 1963): 121; also Huneker, *Iconoclasts*, p. 246; Kaye, *Bernard Shaw*, p. 129; Spink, "The Image of the Artist," *Shaw R* 6(September, 1963): 85; Audrey Williamson, *Bernard Shaw*, p. 117. Henderson (*George Bernard Shaw*, p. 443) quotes a review of an early performance of *Candida* (from *Manchester Guardian*, 15 March 1895) which states that Marchbanks was "got up to look like Shelley." Spink (p. 86) says that Marchbanks is like Douglas, and King ("The Rhetoric of Candida," *MD* 2[September, 1959]: 75) suggests Morris. Burton (*Bernard Shaw*, p. 231) and Bentley ("The Making of a Dramatist," *TDR* 5[September, 1960]: 15) see Shaw as the model.

2. Letter to Beverley Baxter, *Evening Standard* (London), 30 November 1944; reprinted in *A Casebook on "Candida,"* ed. Stephen S. Stanton, p. 159.

3. Augustin Hamon, *The Twentieth Century Molière*, p. 192.

4. Thomas De Quincey, *Confessions of an English Opium-Eater and Other Essays*, ed. A. W. Pollard (London, 1924), p. 23.

5. Ibid., pp. 63, 81.

6. Shaw had earlier in *Love among the Artists* dramatized the idea that the artist must avoid domestic entanglements. In this novel, Edward Conolly (the hero of *The Irrational Knot*) reappears to give Mary Sutherland advice about marriage to a genius; he tells her that "heroes are ill adapted to domestic pur-

poses" and that "a man who is complete in himself needs no wife"; he speaks with authority because he is a genius whose marriage was a failure. In *The Irrational Knot* Shaw anticipates another *Candida* motif when Conolly explains to his wife that he does not object to the poet's love for her. Marian asks, "And do you like men to be in love with me?" He answers, "Yes. It makes the house pleasant for them, it makes them attentive to you, and it gives you a great power for good. When I was a romantic boy, any good woman could have made a saint of me. Let them fall in love with you as much as they please. Afterwards they will seek wives according to a higher standard than if they had never known you. But do not return the compliment, or your influence will become an evil one" (p. 234).

7. Marchbanks has some affinities with the Pre-Raphaelites: in the opening scene of act 3, he has been reading to Candida about an angel; my guess is that Shaw's allusion is to Coventry Patmore's *The Angel in the House*, with its idealization of domestic life. Patmore was a friend of the Pre-Raphaelites and a contributor to *The Germ* and the Pre-Raphaelites read and admired his poetry. Marchbanks uses a medieval literary motif, the "sword between us" (p. 124), in describing his resolve to remain sexually uninvolved with Candida. Neither Candida nor Morell understands what he is talking about.

8. McCabe, *George Bernard Shaw*, p. 181; and Spink, "The Image of the Artist," p. 85. For other unfavorable estimates of Marchbanks's character, see Irvine, *Universe of Bernard Shaw*, p. 174; Auden, "The Fabian Figaro," in *George Bernard Shaw*, ed. Kronenberger, p. 156; Kronenberger, *George Bernard Shaw*, p. xvii; Bentley, "The Making of a Dramatist," *TDR* 5(September, 1960): 15; Stewart, *Eight Modern Writers*, p. 135.

9. North's translation, in *Julius Caesar in Shakespeare, Shaw and the Ancients*, ed. G. H. Harrison (New York, 1960), p. 91. In using this anecdote from Plutarch's *Life*, Shaw modified it by removing the erotic motive, adding comic touches such as the boat's sinking and the bundle's being hoisted up by a crane, and substituting for the "flockbed" a rare and beautiful carpet from the shop of Apollodorus. See George W. Whiting, "The Cleopatra Rug Scene: Another Source," *Shaw R* 3(January, 1960): 15; Whiting suggests that Shaw may have been influenced by Gérome's "Cléopatre apportée à César dans un tapis."

10. For portraits of Morris, see William Sharp, "William Morris: The Man and His Work," *Atlantic Monthly* 78(December, 1896): 772; R. B. Cunningham Graham, "With the North-West Wind," *Saturday Review*, 10 October 1896, pp. 389–90; Ford Madox Ford, "An Old Circle," *Harper's Monthly Magazine* 120(February, 1910): 372. Interestingly, Shaw dresses the childlike, fragile Marchbanks in the rough dress associated with the Pre-Raphaelites: Marchbanks "wears an old blue serge jacket, unbuttoned, over a woollen lawn tennis shirt, with a silk handkerchief for a cravat, trousers matching the jacket, and brown canvas shoes" (*Candida*, p. 91).

11. *Works*, 10:142–43.

12. Shaw uses *amateur* frequently in his novels as a synonym for the dabbler in art, the faddist, the nonartist; see *The Irrational Knot*, p. 10; *Love among the Artists*, pp. 61, 141, 175; *An Unsocial Socialist*, p. 201.

13. Wilde, "Pen, Pencil, and Poison," *Works*, 10:67.

14. *Man and Superman*, p. 151. The Statue uses these identical words in confessing the lies he told women; his defense to Juan is, "I really believed it with all my soul at the moment. I had a heart; not like you" (p. 122). An analysis of Octavius's character would not be complete without noting that Shaw says in the Epistle Dedicatory, "Octavius I take over unaltered from Mozart," and authorizes an actor of Tavy to sing "Dalla sua pace" if he can. Indeed, Shaw's Octavius owes much to Mozart's Don Ottavio, who is also somewhat

fatuous, platitudinous, and weak, and who believes that love cures grief. Don Ottavio, infatuated with Donna Anna, is controlled by her and seeks revenge on Don Giovanni because Anna tells him to; Anna, it may be noted, lies to Ottavio about the details concerning her father's death. Shaw takes the scene in which Ann rejects Tavy's marriage proposal because of her father's recent death almost verbatim from II.iv, of *Don Giovanni*, where Anna answers Ottavio's proposal with, "Oh, Dei! che dite, / In se tristi momente?"

15. Shaw's reference to Wilde's story is not a casual one: the story parallels Octavius's situation in *Man and Superman*. In the story the nightingale idealizes love and is willing to die for love. But the bird is deceived: he sacrifices his life to provide a rose for two true lovers; then the girl rejects the rose for another suitor's jewels, and the discouraged lover throws away the rose, declares love "silly," and resolves to study philosophy. The rose falls into a gutter and is run over by a cart wheel. Octavius's belief in true love is similarly unrealistic: he sacrifices his happiness in the service of love without ever learning the truth about the acquisitive woman and her cynical lover (who, like Wilde's student, renounces love for the sake of metaphysics).

16. Shaw, *William Morris As I Knew Him*, p. xxvii.

17. Henderson, *George Bernard Shaw*, p. 478.

Chapter XII

1. Burton, *Bernard Shaw*, pp. 131–32; Braybrooke, *The Genius of Bernard Shaw*, pp. 53–54; Fuller, *George Bernard Shaw*, p. 57; Stewart, *Eight Modern Writers*, p. 164; Spink, "The Image of the Artist," p. 87; Purdom, *A Guide to the Plays of Bernard Shaw*, p. 103.

2. Winsten, *Days with Bernard Shaw*, p. 83.

3. See especially "What Socialism Will Be Like," *Platform and Pulpit*, pp. 29–30, where Shaw maintains that artists must be pampered by the state. See also "Property and Marriage," in "The Revolutionist's Handbook," *M&S*, pp. 173–78; and preface, *Getting Married*.

4. See the preface of *Overruled*, p. 166: "No necessary and inevitable operation of Human Nature can reasonably be regarded as sinful at all, and . . . a morality which assumes the contrary is an absurd morality, and can be kept in countenance only by hypocrisy."

5. The death of Ftatateeta in *C&C* is an example of a justifiable killing, in Shaw's eyes; see also the preface of *Major Barbara*, p. 239; and the preface of *On the Rocks*, pp. 143–66.

6. *Doctor's Dilemma*, pp. 126–27. Shaw presents a similar dilemma in *Major Barbara* when he brings the good but poor man, Peter Shirley, into conflict with the unscrupulous rich man, Undershaft; in *Major Barbara* Shaw finds for the blackguard, who has world-changing power and no conscience.

7. Shaw characteristically gives no precise information about the kind of art produced by his artists but instead gives only other's reactions to the art. In *Love among the Artists* the quality of Jack's music, of Madame Szczympliça's playing, and of Madge Brailsford's acting is known primarily by the comments of other characters; likewise the name but not the nature of Elinor McQuinch's novel is given in *The Irrational Knot*, and in *Candida*, Candida, not the audience, has heard Marchbanks's poetry.

8. Henderson, *George Bernard Shaw*, p. xxix. Stanley Weintraub says that Beardsley provided Shaw with Dubedat's profession and his fatal illness (*Beardsley*, p. 91).

9. Oswald Doughty, *A Victorian Romantic: Dante Gabriel Rossetti* (London, 1960), pp. 157–58. Doughty says that Rossetti's treatment of MacCracken was typical of his dealings with his patrons.

10. Henderson, *George Bernard Shaw*, p. xxix.

11. Reprinted in *Independent Shavian* 3(Spring, 1965) : 34, from *Kaizo*, April, 1933.

12. Pearson, *G.B.S., A Full Length Portrait*, pp. 102, 203.

13. Ibid., p. 104; Henderson, *George Bernard Shaw*, p. 608. Shaw furthermore said that he knew others, specifically two clergymen and a retired colonel, who, like Dubedat, had no "aggressive vices" but were consciousless regarding money and sex (Pearson, *G.B.S., A Full Length Portrait*, p. 104). Winsten (*Days with Bernard Shaw*, p. 84) says that Shaw dismissed "rather petulantly" the question of why he portrayed Dubedat as an artist, when the original was a scientist. There are a number of feasible reasons for Shaw's irritation at Winsten's question, one of which is that the character of Dubedat was only suggested by Aveling and was never meant to be a faithful portrait, another is that Aveling is not the only source for the portrait.

14. In *Richard Wagner's Prose Works,* trans. William Ashton Ellis (London, 1898), 7:66–67.

15. Ibid., 7:74.

16. Ibid., 7:137–39.

17. Ellehauge, *The Position of Bernard Shaw in European Drama and Philosophy*, p. 293.

18. "An End in Paris," *Richard Wagner's Prose Works*, 7:50–51.

19. Preface, *Dark Lady*, p. 212. Shaw dramatizes this pride in *Dark Lady*, pp. 237–38, in Shakespear's outburst against the suggestion that he is "a base-born servant."

20. P. 241. The preface of *Dark Lady* (p. 219) also stresses Shakespeare's artistic pride: " 'Not marble, nor the gilded monuments / Of princes, shall out-live this powerful rhyme' is only one out of a dozen passages in which he (possibly with a keen sense of the fun of scandalizing the modern coughers) proclaimed his place and his power in 'the wide world dreaming of things to come.' "

Chapter XIII

1. Quoted in Winsten, *Days with Bernard Shaw*, p. 31.

2. *Love among the Artists*, p. 94. When accused of impatience, Jack recoils, saying, " 'My impatience! . . . I, who have hardened myself into a stone statue of dogged patience, impatient!' He glared at her; ground his teeth; and continued vehemently" (*Love among the Artists*, p. 95). For Cyril Scott's similar reaction to criticism of his irascibility, see above, p. 89.

3. Robert Hogan ("The Novels of Bernard Shaw," *ELT* 8[1965]: 83) calls Jack "a Henry Higgins of genius." The course of the students' training in *Love among the Artists* and *Pygmalion* is the same. After Madge learns "to speak the English language with purity and distinctness" (p. 101), she has to acquire a "complete method" of acting by practice and study; after she has perfected the method, she begins "to think of taking a pupil, feeling that she could make an actress of any girl, the matter being merely one of training" (p. 121). Eliza must perfect the art of social intercourse by patient and studious practice. She succeeds so well that Pickering says that her style is almost too

good, i.e., better than the real thing, for many real aristocrats "think style comes by nature to people in their position, and so they never learn. Theres always something professional about doing a thing superlatively well" (p. 266). And like Madge, Eliza threatens to take a pupil herself (p. 293). Finally, Madge's confession of love for Jack brings a lecture on the art based on shamming and the art based on truth, just as Eliza's bid for approval brings a lecture on life based on sensual and romantic ideals and a life based on ascetic and aesthetic ideals.

4. *Pygmalion*, p. 296. See above, p. 27.

5. Ibid., p. 216. Note the woman / nurse and the man / child comparison again.

6. Pater, *Works*, 4:89, 98, 106.

7. *As Far As Thought Can Reach*, p. 219. Winsten (*Days with Bernard Shaw*, pp. 302–3, and *Shaw's Corner*, p. 167), reports that Shaw disliked both Yeats's "Eastern affectations" and his poetry. Ervine (*Bernard Shaw*, p. 189) says that Shaw thought Yeats, because of his "flowing dark garments" and "air of artistic disarray and transcendental abstraction," a better model than Wilde for Gilbert's Bunthorne in *Patience*.

Chapter XIV

1. Henry James, "The Art of Fiction," *Partial Portraits*, pp. 387–88.

2. Winsten, *Days with Bernard Shaw*, pp. 23, 184.

3. "The Critic as Artist," Wilde, *Works*, p. 233; and *The Autobiography of William Butler Yeats*, p. 93. Dietrich correctly observes that Shaw's mask did not hide reality, for "hypocrisy is pretending to be something you are not, whereas Bernard Shaw pretended to be something he really was" (p. 71).

4. *The Autobiography of William Butler Yeats*, pp. 284–85.

5. Winsten, *Days with Bernard Shaw*, p. 57.

6. Hamilton, *Aesthetic Movement in England*, p. 124.

7. Nordau, *Degeneration*, p. 209.

8. "Literature and Art," *Platform and Pulpit*, p. 47; and *Sketches*, pp. 195–96. Ford, "Anarchists and Gray Frieze," discusses Shaw's Pre-Raphaelite dress; John J. Weisert, "Clothes Make the Man," *Shaw R* 4(January, 1961): 30–31, describes Jaeger's Sanitary Woolen System. See also Frank Harris, *Bernard Shaw*, pp. 102–4; W. R. Titterton, *So This Is Shaw*, pp. 24, 55; Pearson, *G. B. S.: A Full-Length Portrait*, pp. 89–90, 163, 270; and Pearson, *G. B. S.: A Postscript*, p. 83, for further description of Shaw's dress.

9. *The New Republic* 29(25 January and 22 February 1922): 241, 361.

10. Jackson, *Bernard Shaw*, p. 85.

11. Quoted in Joseph R. Dunlap, "The Typographical Shaw: GBS and the Revival of Printing," *Shavian* 2(February, 1961): 8. See also Joseph R. Dunlap, "A Note on Shaw's 'Formula' and Pre-Kelmscott Printing," *Independent Shavian* 2(Winter, 1963–64): 20.

12. Holbrook Jackson, "Robert Bridges, George Moore, Bernard Shaw and Printing," *The Fleuron: A Journal of Typography*, no. 4(1925): 43–53. Other studies of Shaw's typography are James Shand, "Author and Printer: G.B.S. and R. & R. C.: 1898–1948," *Alphabet and Image*, no. 8(December, 1948), 3–38; Dunlap, "The Typographical Shaw"; Dunlap, "A Note on Shaw's 'Formula' . . . Printing"; Dunlap, "Morrisian and Shavian Typography: A Few Illustrations," *Independent Shavian* 3(Fall, 1964): 6–7; and Dunlap, "Richards, Scott, Ibsen

and Shaw, or Leaves from a Typographical Family Tree," *Independent Shavian* 3(Spring, 1965): 44–46. One could cite as other instances of Shaw's aesthetic sensitivity his demand for correctly and beautifully pronounced English, and his respect for a beautiful handwriting.

13. Winsten, *Shaw's Corner*, p. 182.

14. Ervine, *Bernard Shaw*, pp. 100–103.

15. Henderson, *George Bernard Shaw*, p. 419; Janet Dunbar, *Mrs. G. B. S.*, pp. 145–46 ff.

16. Letter to Rugby boys, in Riding, "The *Candida* Secret," *Spectator* 185 (17 November 1950): 506.

17. Henderson, *George Bernard Shaw*, p. 820.

18. Shaw, "Mr. Bernard Shaw's Works of Fiction," *Selected Non-Dramatic Writings of Bernard Shaw*, p. 314.

19. Winsten, *Days with Bernard Shaw*, p. 299.

20. In *Bernard Shaw: Collected Letters*, p. 596.

21. Both are reprinted in the Constable *The Black Girl in Search of God, and Some Lesser Tales.*

22. Winsten, *Shaw's Corner*, p. 14.

Bibliography

Works by Shaw

Advice to a Young Critic, and Other Letters. Edited by E. J. West. New York: Crown, 1955.

"Art Corner" (monthly review article), *Our Corner*, from 1 June 1885, to 1 September 1886.

"Author's Preface, The," *Widowers' Houses: A Comedy by G. Bernard Shaw.* London: Henry and Co., 1893 (contains three appendices by Shaw).

Bernard Shaw and Mrs. Patrick Campbell: Their Correspondence. Edited by Alan Dent. New York: Knopf, 1952.

Bernard Shaw: Collected Letters, 1874–1897. Edited by Dan H. Laurence. London: Max Reinhardt, 1965.

Bernard Shaw's Letters to Granville Barker. Edited by C. B. Purdom. New York: Theatre Arts Books, 1957.

Casebook on "Candida," A. Edited by Stephen S. Stanton. New York: Thomas Y. Crowell, 1962.

Ellen Terry and Bernard Shaw: A Correspondence. Edited by Christopher St. John [Christabel Marshall]. New York: Putnam's, 1931.

"English Academy of Letters, An: A Correspondence of 1897," *Shaw R* 6(January, 1963): 16–17, 21–22. (Letters to *Academy*, November, 1897.)

Florence Farr, Bernard Shaw, W. B. Yeats: Letters. Edited by Clifford Bax. New York: Dodd, Mead, 1942.

How to Become a Musical Critic. Edited by Dan H. Laurence. New York: Hill & Wang, 1961.

"In the Picture Galleries: The Holman Hunt Exhibition," "The New Galley—the Kakemonos in Bond Street," "Arts and Crafts," and "The New English Art Club—Monet at the Goupil Gallery," reprinted in "Shaw on Art," by Jack Kalmar, *MD* 2(September, 1959): 147–59. (Reprinted from *The World*, 24 March 1886; 16 May 1888; 3 October 1888; and 24 April 1889, respectively.)

"J. M. Strudwick," *Art Journal* 53(April, 1891): 97–101.

"The Nun and the Dramatist. George Bernard Shaw to the Abbess of Stanbrook," *Atlantic Monthly* 198(July, August, 1956): 27–34, 69–76.

Platform and Pulpit. Edited by Dan H. Laurence. New York: Hill & Wang, 1961.

Preface to *Three Plays by Brieux, Member of the French Academy.* English Versions by Mrs. Bernard Shaw, St. John Hankin, and John Pollock. New York: Brentano's, 1913.

Religious Speeches of Bernard Shaw, The. Edited by Warren S. Smith. University Park: Pennsylvania State University Press, 1963.

177

Selected Non-Dramatic Writings of Bernard Shaw. Edited by Dan H. Laurence. New York: Houghton Mifflin, 1965.

Shaw on Shakespeare: An Anthology of Bernard Shaw's Writings on the Plays and Production of Shakespeare. Edited by Edwin Wilson. New York: Dutton, 1961.

Shaw on Theatre. Edited by E. J. West. New York: Hill & Wang, 1959.

To a Young Actress: The Letters of Bernard Shaw to Molly Tompkins. Edited by Peter Tompkins. New York: Clarkson N. Potter, 1960.

"Two Shaw Letters, " *MLR* 53 (October, 1958) : 548–50.

William Morris As I Knew Him. New York: Dodd, Mead, 1936. (Also in *William Morris: Artist, Writer, Socialist,* ed. May Morris, ix–xl.)

The Works of Bernard Shaw. Standard Edition. 36 vols. London: Constable, 1931–52.

Works about Shaw

Abbott, Anthony. *Shaw and Christianity.* New York: Seabury, 1965.

Adler, Jacob H. "Ibsen, Shaw and *Candida,*" *JEGP* 59 (January, 1960) : 50–58.

Albert, Sidney P. "Bernard Shaw: The Artist as Philosopher," *JAAC* 14 (June, 1956) : 419–38.

Archer, William. *English Dramatists of To-Day.* London: Sampson Low Marston, Searle, & Rivington, 1882.

Arnot, Page. Speech on Morris and Shaw to The Shaw Society and William Morris Society, 11 May 1956, abstracted in *Shavian* 1 (May, 1957) : 12–13.

Bentley, Eric. *Bernard Shaw, 1856–1950.* Rev. ed. Norfolk, Conn.: New Directions, 1957. London: Methuen, 1967. Reprinted.

———. *A Century of Hero-Worship: A Study of the Idea of Heroism in Carlyle and Nietzsche with Notes on Other Hero-Worshipers of Modern Times.* Philadelphia: Lippincott, 1944.

———. "The Making of a Dramatist (1892–1903)," *TDR,* September, 1960, pp. 3–21.

———. *The Playwright as Thinker.* New York: Harcourt, Brace, 1946.

Bentley, Joseph. "Tanner's Decision to Marry in *Man and Superman,*" *Shaw R* 11 (January, 1968) : 26–28.

Bissell, Claude T. "The Novels of Bernard Shaw," *UTQ* 17 (October, 1947) : 38–51.

Blanch, Robert J. "The Myth of Don Juan in *Man and Superman,*" *Revue des Langues Vivantes* 33 (1967) : 158–63.

Braybrooke, Patrick. *The Genius of Bernard Shaw.* Philadelphia: Lippincott, 1925.

Broad, C. Lewis and Violet M. *Dictionary to the Plays and Novels of Bernard Shaw with Bibliography of his Works and of the Literature*

Concerning Him with a Record of the Principal Shavian Play Productions. London: A & C Black, 1929.

Brooks, Harold F. " 'Pygmalion' and 'When We Dead Awaken,' " *N&Q*, n.s., 7 (December, 1960) : 469–71.

Brown, Ivor. *Shaw in His Time.* London: Nelson, 1965.

Burton, Richard. *Bernard Shaw: The Man and the Mask.* New York: Holt, 1916.

Carpenter, Charles A., Jr. *Bernard Shaw and the Art of Destroying Ideals: The Early Plays.* Madison: University of Wisconsin Press, 1969.

Chesterton, Gilbert K. *George Bernard Shaw.* New York: Hill & Wang, 1956.

Colbourne, Maurice. *The Real Bernard Shaw.* London: Dent, 1939.

Couchman, Gordon W. "Comic Catharsis in *Caesar and Cleopatra*," *Shaw R* 3 (January, 1960) : 11–14.

Crane, Milton. "Pymalion: Bernard Shaw's Dramatic Theory and Practice," *PMLA* 66 (December, 1951) : 879–85.

Crompton, Louis. *Shaw the Dramatist.* Lincoln: University of Nebraska Press, 1969.

Deacon, Renée M. *Bernard Shaw As Artist-Philosopher: An Exposition of Shavianism.* London: A. C. Fifield, 1910.

Dietrich, R. F. *Portrait of the Artist as a Young Superman: A Study of Shaw's Novels.* Gainesville: University of Florida Press, 1969.

Duerksen, Roland A. "Shelley and Shaw," *PMLA* 78 (March, 1963) : 114–27.

Dunbar, Janet. *Mrs. G. B. S.: A Portrait.* New York: Harper & Row, 1963.

Dunkel, Wilbur D. "The Essence of Shaw's Dramaturgy," *CE* 10 (March, 1949) : 307–12.

Dunlap, Joseph R. "Morrisian and Shavian Typography: A Few Illustrations," *Independent Shavian* 3 (Fall, 1964) : 6–7.

———. "A Note on Shaw's 'Formula' and Pre-Kelmscott Printing," *Independent Shavian* 2 (Winter, 1963–64) : 20.

———. "Richards, Scott, Ibsen, and Shaw, or Leaves from a Typographical Family Tree," *Independent Shavian* 3 (Spring, 1965) : 44–46.

———. "The Typographical Shaw: GBS and the Revival of Printing," *Shavian* 2 (February, 1961) : 8–9.

Ellehauge, Martin. *The Position of Bernard Shaw in European Drama and Philosophy.* Copenhagen: Levin & Munksgaard, 1931.

Ervine, St. John. *Bernard Shaw: His Life, Work and Friends.* London: Constable, 1956.

Fiske, Irving. *Bernard Shaw's Debt to William Blake.* Shavian Tract No. 2. London: Shaw Society, 1951.

Foster, Brian. "A Shavian Allusion," *N&Q*, n.s., 8 (March, 1961) : 106–7.

Fromm, Harold. *Bernard Shaw and the Theater of the Nineties: A Study of Shaw's Dramatic Criticism.* Lawrence: University of Kansas Press, 1967.

Fuller, Edmund. *George Bernard Shaw: Critic of Western Morale.* Twentieth Century Library. Edited by Hiram Haydn. New York: Scribner's, 1950.

Gassner, John. "Bernard Shaw and the Making of the Modern Mind," *CE* 23 (April, 1962): 517–25.

———. "The Puritan in Hell," *Theatre Arts* 36 (April, 1952): 67–70.

———. "Shaw as a Drama Critic," *Theatre Arts* 36 (May, 1951): 26–29, 91–95.

———. "Shaw on Shakespeare," *Independent Shavian* 2 (Fall, 1963): 1, 3–5; (Winter, 1963–64): 13, 15, 23–24.

Gilkes, A. N. "Candour about *Candida,*" *Fortnightly,* n.s., 171 (February, 1952): 122–27.

Glicksberg, Charles I. "Shaw the Novelist," *Pr S* 25 (Spring, 1951): 1–9.

Goodman, Phyllis M. "Beethoven as the Prototype of Owen Jack," *Shaw R* 8 (January, 1965): 12–24.

Hamon, Augustin. *The Twentieth Century Molière: Bernard Shaw.* Translated by Eden and Cedar Paul. London: Allen & Unwin, 1915.

Harris, Frank. *Bernard Shaw: An Unauthorized Biography Based on First Hand Information.* New York: Simon and Schuster, 1931.

Henderson, Archibald. *George Bernard Shaw: Man of the Century.* New York: Appleton-Century-Crofts, 1956.

———. "The Philosophy of Bernard Shaw," *Atlantic Monthly* 103 (February, 1909): 227–34.

———. "Shaw's Novels: And Why They Failed," *Shaw Bulletin* 1 (May, 1955): 11–18. (Reprinted from *DR* 34 [Winter, 1954–55]: 373–82.)

———. *Table-Talk of G. B. S.: Conversations on Things in General between George Bernard Shaw and his Biographer.* New York: Harper, 1925.

Henson, Janice. "Bernard Shaw's Contribution to the Wagner Controversy in England," *Shaw R* 4 (January, 1961): 21–26.

Hogan, Robert. "The Novels of Bernard Shaw," *ELT* 8 (1965): 63–114.

Holt, Charles Loyd. " 'Candida': The Music of Ideas," *Shaw R* 9 (January, 1966): 2–14.

———. "Mozart, Shaw and *Man and Superman,*" *Shaw R* 9 (September, 1966): 102–16.

Howe, P. P. *Bernard Shaw: A Critical Study.* London: Martin Secker, 1915.

Huneker, James. *Iconoclasts: A Book of Dramatists.* New York: Scribner's, 1909.

Irvine, William. "Shaw's Quintessence of Ibsenism," *SAQ* 46 (April, 1947): 252–62.

———. *The Universe of Bernard Shaw.* New York: Whittlesey House (a division of McGraw-Hill), 1949. (Also New York: Russell & Russell, 1968.)

Jackson, Holbrook. *Bernard Shaw*. London: Grant Richards, 1907.

———. "Robert Bridges, George Moore, Bernard Shaw and Printing," *The Fleuron: A Journal of Typography*, no. 4 (1925), pp. 43–53.

James, Eugene Nelson. "The Critic as Dramatist: Bernard Shaw, 1895–98," *Shaw R* 5(September, 1962): 97–108.

Joad, C. E. M. *Shaw*. London: Gollancz, 1949.

Jones, Howard M. "Shaw as a Victorian," *VS* 1:165–72.

Kalmar, Jack, "Shaw on Art," *MD* 2(September, 1959): 147–59.

Kaufmann, R. J. (ed.) *George Bernard Shaw*. Englewood Cliffs, N.J.: Prentice-Hall, 1965.

Kaye, Julian B. *Bernard Shaw and the Nineteenth-Century Tradition*. Norman: University of Oklahoma Press, 1958.

King, Walter N. "The Rhetoric of *Candida*," *MD* 2(September, 1959): 71–83.

Kornbluth, Martin L. "Shaw and Restoration Comedy," *Shaw Bulletin* 2(January, 1958): 9–17.

Kronenberger, Louis, ed. *George Bernard Shaw: A Critical Survey*. Cleveland: World, 1953.

Laurence, Dan H. "Bernard Shaw and the Pall Mall Gazette: II," *Shaw Bulletin* 1(September, 1954): 8–10.

———. "Genesis of a Dramatic Critic," *MD* 2(September, 1959): 178–83.

Lauter, Paul. " 'Candida' and 'Pygmalion': Shaw's Subversion of Stereotypes," *Shaw R* 3(September, 1960): 14–19.

Leary, Daniel J. "The Moral Dialectic in *Caesar and Cleopatra*," *Shaw R* 5(May, 1962): 42–53.

———. "Shaw's Use of Stylized Characters and Speech in *Man and Superman*," *MD* 5(February, 1963): 477–90.

Lerner, Alan Jay. "Pygmalion and My Fair Lady," *Shaw Bulletin* 1(November, 1956): 4–7.

Mander, Raymond, and Joe Mitchenson. *Theatrical Companion to Shaw: A Pictorial Record of the First Performance of the Plays of George Bernard Shaw*. London: Rockliff, 1954.

Matlaw, Myron. "The Denouement of *Pygmalion*," *MD* 1(May, 1958): 29–34.

———. "Will Higgins Marry Eliza?" *Shavian*, no. 12(May, 1958), pp. 14–19.

Mayer, David. "The Case for Harlequin: A Footnote on Shaw's Dramatic Method," *MD* 3(May, 1960): 60–74.

McCabe, Joseph. *George Bernard Shaw: A Critical Study*. London: Kegan Paul, Trench, Trübner, 1914.

McDowell, Frederick P. W. "Another Look at Bernard Shaw: A Reassess-

ment of His Dramatic Theory, His Practice, and His Achievement,"
Dram S 1(May, 1961): 34–53.

Meisel, Martin. "Cleopatra and 'The Flight into Egypt,' " *Shaw R* 7(May, 1964): 62–63.

———. *Shaw and the Nineteenth-Century Theater.* Princeton, N.J.: Princeton University Press, 1963.

Mencken, Henry L. *George Bernard Shaw: His Plays.* Boston: John W. Luce, 1905.

Mills, Carl Henry. "*Man and Superman* and The Don Juan Legend," *CL* 19(Summer, 1967): 216–25.

Mills, John A. *Language and Laughter: Comic Diction in the Plays of George Bernard Shaw.* Tuscon: University of Arizona Press, 1968.

Minney, R. J. *Recollections of George Bernard Shaw.* New York: Prentice-Hall, 1968.

Morgan, Margery M. " 'Back to Methuselah': The Poet and the City," *Essays and Studies,* n.s., 13(1960): 82–98.

Morse, David. "Shaw, the Victorian," *Encounter* 22(February, 1964): 78–80.

Nethercot, Arthur H. "Bernard Shaw, Ladies and Gentlemen," *MD* 2(September, 1959): 84–98.

———. *Men and Supermen: The Shavian Portrait Gallery.* Cambridge, Mass.: Harvard University Press, 1954. Reprinted. Bronx, N.Y.: Benjamin Blom, 1965.

———. "The Quintessence of Idealism; or, The Slaves of Duty," *PMLA* 62(September, 1957): 844–59.

———. "The Schizophrenia of Bernard Shaw," *A Sch* 21(Autumn, 1952): 455–67.

———. "Shaw's Women and the Truth about Candida" (Speech of 11 Sept. 1953; summarized by Barbara Smoker), *Shavian,* n.s., no. 1 (December, 1953), pp. 12–13.

Norwood, Gilbert. *Euripides & Mr. Bernard Shaw.* London: St. Catherine Press, 1913.

O'Conor, Beatrice. "G. B. S. and William Morris," *New Statesman and Nation* 7(10 November 1934): 660.

O'Donnell, Norbert F. "The Conflict of Wills in Shaw's Tragi-comedy," *MD* 4(February, 1962): 413–25.

———. "Doctor Ridgeon's Deceptive Dilemma," *Shaw R* 2(January, 1959): 1–5.

———. "On the 'Unpleasantness' of *Pygmalion,*" *Shaw Bulletin* 1(May, 1955): 7–10.

O'Donovan, John. *Shaw and the Charlatan Genius.* London: Oxford University Press, 1965.

Ohmann, Richard M. *Shaw: The Style and the Man.* Middletown, Conn.: Wesleyan University Press, 1962.

Palmer, John. *George Bernard Shaw, Harlequin or Patriot?* New York: Century, 1915.

Park, Bruce R. "A Mote in the Critic's Eye: Bernard Shaw and Comedy," *Texas Studies in English* 37(1958): 195–210.

Patch, Blanche. *Thirty Years with G. B. S.* London: Gollancz, 1951.

Pearson, Hesketh. *G. B. S., a Full Length Portrait.* 2d ed. New York: Harper, 1942.

——. *G. B. S.: A Postscript.* New York: Harper, 1950.

——. "A Pygmalion Pickle: Beerbohm Tree, Mrs. Pat and G. B. S.," *Theatre Arts* 40(December, 1956): 29–31, 82–85.

Purdom, C. B. *A Guide to the Plays of Bernard Shaw.* London: Methuen, 1963. Reprinted. New York: Apollo Editions, 1965.

Rattray, R. F. *Bernard Shaw: A Chronicle and an Introduction.* London: Duckworth, 1934.

Reinert, Otto. "Old History and New: Anachronism in *Caesar and Cleopatra,*" *MD* 3(May, 1960): 37–41.

Rider, Dan. *Adventures with Bernard Shaw.* London: Morley & Mitchell, n.d.

Riding, George A. "The *Candida* Secret," *Spectator* 185(17 November 1950): 506.

Rosset, B. C. *Shaw of Dublin: The Formative Years.* University Park, Pa.: Pennsylvania State University Press, 1964.

Ruff, William. "Shaw on Wilde and Morris: A Clarification," *Shaw R* 11(January, 1968): 32–33.

Schlauch, Margaret. "Symbolic Figures and the Symbolic Technique of George Bernard Shaw," *Science and Society* 21(Summer, 1957): 210–21.

Shand, James. "Author and Printer: G. B. S. and R. & R. C.: 1898–1948," *Alphabet and Image,* no. 8 (December, 1948), pp. 3–38.

Shanks, Edward. *Bernard Shaw.* Writers of the Day. Edited by Bertram Christian. London: Nisbet, 1924.

Sherard, Robert Barborough. *Bernard Shaw, Frank Harris, & Oscar Wilde.* London: T. Werner Laurie, 1937.

Sidnell, M. J. "John Bull's Other Island—Yeats and Shaw," *MD* 11 (December, 1968): 245–51.

Smith, P. Percy. "A Shavian Tragedy: The Doctor's Dilemma," in *The Image of the Work: Essays in Criticism,* by B. H. Lehman et al. Berkeley: University of California Press, 1955.

——. *The Unrepentant Pilgrim.* Boston: Houghton Mifflin, 1966.

Smith, Warren S. "The Bishop, the Dancer, and Bernard Shaw," *Shaw R* 3(January, 1960): 2–10.

Smith, Winifred. "Bernard Shaw and his Critics (1892–1938)," *Poet Lore* 47(Spring, 1941): 76–83.

Spink, Judith B. "The Image of the Artist in the Plays of Bernard Shaw," *Shaw R* 6(September, 1963): 82–88.

Stewart, J. I. M. *Eight Modern Writers.* Oxford: At the Clarendon Press, 1963.

Stockholder, Fred E. "Shaw's Drawing-Room Hell: A Reading of *Man and Superman,*" *Shaw R* 11(May, 1968): 42–51.

Stokes, E. E., Jr. "Bernard Shaw and Nineteenth Century Thought," *Shaw R* 2(January, 1959): 19–21.

———. "Shaw and William Morris," *Shaw Bulletin* 1(Summer, 1953): 16–19.

Strauss, E. *Bernard Shaw: Art and Socialism.* London: Gollancz, 1942.

Titterton, W. R. *So This Is Shaw.* London: Douglas Organ, 1945.

Wagenknecht, Edward. *A Guide to Bernard Shaw.* New York: Appleton, 1929.

Ward, A. C. *Bernard Shaw.* Men and Books. London: Longmans, Green, 1951.

Watson, Barbara Bellow. *A Shavian Guide to the Intelligent Woman.* New York: Norton, 1964.

Weintraub, Stanley. "'Humors' Names in Shaw's Prentice Novels," *Names* 5(December, 1957): 222–25.

———. *Private Shaw and Public Shaw.* London: Cape, 1963.

Weisert, John J. "Clothes Make the Man," *Shaw R* 4(January, 1961): 30–31.

Whitehead, George. *Bernard Shaw Explained: A Critical Exposition of the Shavian Religion.* London: Watts, 1925.

Whiting, George W. "The Cleopatra Rug Scene: Another Source," *Shaw R* 3(January, 1960): 15–17.

Williamson, Audrey. *Bernard Shaw: Man and Writer.* New York: Crowell-Collier, 1963.

Wilson, Angus. "The Living Dead—IV. Bernard Shaw," *London Magazine* 3(December, 1956): 53–58.

Wilson, Edmund. "Bernard Shaw at Eighty," in *The Triple Thinkers: Twelve Essays on Literary Subjects.* Rev. ed. New York: Oxford University Press, 1948.

Winsten, Stephen. *Days with Bernard Shaw.* New York: Vanguard Press, 1949.

———. *Shaw's Corner.* New York: Roy Publishers, 1952.

Woodbridge, Homer E. *George Bernard Shaw: Creative Artist.* Crosscurrents: Modern Critiques. Edited by Harry T. Moore. Carbondale: Southern Illinois University Press, 1953.

Young, Stark. *Immortal Shadows.* New York: Scribner's, 1948.

Works by the Aesthetes

Arnold, Matthew. *Culture and Anarchy.* Edited by J. Dover Wilson. Cambridge: At the University Press, 1960.

BIBLIOGRAPHY

Beardsley, Aubrey. *Under the Hill and Other Essays in Prose and Verse.* Publisher's note by John Lane. 3d ed. London: John Lane, 1921.

Beckson, Karl. *Aesthetes and Decadents of the 1890's: An Anthology of British Poetry and Prose.* New York: Vintage Books, 1966.

Davidson, Donald (ed.). *British Poetry of the Eighteen-Nineties.* Series in Literature. Edited by Robert Shafer. Garden City, N.Y.: Doubleday, Doran, 1937.

Dowson, Ernest. *The Poetical Works of Ernest Christopher Dowson.* Edited by Desmond Flower. London: Cassell, 1950.

————. *The Stories of Ernest Dowson.* Edited by Mark Longaker. New York: Barnes, 1960.

Dowson, Ernest, and Arthur Moore. *A Comedy of Masks: A Novel.* Appleton's Town and Country Library, No. 124. New York: Appleton, 1893.

Germ, The: Thoughts towards Nature in Poetry, Literature, and Art. Introduction by William Michael Rossetti. New York: AMS Press, 1965.

Hunt, W. Holman, "The Ideals of Art," *New Review* 4(May, 1891): 420-31.

————. *Pre-Raphaelitism and the Pre-Raphaelite Brotherhood.* 2 vols. New York: Macmillan, 1905-6.

James, Henry. *The Complete Tales of Henry James.* Edited by Leon Edel. 12 vols. Philadelphia: Lippincott, 1961-64.

————. *Literary Reviews and Essays on American, English, and French Literature.* Edited by Albert Mordell. New York: Grove, 1957.

————. *Partial Portraits.* New York: Macmillan, 1888.

————. *Views and Reviews.* Edited by Le Roy Phillips. Boston: Ball, 1908.

Moore, George. *The Collected Works of George Moore.* The Carra Edition. 21 vols. New York: Boni & Liveright, 1922-24.

————. *A Mere Accident.* Vizetelly's One-Volume Novels, XXVI. London: Vizetelly, 1887.

Morris, William. *The Collected Works of William Morris.* Edited by May Morris. 24 vols. London: Longmans, Green, 1910-15.

————. Review of *Poems,* by Dante Gabriel Rossetti. *Academy,* 14 May 1870, pp. 199-200.

————. *William Morris: Artist, Writer, Socialist.* Edited by May Morris. 2 vols. Oxford: Basil Blackwell, 1936.

Pater, Walter. *The Works of Walter Pater.* New Library Edition. 10 vols. London: Macmillan, 1910.

Peters, Robert L., ed. *Victorians on Literature and Art.* New York: Appleton-Century-Crofts, 1961.

Rossetti, Dante Gabriel. *The Collected Works of Dante Gabriel Rosetti.* Edited by William M. Rossetti. 2 vols. London: Ellis and Elvey, 1897.

———. *Dante Gabriel Rossetti: His Family Letters.* With a Memoir by William Michael Rossetti. 2 vols. Boston: Roberts, 1895.

———. *Letters of Dante Gabriel Rossetti to William Allingham, 1854–1870.* Edited by George Birkbeck Hill. London: Unwin, 1897.

———. *Rossetti Papers, 1862 to 1870.* Edited by William Michael Rossetti. London: Sand, 1903.

Rossetti, William Michael, ed. *Praeraphaelite Diaries and Letters.* London: Hurst and Blackett, 1900.

———, ed. *Ruskin: Rossetti: Preraphaelitism. Papers 1854 to 1862.* London: Allen, 1899.

Ruskin, John. *The Works of John Ruskin.* Edited by E. T. Cook and Alexander Wedderburn. Library Edition. London: Allen, 1903–12.

Savoy, The: An Illustrated Quarterly. Edited by Arthur Symons. 8 nos. London: Leonard Smithers, January–December, 1896 (title changes, with no. 3, to *The Savoy: An Illustrated Monthly*).

Secker, Martin, ed. *The Eighteen-Nineties: A Period Anthology in Prose and Verse.* Introduction by John Betjeman. London: Richards, 1948.

Stanford, Derek, ed. *Poets of the 'Nineties: A Biographical Anthology.* London: Baker, 1965.

Swinburne, Algernon Charles. *The Complete Works of Algernon Charles Swinburne.* Edited by Sir Edmund Gosse and Thomas James Wise. Bonchurch Edition. 20 vols. London: Heinemann, 1925–27.

Symons, A. J. A., ed. *An Anthology of 'Nineties' Verse.* London: Mathews & Marrot, 1928.

Symons, Arthur. *Aubrey Beardsley.* London: At the Sign of the Unicorn, 1898.

———. *Dramatis Personae.* Indianapolis: Bobbs-Merrill, 1923.

———. "Modernity in Verse," in *The Bibelot* 13:261–85.

———. "Morris as Poet," *Saturday Review* 82(10 October 1896): 387–88.

———. "Mr. Ernest Dowson," *Athenæum*, 3 March 1900, p. 274.

———. *The Romantic Movement in English Poetry.* New York: Dutton, 1909.

———. *Studies in Prose and Verse.* New York: Dutton, 1922.

———. *The Symbolist Movement in Literature.* London: Constable, 1911.

Weintraub, Stanley, ed. *The Savoy, Nineties Experiment.* University Park: Pennsylvania State University Press, 1966.

———, ed. *The Yellow Book: Quintessence of the Nineties.* Garden City, N.Y.: Doubleday, 1964.

Whistler, James McNeill. *The Gentle Art of Making Enemies* (1890). New York: Dover, 1967.

Wilde, Oscar. *The Works of Oscar Wilde.* Sunflower Edition. 15 vols. New York: Lamb, 1909.

Yeats, William Butler. *The Autobiography of William Butler Yeats, Consisting of Reveries over Childhood and Youth, The Trembling of the Veil, and Dramatis Personae.* New York: Macmillan, 1953.

The Yellow Book: An Illustrated Quarterly. Edited by Henry Harland and A. Beardsley. 13 vols. London: Mathews and John Lane, April, 1894–April, 1897. (Beardsley editor of first 4 vols. only; Mathews publisher of first 2 vols. only.)

Works about the Aesthetes

(No attempt has been made to list works about individual aesthetes.)

Allen, Grant. "The New Hedonism," *Fortnightly Review,* n.s., 55(1 March 1894): 377–92.

Archer, William. *Poets of the Younger Generation.* London: John Lane, 1902.

Beers, Henry A. "The Pre-Raphaelites," *A History of English Romanticism in the Nineteenth Century.* New York: Holt, 1901.

Bell, Clive. "The Creed of an Aesthete," *New Republic* 29(25 January 1922): 241–42.

Bibelot, The: A Reprint of Poetry and Prose for Book Lovers, Chosen in Part from Scarce Editions and Sources Not Generally Known. 21 vols. Portland, Me.: Mosher, 1895–1915.

[Buchanan, Robert]. "The Fleshly School of Poetry," in *Notorious Literary Attacks.* Edited by Albert Mordell. New York: Boni & Liveright, 1926.

Buckley, Jerome Hamilton. *The Victorian Temper, A Study in Literary Culture.* Cambridge, Mass.: Harvard University Press, 1951.

———. *The Triumph of Time: A Study of the Victorian Concepts of Time, History, Progress, and Decadence.* Cambridge, Mass.: Harvard University Press, 1966.

Burdett, Osbert. *The Beardsley Period, An Essay in Perspective.* London: John Lane, 1925.

Cassidy, J. A. "Robert Buchanan and the Fleshly Controversy," *PMLA* 67(March, 1952): 65–93.

Charlesworth, Barbara. *Dark Passages: The Decadent Consciousness in Victorian Literature.* Madison: The University of Wisconsin Press, 1965.

Chesterton, G. K. *The Victorian Age in Literature.* New York: Holt, 1913.

———. "Writing 'Finis' to Decadence," *Independent* 39(15 January 1917): 100.

"Contemporary Poets and Versifiers," *Edinburgh Review* 177(October, 1893): 469–99.

Cruse, Amy. "The Aesthetes," in *The Victorians and Their Books.* London: Allen & Unwin, 1935.

DeArmond, Anna Janney. "What Is Pre-Raphaelitism in Poetry?" *Delaware Notes*, 19th series (1946), pp. 67–88.

Decker, Clarence R. "The Aesthetic Revolt against Naturalism in Victorian Criticism," *PMLA* 53 (September, 1938): 844–56.

Dyson, A. E. "The Socialist Aesthete," *Listener* 66 (24 August 1961): 273–74.

Eckhoff, Lorentz. *The Aesthetic Movement in English Literature*. Oslo: Oslo University Press, 1959.

Egan, Rose Frances. "The Genesis of the Theory of 'Art for Art's Sake' in Germany and in England," *Smith College Studies in Modern Languages* 2 (July, 1921); 5 (April, 1924).

Farmer, Albert J. *Le Mouvement esthétique et "décadent" en Angleterre (1873–1900)*. Bibliothèque de la Revue de Littérature Comparée., Vol. 75. Edited by F. Baldensperger and P. Hazard. Paris: Librairie Ancienne Honoré Champion, 1931.

Fletcher, Ian. "The 1890's: A Lost Decade," *VS* 4 (June, 1961): 345–54.

————. "Bedford Park: Aesthete's Elysium?" in *Romantic Mythologies*. London: Routledge and K. Paul, 1967.

Ford, Ford Madox. *See* Hueffer, Ford Madox.

Fredeman, William E. *Pre-Raphaelitism: A Bibliocritical Study*. Cambridge, Mass.: Harvard University Press, 1965.

"French and English Pictures," *Cornhill* 40 (July, 1879): 92–106.

Gaunt, William. *The Aesthetic Adventure*. Pelican Books, A386. Harmondsworth, Middlesex: Penguin, n.d.

Gerber, Helmut E. "The Nineties: Beginning, End, or Transition?" in *Edwardians and Late Victorians*, edited by Richard Ellman. English Institute Essays, 1959. New York: Columbia University Press, 1960.

Gilbert, W. S. *Patience; or, Bunthorne's Bride*, in *H. M. S. Pinafore and Six Other Savoy Operas*. Garden City, N.Y.: Doubleday, 1961.

"Gospel of Aestheticism, The," *Nation* 33 (3 November 1881): 357–58.

Hamilton, Walter. *The Aesthetic Movement in England*. 3d ed. London: Reeves & Turner, 1882.

Harris, Wendell. "Innocent Decadence: The Poetry of the *Savoy*," *PMLA* 77 (December, 1962): 629–36.

Harrison, Frederic. "The Aesthete," in *The Choice of Books and Other Literary Pieces*. London: Macmillan, 1886.

[Hichens, Robert]. *The Green Carnation*. New York: Appleton, 1894.

Hicks, Granville. *Figures of Transition: A Study of British Literature at the End of the Nineteenth Century*. New York: Macmillan, 1939.

HQ. *See* Q[uilter], H[arry].

Hough, Graham. *The Last Romantics*. London: Duckworth, 1949. Reprinted University Paperbacks. London: Methuen, 1961.

Hueffer, Ford Madox [Ford Madox Ford]. *Memories and Impressions: A Study in Atmospheres*. New York: Harper, 1911.

Jackson, Holbrook. *The Eighteen Nineties: A Review of Art and Ideas at the Close of the Nineteenth Century.* New York: Knopf, 1925. Reprinted New York: Capricorn, 1966.

Johnson, R. V. *Aestheticism.* The Critical Idiom, No. 3. Edited by John D. Jump. London: Methuen, 1969.

Kennedy, J. M. *English Literature, 1880–1905.* Boston: Small, Maynard, 1913.

Le Gallienne, Richard. *The Romantic '90s.* London: Putnam's, 1926.

––––––. "What's Wrong with the Eighteen-Nineties?" *Bookman* (New York), 54(September, 1921): 1–7.

Lester, John A., Jr. *Journey through Despair 1880–1914: Transformations in British Literary Culture.* Princeton, N.J.: Princeton University Press, 1968.

Mallock, William Hurrell. *The New Republic: Or Culture, Faith, and Philosophy in an English Country House* (1877). Edited by J. Max Patrick. Gainesville: University of Florida Press, 1950.

March-Phillips, L. "Pre-Raphaelitism and the Present," *Contemporary Review* 89(May, 1906): 704–13.

Millais, John Guille, ed. *The Life and Letters of Sir John Millais.* 2 vols. New York: Stokes, 1899.

"Mr. Cimabue Brown on the Defensive," *Belgravia: An Illustrated London Magazine* 45(September, 1881): 284–97.

"Mr. Gilbert's Satire" (Review of *Patience*), *Academy*, 30 April 1881, pp. 326–27.

More, Paul Elmer. "A Naughty Decade," *Nation* 98(14 May 1914): 566–68; (21 May 1914): 590–600.

Muddiman, Bernard. *The Men of the Nineties.* London: Danielson, 1920.

Murdoch, W. G. Blaikie. *The Renaissance of the Nineties.* London: Moring, 1911.

Nordau, Max. *Degeneration.* Translated from 2d ed. New York: Appleton, 1905.

Peckham, Morse. *Beyond the Tragic Vision: The Quest for Identity in the Nineteenth Century.* New York: Braziller, 1962.

Peters, Robert L. "Toward an 'Un-Definition' of Decadent as Applied to British Literature of the Nineteenth Century," *JAAC* 18(December, 1959): 258–64.

Plowman, Thomas F. "The Aesthetes; the Story of a Nineteenth-Century Cult," *Pall Mall Magazine* 5(January, 1895): 27–44.

Punch, or The London Charivara. Vols. 76–83 (1879–82).

Q[uilter], H[arry]. "The Apologia of Art," *Cornhill Magazine* 40(November, 1879): 533–48.

Quilter, Harry. "The Gospel of Intensity," *Contemporary Review* 67(June, 1895): 761–82.

Raymond, E. T. *Portraits of the Nineties.* London: Unwin, 1921.

Reckitt, Maurice B. "When Did 'Victorianism' End?" *VS* 1:268–71.

Richardson, Dorothy. "Saintsbury and Art for Art's Sake in England," *PMLA* 59 (March, 1944) : 243–60.

Robinson, James K. "A Neglected Phase of the Aesthetic Movement: English Parnassianism," *PMLA* 68 (September, 1953) : 733–54.

Rosenblatt, Louise. *L'Idée de l'art pour l'art dans la littérature anglaise pendant la période victorienne*. Paris: Librairie Ancienne Honoré Champion, 1931.

Ryals, Clyde de L. "The Nineteenth-Century Cult of Inaction," *TSL* 4 (1959) : 51–60.

————. "Toward a Definition of *Decadent* as Applied to British Literature of the Nineteenth Century," *JAAC* 17 (September, 1958) : 85–92.

Saintsbury, George. *A Short History of English Literature* (1898). London: Macmillan, 1925.

Scott, William Bell. *Autobiographical Notes of the Life of William Bell Scott and Notices of his Artistic and Poetic Circle of Friends. 1830 to 1882*. Edited by W. Minto. 2 vols. New York: Harper, 1892.

Smith, Warren S. *The London Heretics, 1870–1914*. New York: Dodd, Mead, 1968.

Stutfield, Hugh E. M. "Tommyrotics," *Blackwood's Edinburgh Magazine* 157 (June, 1895) : 833–45.

Wedmore, Frederick. "The New Satire" (Review of *The Colonel*) *Academy*, 12 February 1881, pp. 125–26.

Wellek, René. *The Later Nineteenth Century*. A History of Modern Criticism: 1750–1950, Vol. 4. New Haven: Yale University Press, 1965.

Wilcox, John. "The Beginnings of *l'art pour l'art*," *JAAC* 11 (June, 1953) : 360–77.

Wright, Cuthbert. "Out of Harm's Way: Some Notes on the Esthetic Movement of the 'Nineties,'" *Bookman* (New York) 70 (November 1929) : 234–43.

Index

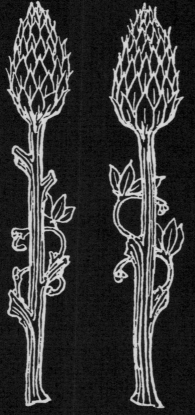